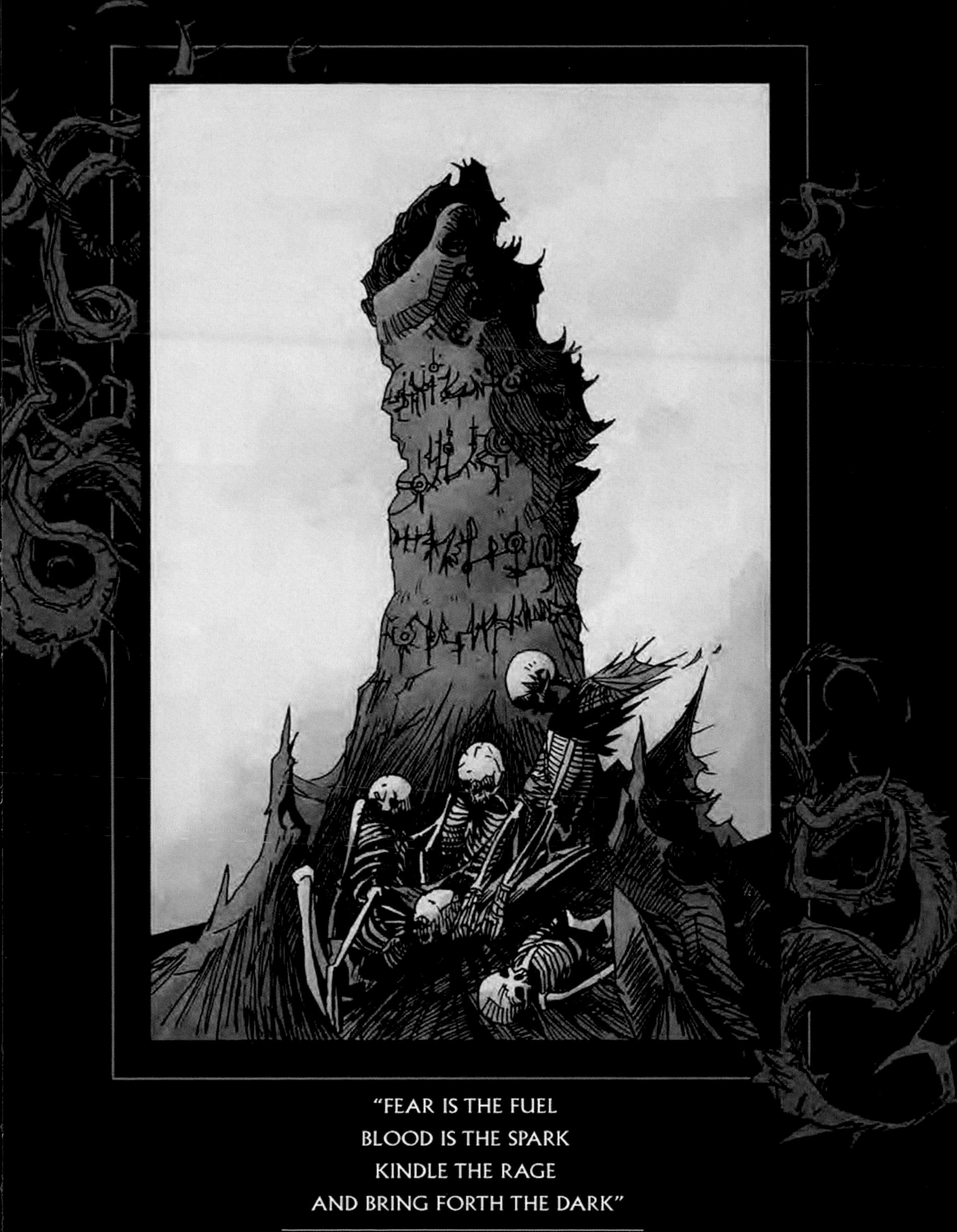

"FEAR IS THE FUEL
BLOOD IS THE SPARK
KINDLE THE RAGE
AND BRING FORTH THE DARK"

DIABLO®

SWORD OF JUSTICE

Diablo: Sword of Justice
Writers: Aaron Williams and Joseph Lacroix

FOR BLIZZARD ENTERTAINMENT

Senior Vice President, Story and Franchise Development
LYDIA BOTTEGONI

Lead Editor, Publishing
CHLOE FRABONI

Editor
ALLISON IRONS

Producer
BRIANNE MESSINA

Vice President, Global Consumer Products
MATT BEECHER

Director, Consumer Products, Publishing
BYRON PARNELL

Special Thanks
SEAN COPELAND, EVELYN FREDERICKSEN, PHILLIP
HILLENBRAND, DEREK ROSENBERG, DAVID SEEHOLZER,
ANNA WAN, JUSTIN PARKER

FOR DC COMICS

Editor - Original Series: MICHAEL MCCALISTER

Editor: PETER HAMBOUSSI

Design Director - Books: ROBBIN BROSTERMAN

Publication Design: DAMIAN RYLAND

Senior VP - Editor-in-Chief, DC Comics: BOB HARRAS

President: DIANE NELSON

Co-Publishers: DAN DIDIO and JIM LEE

Chief Creative Officer: GEOFF JOHNS

Executive VP - Sales, Marketing and Business
Development: JOHN ROOD

Senior VP -Business and Legal Affairs: AMY GENKINS

Senior VP - Finance: NAIRI GARDINER

VP - Publishing Planning: JEFF BOISON

VP - Art Direction and Design: MARK CHIARELLO

VP - Marketing: JOHN CUNNINGHAM

VP - Editorial Administration: TERRI CUNNINGHAM

Senior VP - Manufacturing and Operations: ALISON GIL

Senior VP - Vertigo & Integrated Publishing: HANK KANALZ

VP - Business and Legal Affairs, Publishing: JAY KOGAN

VP - Business Affairs, Talent: JACK MAHAN

VP - Manufacturing Administration: NICK NAPOLITANO

VP - Book Sales: SUE POHJA

Senior VP - Publicity: COURTNEY SIMMONS

Senior VP - Sales: BOB WAYNE

gear.blizzard.com

ISBN: 978-1-9503-6644-6

10 9 8 7 6 5 4 3 2 1
Manufacturedt in China

DC Comics, 1700 Broadway, New York, NY 10019
A Warner Bros. Entertainment Company.
Printed by RR Donnelley, Salem, VA, USA.
First printing, 5/13/13 ISBN: 978-1-4012-4497-2

DIABLO®

SWORD OF JUSTICE

BLIZZARD ENTERTAINMENT

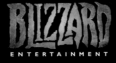

AARON WILLIAMS
WRITER

JOSEPH LACROIX
ARTIST

DAVE STEWART
LEE LOUGHRIDGE
COLORISTS

SAIDA TEMOFONTE
LETTERER

JOSEPH LACROIX
AND
DAVE STEWART
COVERS

MICKY NEILSON
AND
DOUG ALEXANDER
STORY & ART
CONSULTANTS

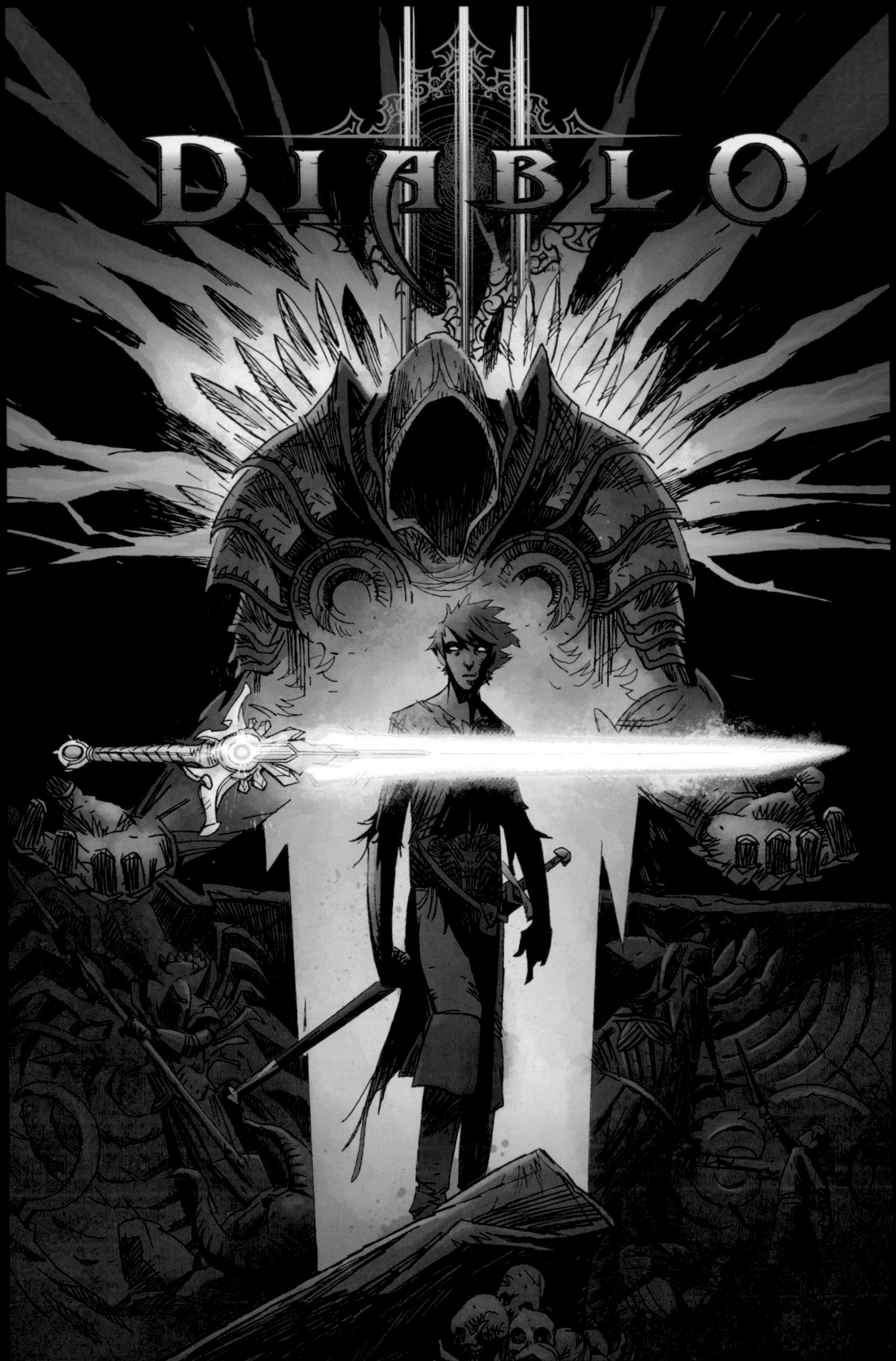
DIABLO

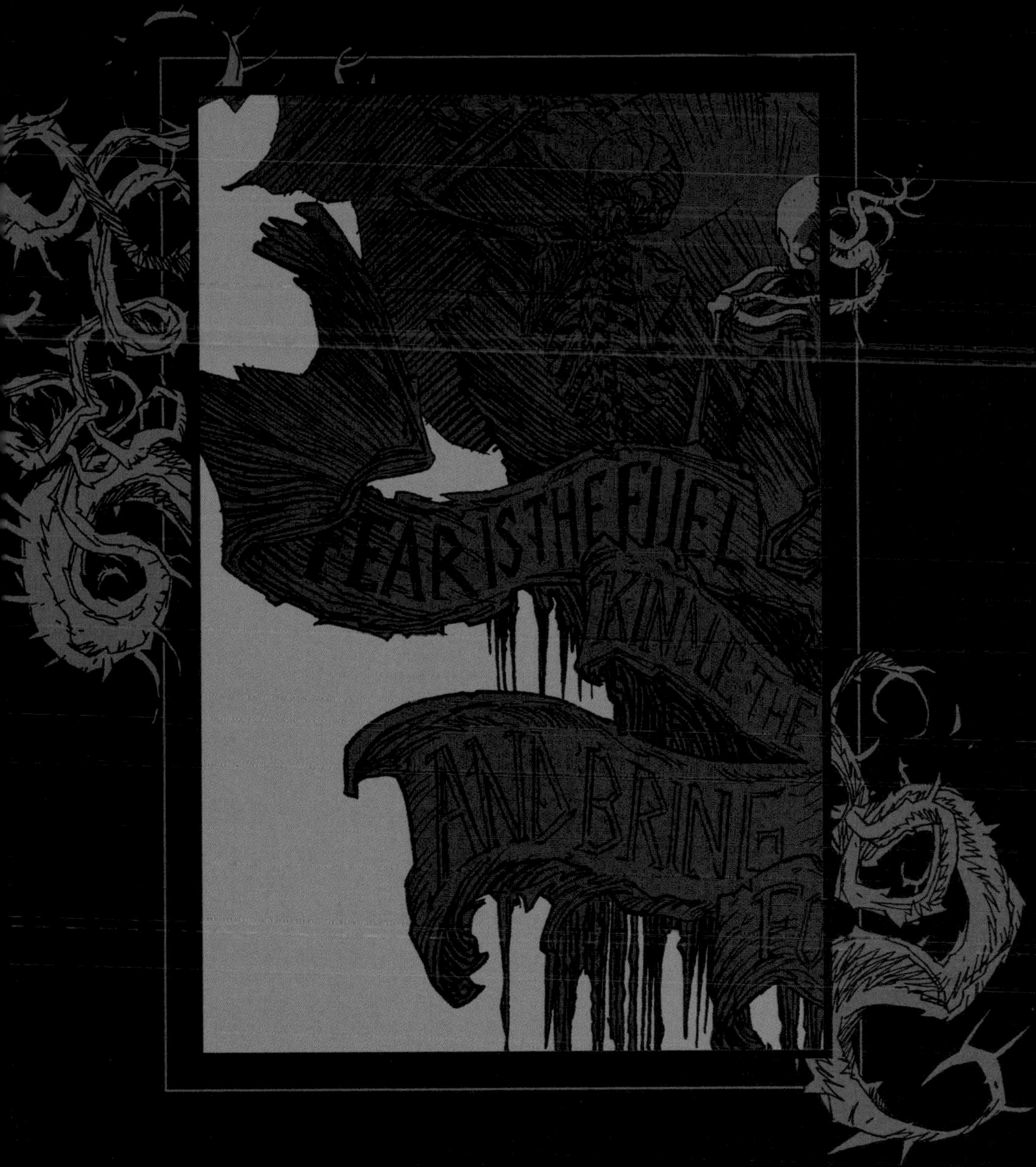
FEAR IS THE FUEL
KINDLE THE
AND BRING

ACT I

AARON WILLIAMS
JOSEPH LACROIX
DAVE STEWART

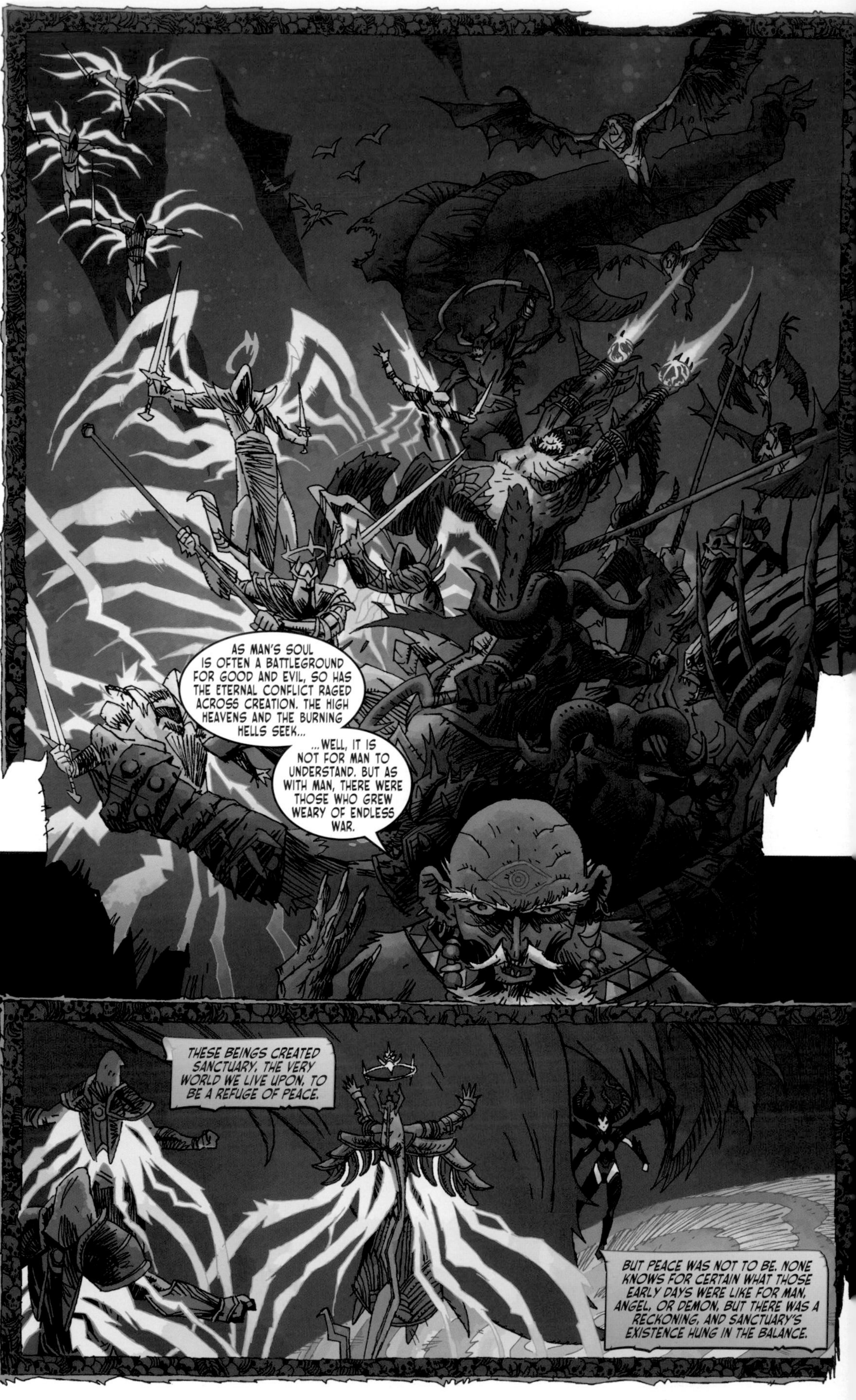
AS MAN'S SOUL IS OFTEN A BATTLEGROUND FOR GOOD AND EVIL, SO HAS THE ETERNAL CONFLICT RAGED ACROSS CREATION. THE HIGH HEAVENS AND THE BURNING HELLS SEEK...
...WELL, IT IS NOT FOR MAN TO UNDERSTAND. BUT AS WITH MAN, THERE WERE THOSE WHO GREW WEARY OF ENDLESS WAR.
THESE BEINGS CREATED SANCTUARY, THE VERY WORLD WE LIVE UPON, TO BE A REFUGE OF PEACE.
BUT PEACE WAS NOT TO BE. NONE KNOWS FOR CERTAIN WHAT THOSE EARLY DAYS WERE LIKE FOR MAN, ANGEL, OR DEMON, BUT THERE WAS A RECKONING, AND SANCTUARY'S EXISTENCE HUNG IN THE BALANCE.

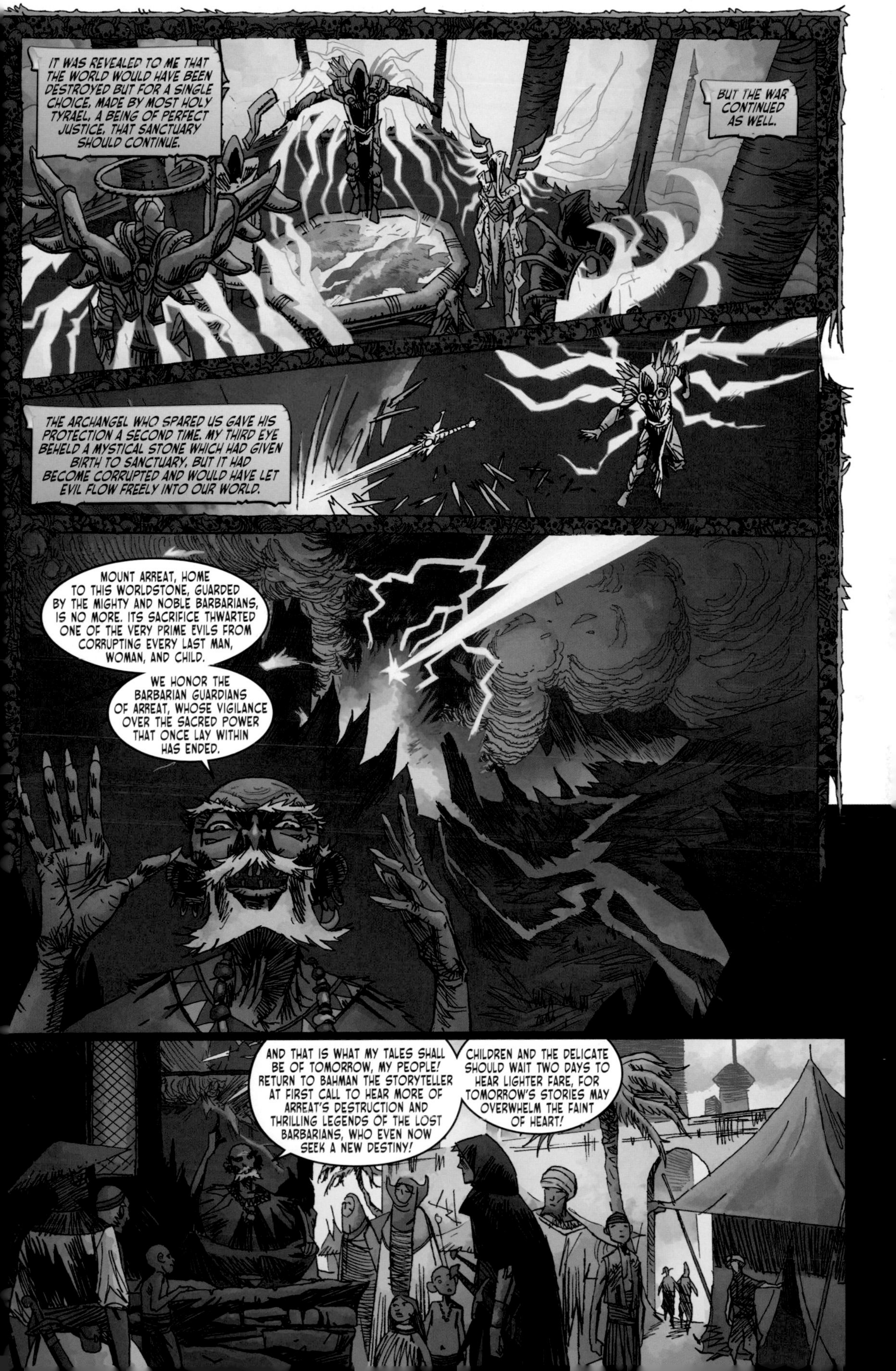
IT WAS REVEALED TO ME THAT THE WORLD WOULD HAVE BEEN DESTROYED BUT FOR A SINGLE CHOICE, MADE BY MOST HOLY TYRAEL, A BEING OF PERFECT JUSTICE, THAT SANCTUARY SHOULD CONTINUE.
BUT THE WAR CONTINUED AS WELL.
THE ARCHANGEL WHO SPARED US GAVE HIS PROTECTION A SECOND TIME. MY THIRD EYE BEHELD A MYSTICAL STONE WHICH HAD GIVEN BIRTH TO SANCTUARY, BUT IT HAD BECOME CORRUPTED AND WOULD HAVE LET EVIL FLOW FREELY INTO OUR WORLD.
MOUNT ARREAT, HOME TO THIS WORLDSTONE, GUARDED BY THE MIGHTY AND NOBLE BARBARIANS, IS NO MORE. ITS SACRIFICE THWARTED ONE OF THE VERY PRIME EVILS FROM CORRUPTING EVERY LAST MAN, WOMAN, AND CHILD.
WE HONOR THE BARBARIAN GUARDIANS OF ARREAT, WHOSE VIGILANCE OVER THE SACRED POWER THAT ONCE LAY WITHIN HAS ENDED.
AND THAT IS WHAT MY TALES SHALL BE OF TOMORROW, MY PEOPLE! RETURN TO BAHMAN THE STORYTELLER AT FIRST CALL TO HEAR MORE OF ARREAT'S DESTRUCTION AND THRILLING LEGENDS OF THE LOST BARBARIANS, WHO EVEN NOW SEEK A NEW DESTINY!
CHILDREN AND THE DELICATE SHOULD WAIT TWO DAYS TO HEAR LIGHTER FARE, FOR TOMORROW'S STORIES MAY OVERWHELM THE FAINT OF HEART!

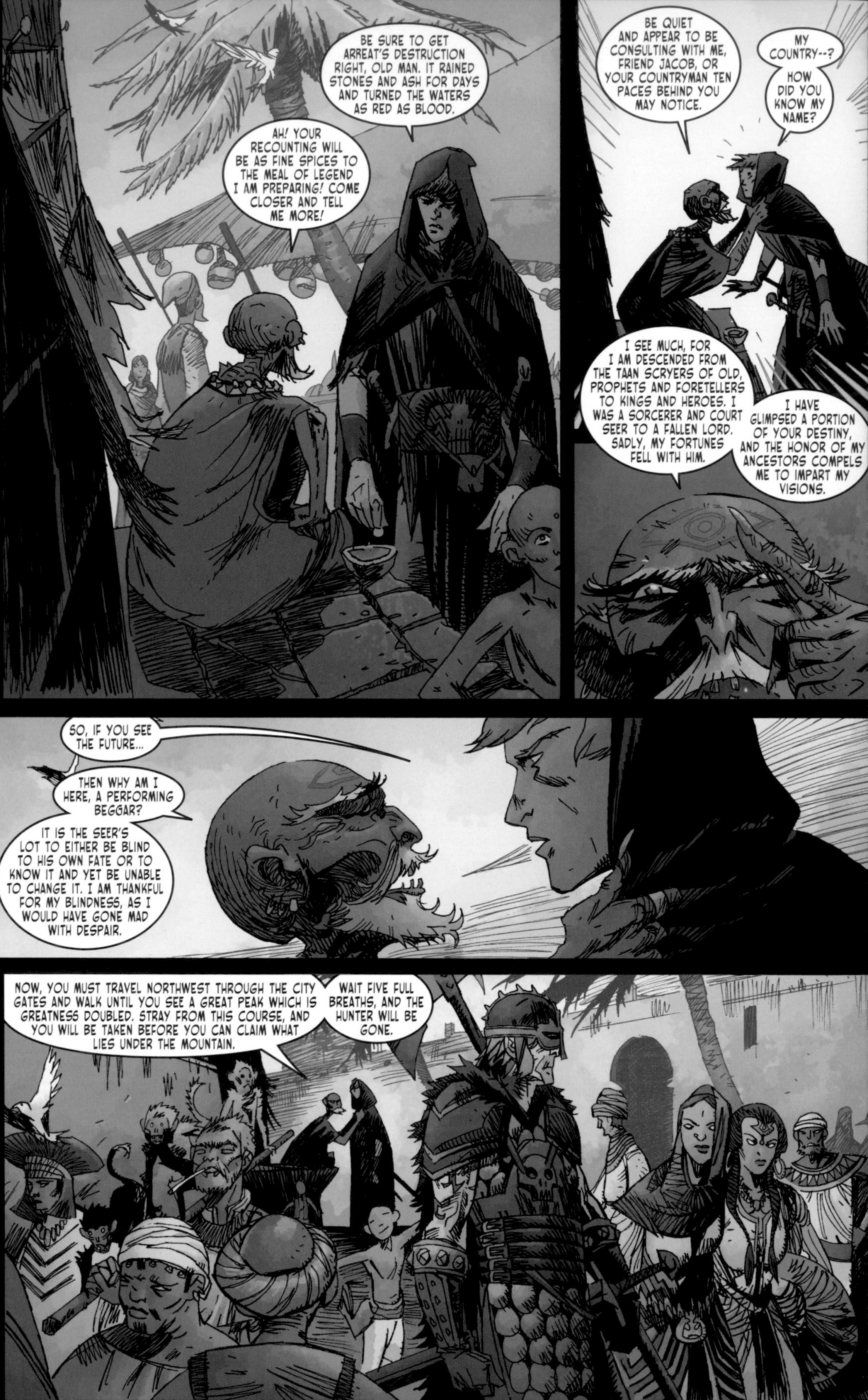
BE SURE TO GET ARREAT'S DESTRUCTION RIGHT, OLD MAN. IT RAINED STONES AND ASH FOR DAYS AND TURNED THE WATERS AS RED AS BLOOD.
AH! YOUR RECOUNTING WILL BE AS FINE SPICES TO THE MEAL OF LEGEND I AM PREPARING! COME CLOSER AND TELL ME MORE!
BE QUIET AND APPEAR TO BE CONSULTING WITH ME, FRIEND JACOB, OR YOUR COUNTRYMAN TEN PACES BEHIND YOU MAY NOTICE.
MY COUNTRY--?
HOW DID YOU KNOW MY NAME?
I SEE MUCH, FOR I AM DESCENDED FROM THE TAAN SCRYERS OF OLD, PROPHETS AND FORETELLERS TO KINGS AND HEROES. I WAS A SORCERER AND COURT SEER TO A FALLEN LORD. SADLY, MY FORTUNES FELL WITH HIM.
I HAVE GLIMPSED A PORTION OF YOUR DESTINY, AND THE HONOR OF MY ANCESTORS COMPELS ME TO IMPART MY VISIONS.
SO, IF YOU SEE THE FUTURE...
THEN WHY AM I HERE, A PERFORMING BEGGAR?
IT IS THE SEER'S LOT TO EITHER BE BLIND TO HIS OWN FATE OR TO KNOW IT AND YET BE UNABLE TO CHANGE IT. I AM THANKFUL FOR MY BLINDNESS, AS I WOULD HAVE GONE MAD WITH DESPAIR.
NOW, YOU MUST TRAVEL NORTHWEST THROUGH THE CITY GATES AND WALK UNTIL YOU SEE A GREAT PEAK WHICH IS GREATNESS DOUBLED. STRAY FROM THIS COURSE, AND YOU WILL BE TAKEN BEFORE YOU CAN CLAIM WHAT LIES UNDER THE MOUNTAIN.
WAIT FIVE FULL BREATHS, AND THE HUNTER WILL BE GONE.

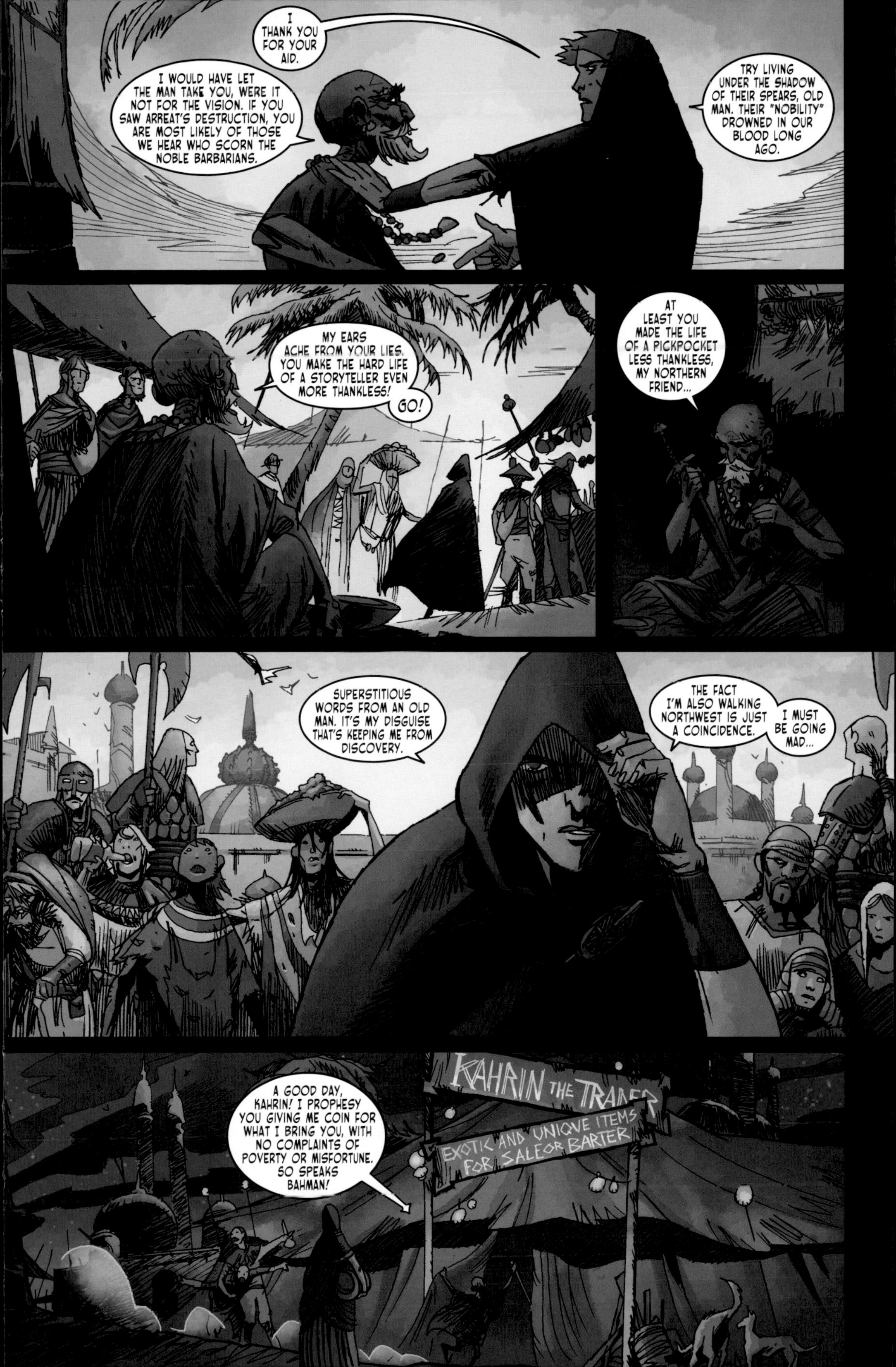
I THANK YOU FOR YOUR AID.
I WOULD HAVE LET THE MAN TAKE YOU, WERE IT NOT FOR THE VISION. IF YOU SAW ARREAT'S DESTRUCTION, YOU ARE MOST LIKELY OF THOSE WE HEAR WHO SCORN THE NOBLE BARBARIANS.
TRY LIVING UNDER THE SHADOW OF THEIR SPEARS, OLD MAN. THEIR "NOBILITY" DROWNED IN OUR BLOOD LONG AGO.
MY EARS ACHE FROM YOUR LIES. YOU MAKE THE HARD LIFE OF A STORYTELLER EVEN MORE THANKLESS!
GO!
AT LEAST YOU MADE THE LIFE OF A PICKPOCKET LESS THANKLESS, MY NORTHERN FRIEND...
SUPERSTITIOUS WORDS FROM AN OLD MAN. IT'S MY DISGUISE THAT'S KEEPING ME FROM DISCOVERY.
THE FACT I'M ALSO WALKING NORTHWEST IS JUST A COINCIDENCE.
I MUST BE GOING MAD...
KAHRIN THE TRADER
EXOTIC AND UNIQUE ITEMS FOR SALE OR BARTER
A GOOD DAY, KAHRIN! I PROPHESY YOU GIVING ME COIN FOR WHAT I BRING YOU, WITH NO COMPLAINTS OF POVERTY OR MISFORTUNE. SO SPEAKS BAHMAN!

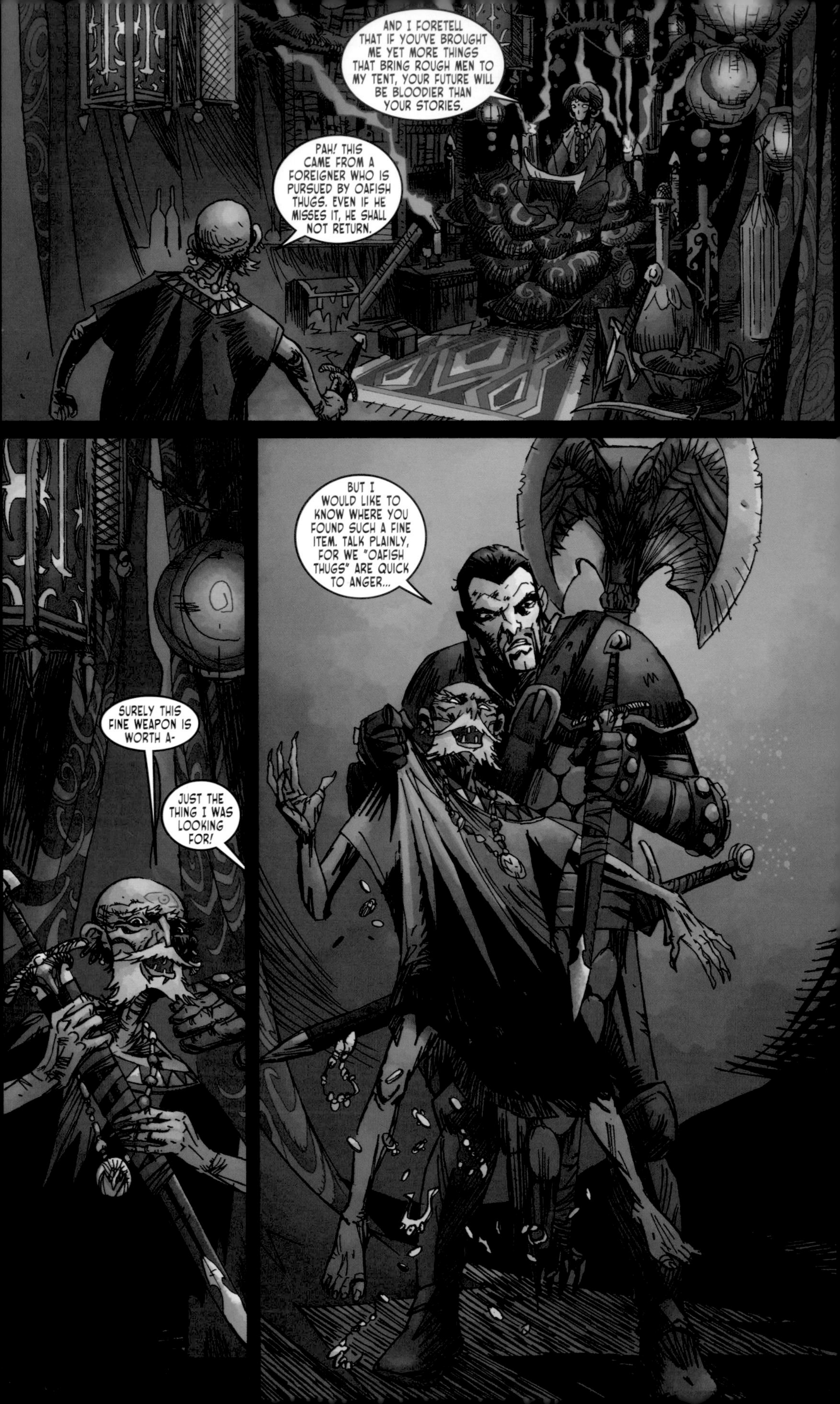
AND I FORETELL THAT IF YOU'VE BROUGHT ME YET MORE THINGS THAT BRING ROUGH MEN TO MY TENT, YOUR FUTURE WILL BE BLOODIER THAN YOUR STORIES.
PAH! THIS CAME FROM A FOREIGNER WHO IS PURSUED BY OAFISH THUGS. EVEN IF HE MISSES IT, HE SHALL NOT RETURN.
SURELY THIS FINE WEAPON IS WORTH A-
JUST THE THING I WAS LOOKING FOR!
BUT I WOULD LIKE TO KNOW WHERE YOU FOUND SUCH A FINE ITEM. TALK PLAINLY, FOR WE "OAFISH THUGS" ARE QUICK TO ANGER...

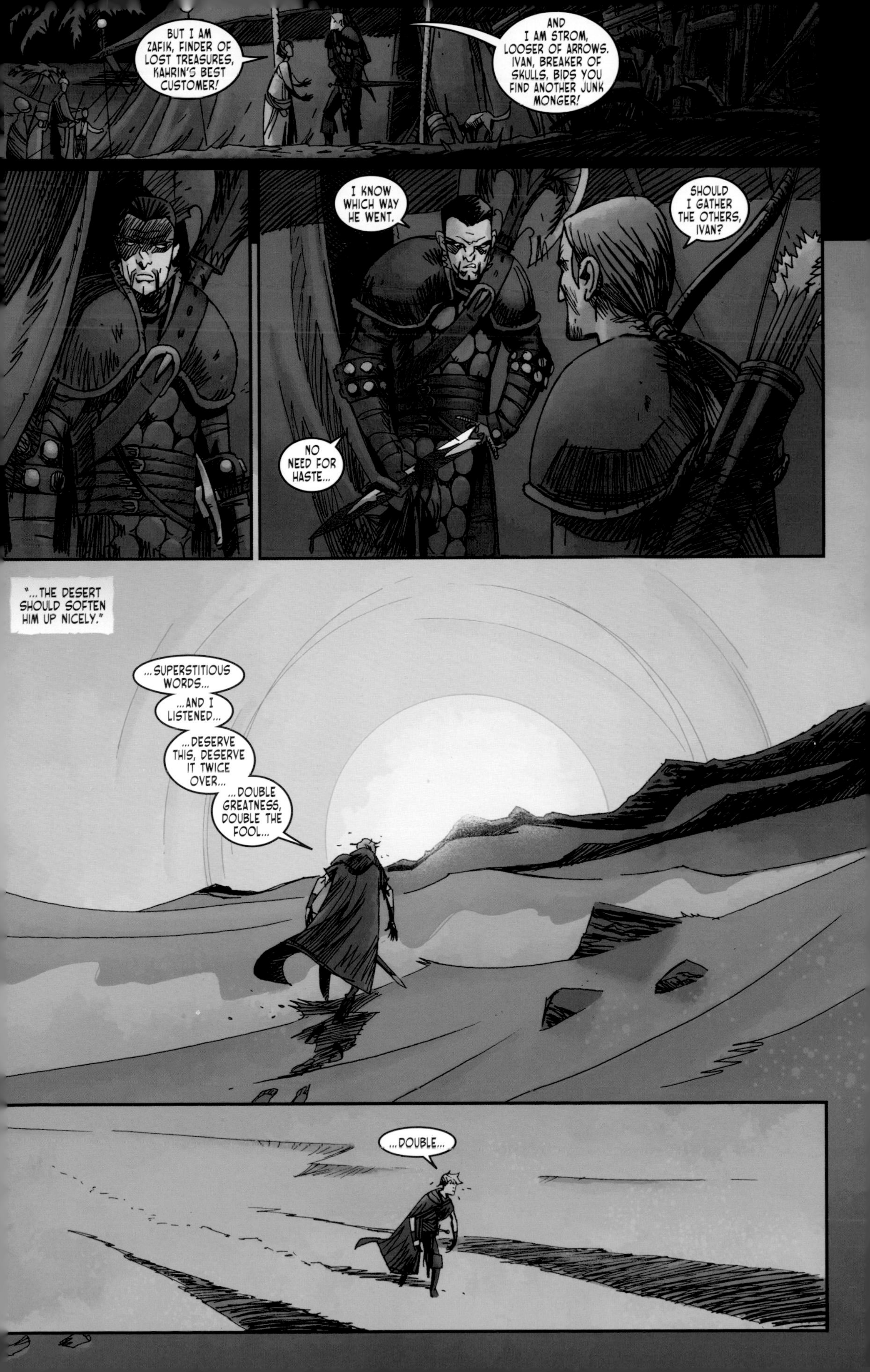
BUT I AM ZAFIK, FINDER OF LOST TREASURES, KAHRIN'S BEST CUSTOMER!
AND I AM STROM, LOOSER OF ARROWS. IVAN, BREAKER OF SKULLS, BIDS YOU FIND ANOTHER JUNK MONGER!
I KNOW WHICH WAY HE WENT.
SHOULD I GATHER THE OTHERS, IVAN?
NO NEED FOR HASTE...
"...THE DESERT SHOULD SOFTEN HIM UP NICELY."
...SUPERSTITIOUS WORDS...
...AND I LISTENED...
...DESERVE THIS, DESERVE IT TWICE OVER...
...DOUBLE GREATNESS, DOUBLE THE FOOL...
...DOUBLE...

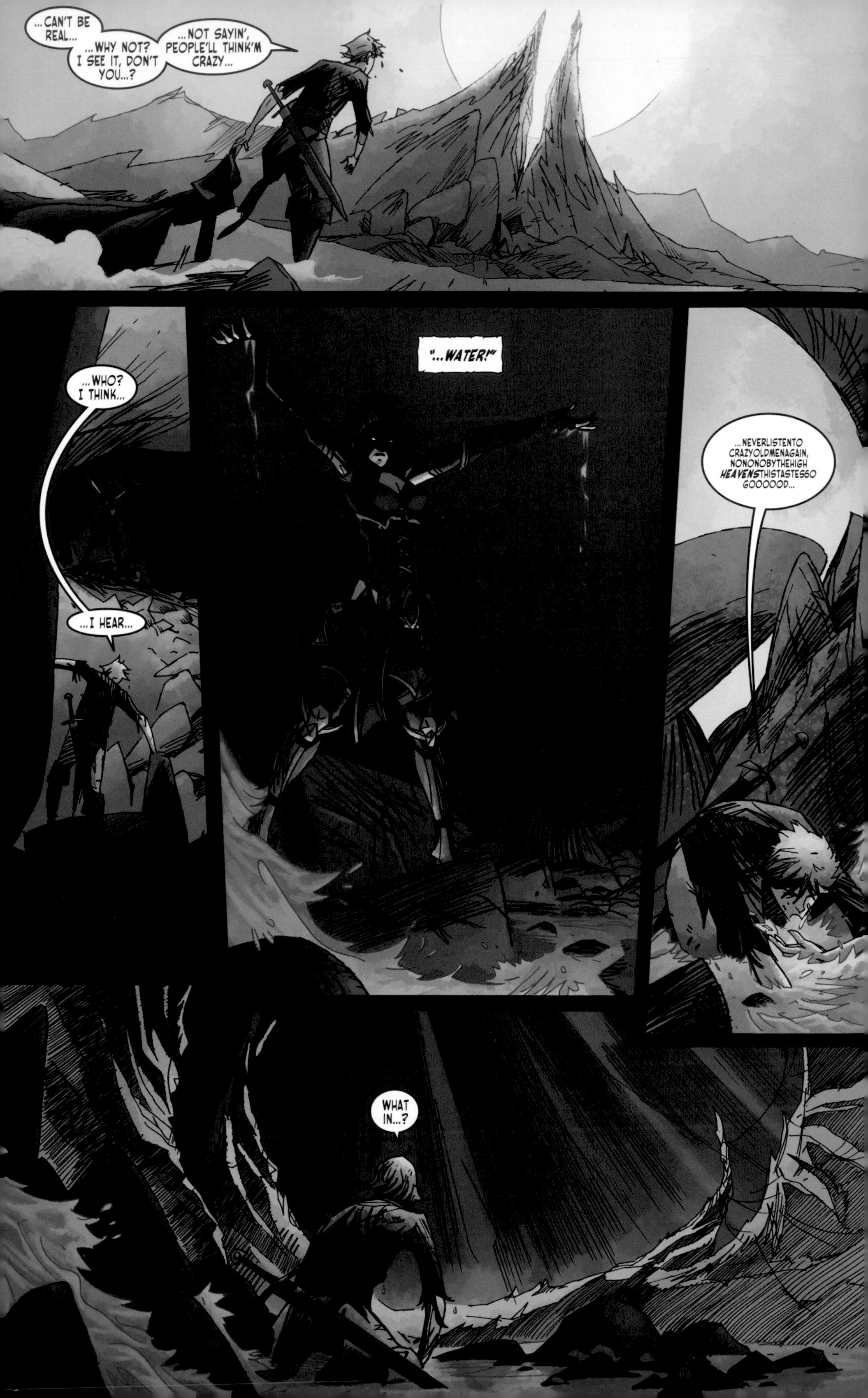
...CAN'T BE REAL...
...WHY NOT? I SEE IT, DON'T YOU...?
...NOT SAYIN', PEOPLE'LL THINK'M CRAZY...
...WHO? I THINK...
...I HEAR...
"...WATER!"
...NEVERLISTENTO CRAZYOLDMENAGAIN, NONONOBYTHEHIGH HEAVENSTHISTASTESSO GOOOOOD...
WHAT IN...?

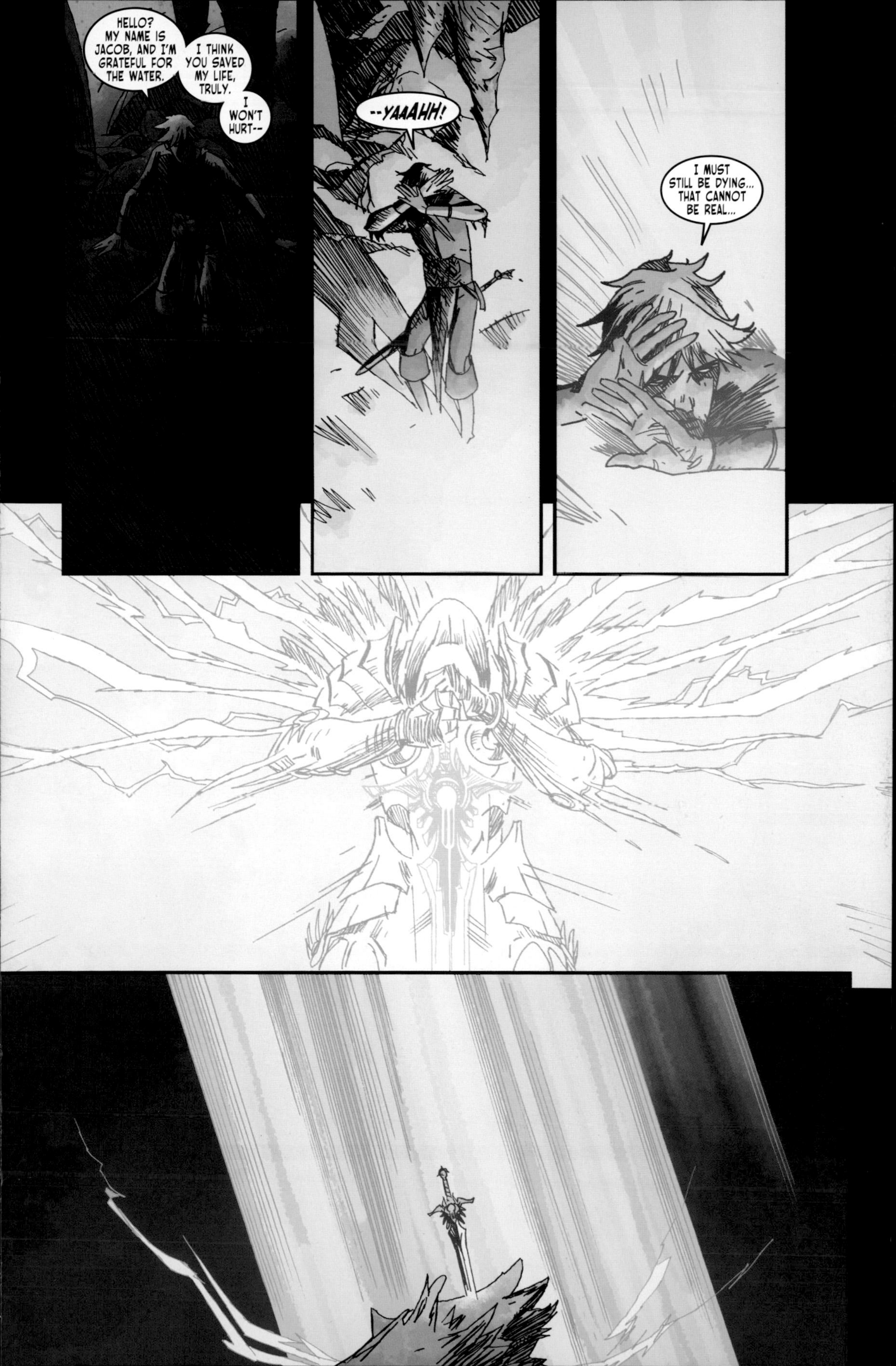
HELLO? MY NAME IS JACOB, AND I'M GRATEFUL FOR THE WATER.
I THINK YOU SAVED MY LIFE, TRULY.
I WON'T HURT--
--YAAAHH!
I MUST STILL BE DYING... THAT CANNOT BE REAL...

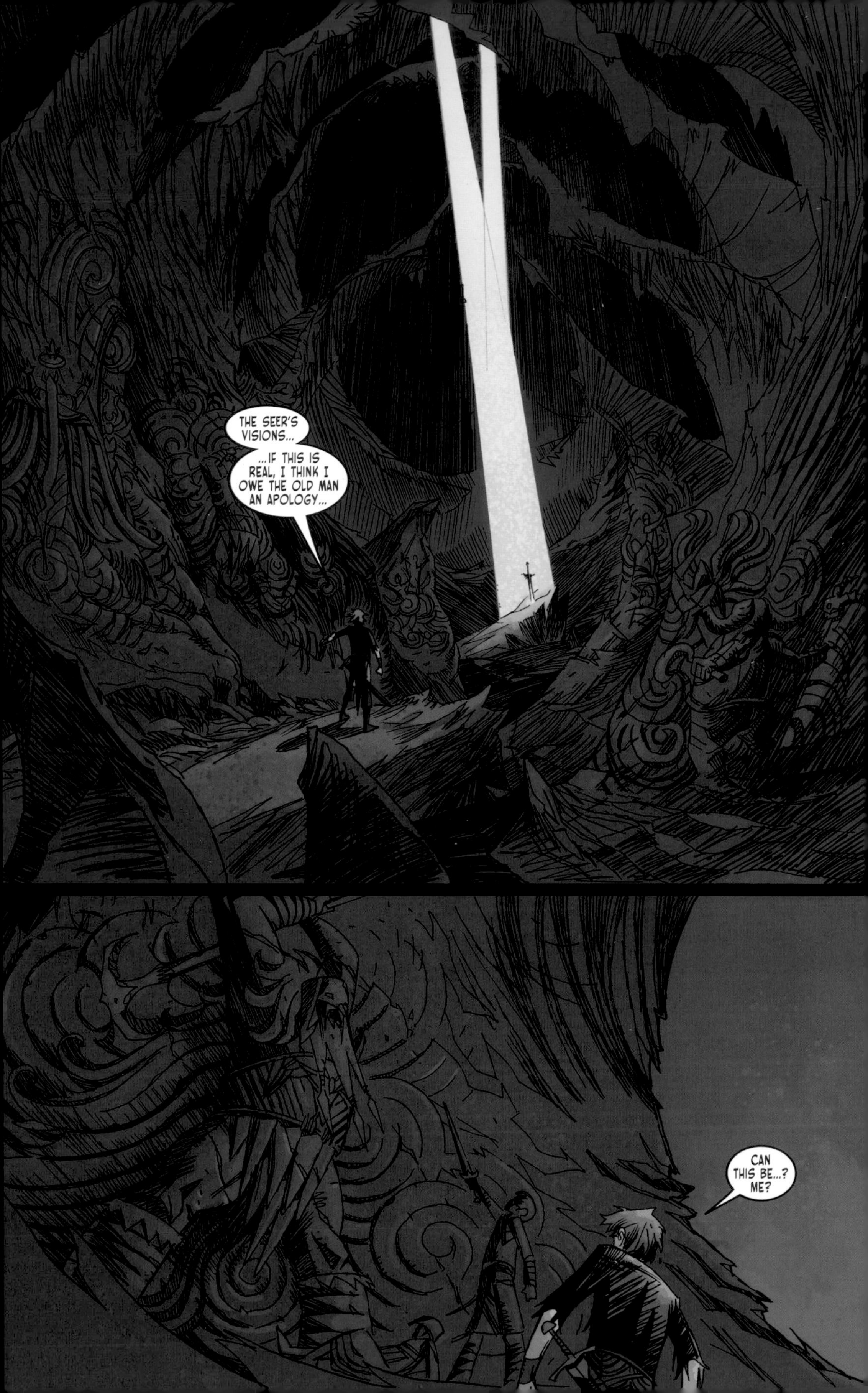
THE SEER'S VISIONS...
...IF THIS IS REAL, I THINK I OWE THE OLD MAN AN APOLOGY...
CAN THIS BE...? ME?

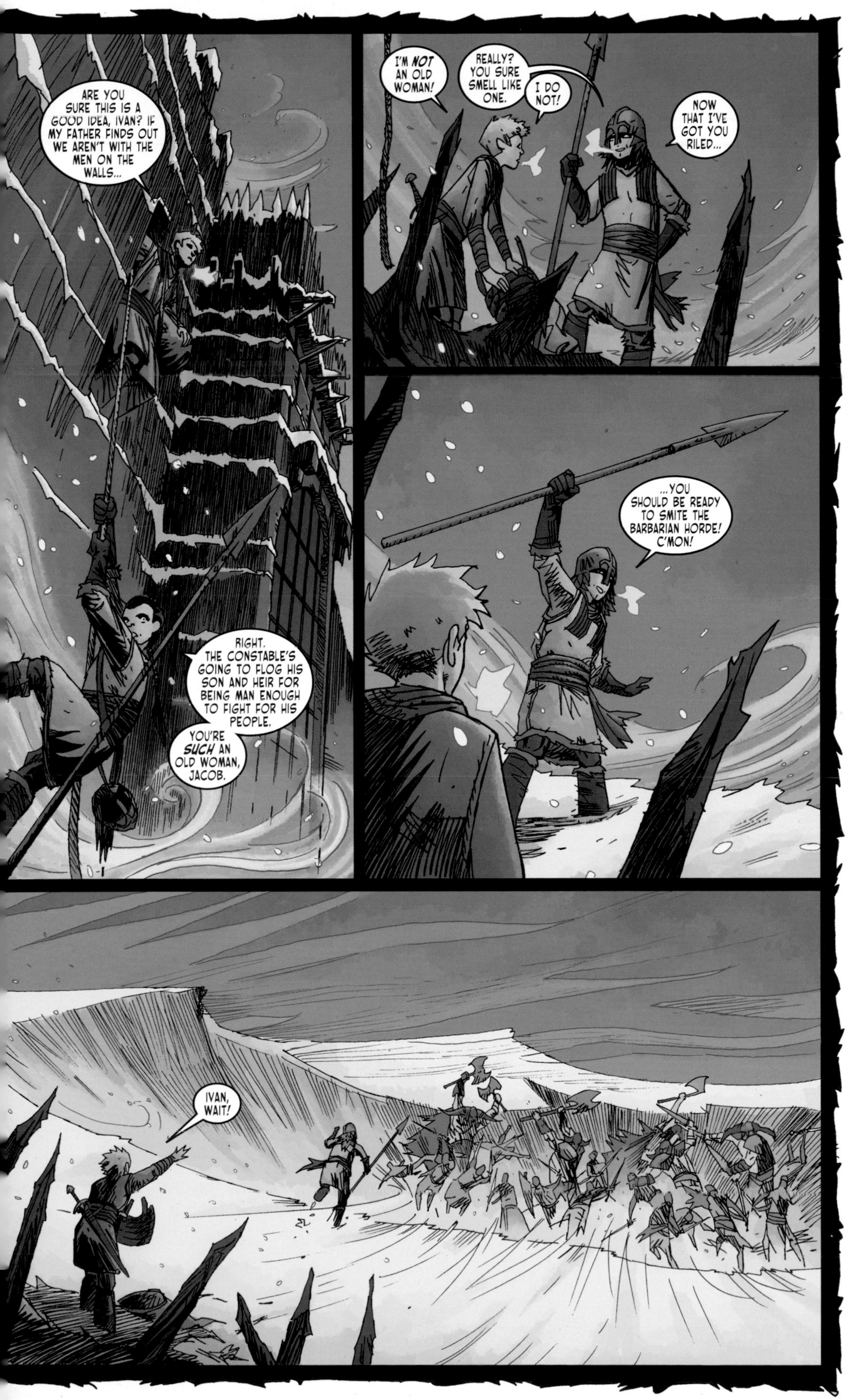
ARE YOU SURE THIS IS A GOOD IDEA, IVAN? IF MY FATHER FINDS OUT WE AREN'T WITH THE MEN ON THE WALLS...
RIGHT. THE CONSTABLE'S GOING TO FLOG HIS SON AND HEIR FOR BEING MAN ENOUGH TO FIGHT FOR HIS PEOPLE.
YOU'RE SUCH AN OLD WOMAN, JACOB.
I'M NOT AN OLD WOMAN!
REALLY? YOU SURE SMELL LIKE ONE.
I DO NOT!
NOW THAT I'VE GOT YOU RILED...
...YOU SHOULD BE READY TO SMITE THE BARBARIAN HORDE! C'MON!
IVAN, WAIT!

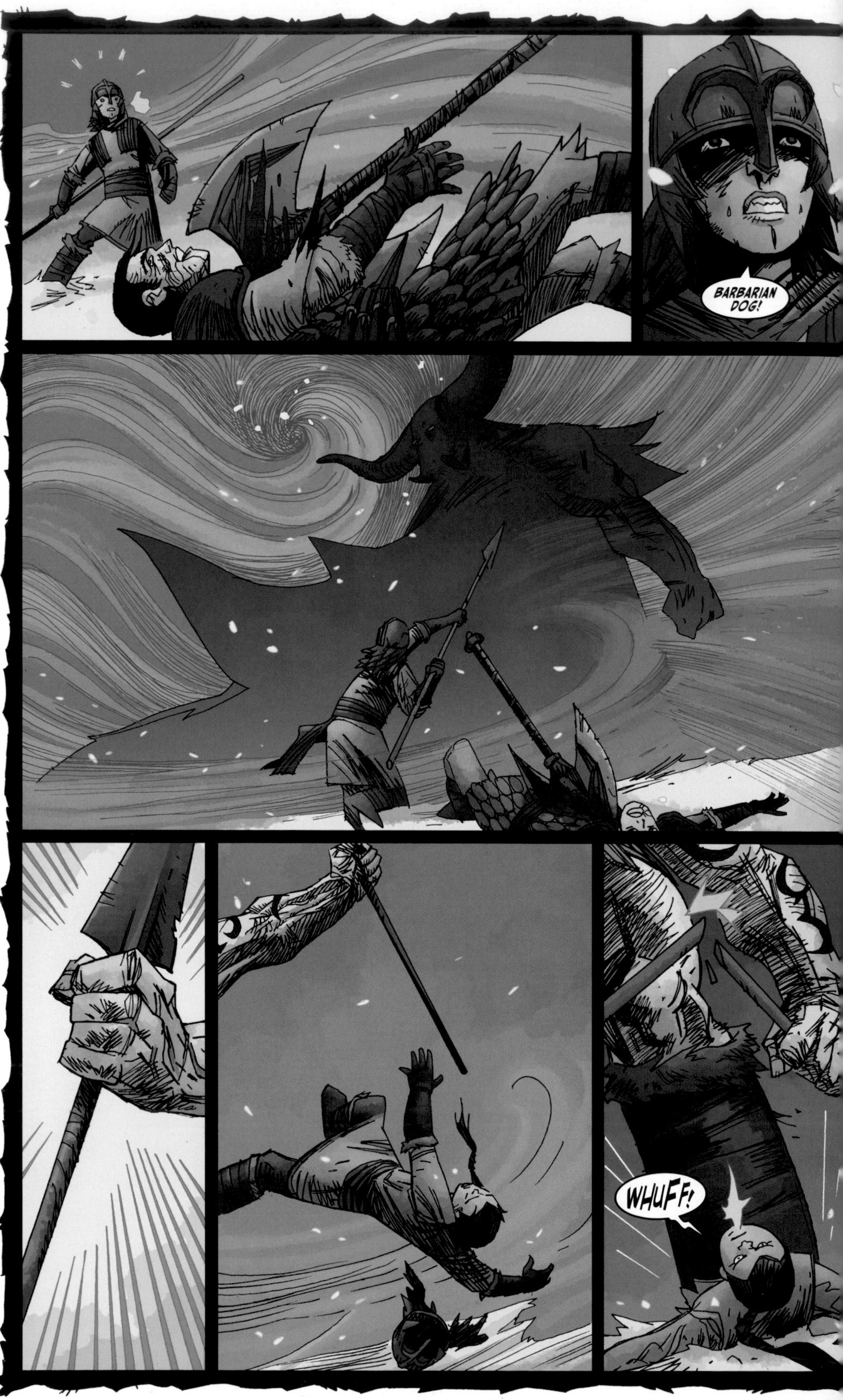
BARBARIAN DOG!
WHUFF!

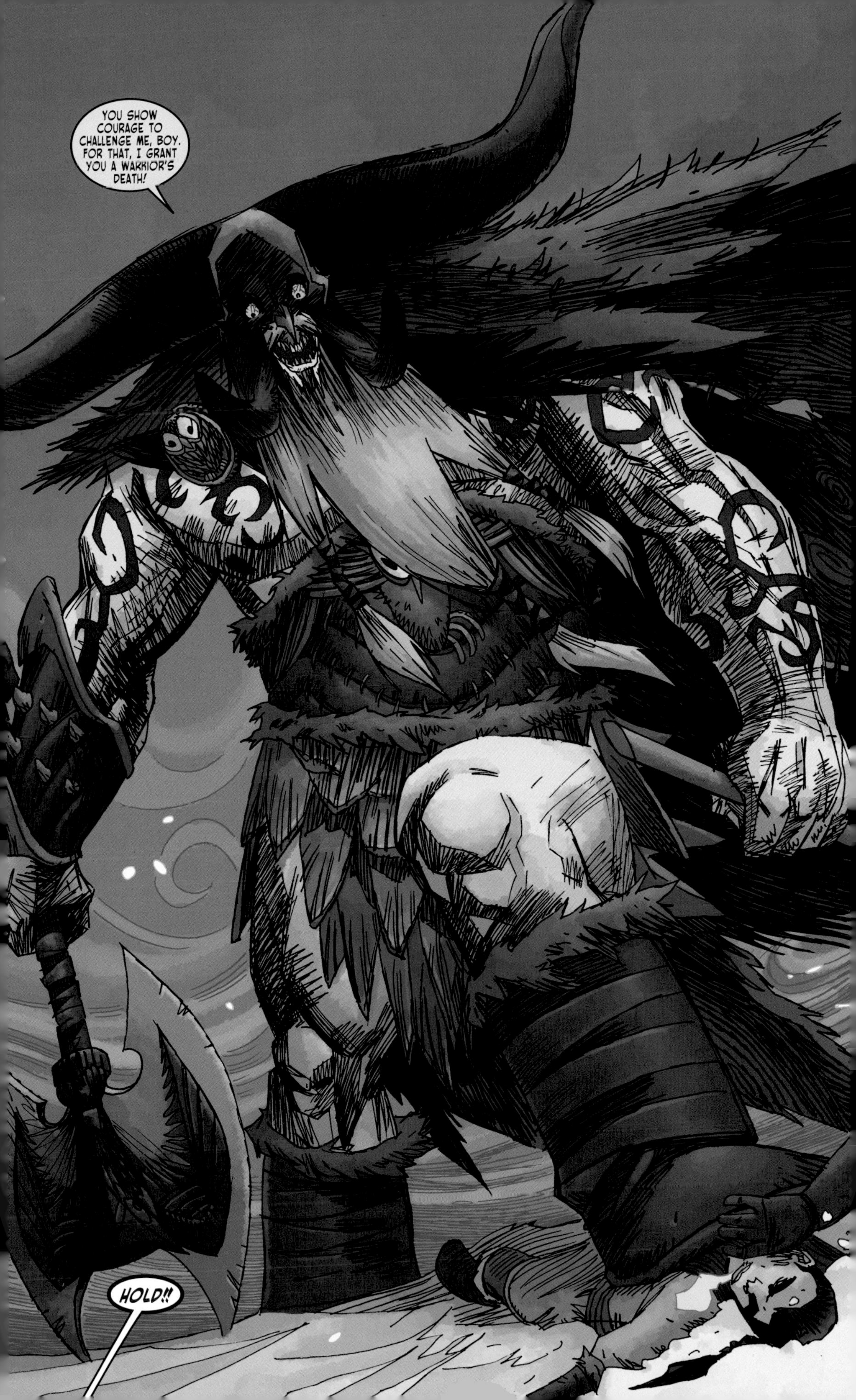
YOU SHOW COURAGE TO CHALLENGE ME, BOY. FOR THAT, I GRANT YOU A WARRIOR'S DEATH!
HOLD!!

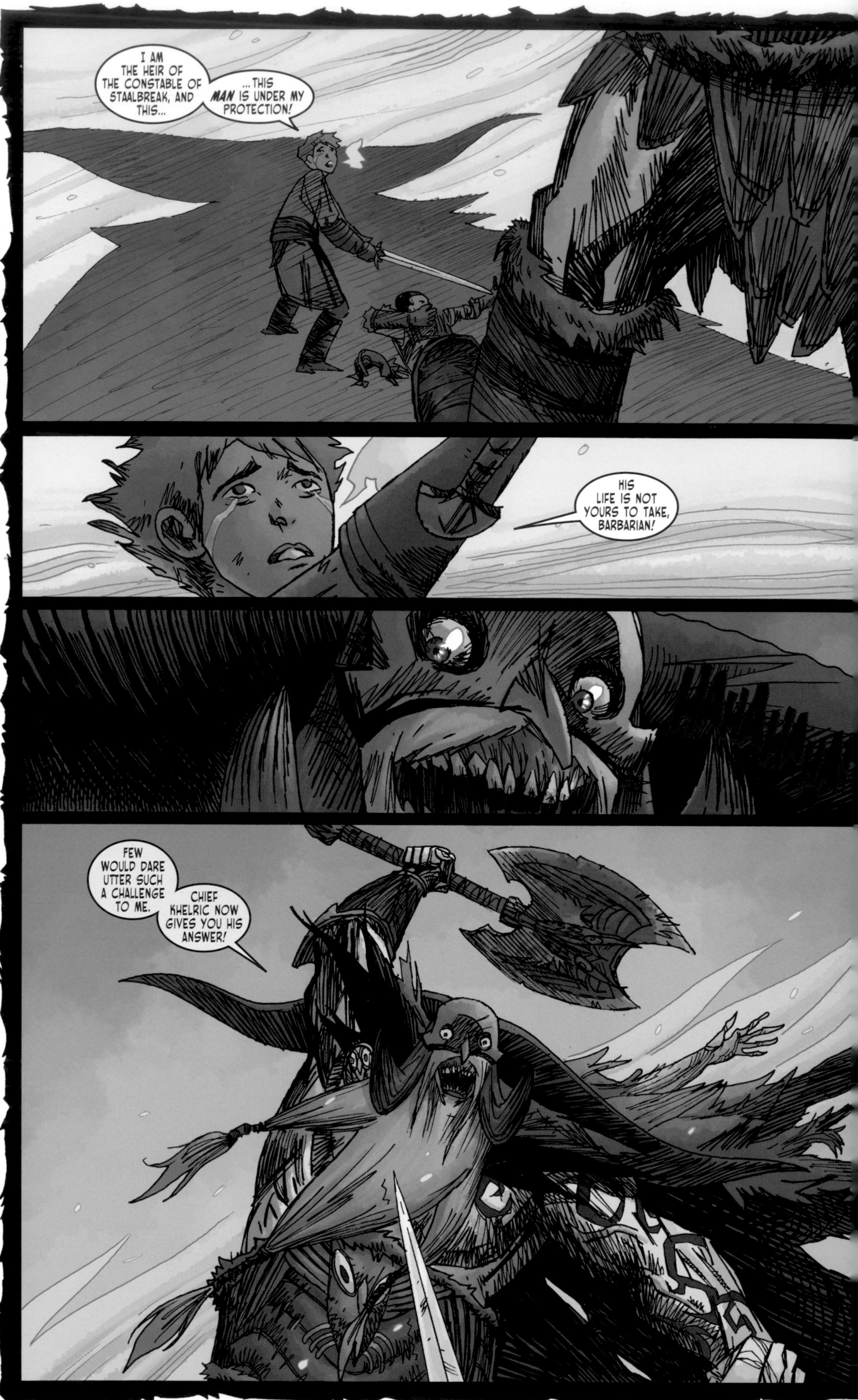
I AM THE HEIR OF THE CONSTABLE OF STAALBREAK, AND THIS...
...THIS MAN IS UNDER MY PROTECTION!
HIS LIFE IS NOT YOURS TO TAKE, BARBARIAN!
FEW WOULD DARE UTTER SUCH A CHALLENGE TO ME.
CHIEF KHELRIC NOW GIVES YOU HIS ANSWER!

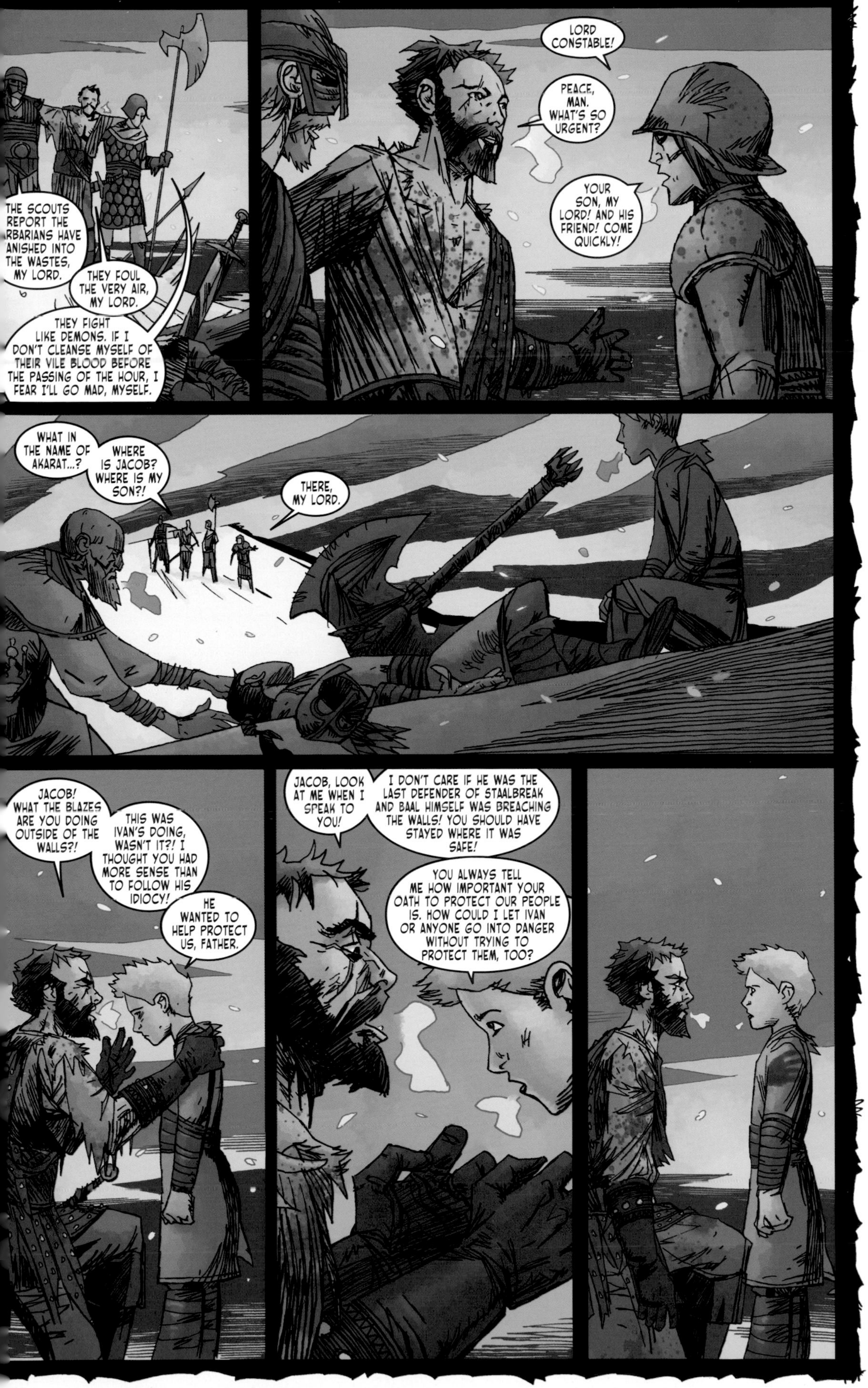
THE SCOUTS REPORT THE ARBARIANS HAVE ANISHED INTO THE WASTES, MY LORD.
THEY FOUL THE VERY AIR, MY LORD.
THEY FIGHT LIKE DEMONS. IF I DON'T CLEANSE MYSELF OF THEIR VILE BLOOD BEFORE THE PASSING OF THE HOUR, I FEAR I'LL GO MAD, MYSELF.
LORD CONSTABLE!
PEACE, MAN. WHAT'S SO URGENT?
YOUR SON, MY LORD! AND HIS FRIEND! COME QUICKLY!
WHAT IN THE NAME OF AKARAT...?
WHERE IS JACOB? WHERE IS MY SON?!
THERE, MY LORD.
JACOB! WHAT THE BLAZES ARE YOU DOING OUTSIDE OF THE WALLS?!
THIS WAS IVAN'S DOING, WASN'T IT?! I THOUGHT YOU HAD MORE SENSE THAN TO FOLLOW HIS IDIOCY!
HE WANTED TO HELP PROTECT US, FATHER.
JACOB, LOOK AT ME WHEN I SPEAK TO YOU!
I DON'T CARE IF HE WAS THE LAST DEFENDER OF STAALBREAK AND BAAL HIMSELF WAS BREACHING THE WALLS! YOU SHOULD HAVE STAYED WHERE IT WAS SAFE!
YOU ALWAYS TELL ME HOW IMPORTANT YOUR OATH TO PROTECT OUR PEOPLE IS. HOW COULD I LET IVAN OR ANYONE GO INTO DANGER WITHOUT TRYING TO PROTECT THEM, TOO?

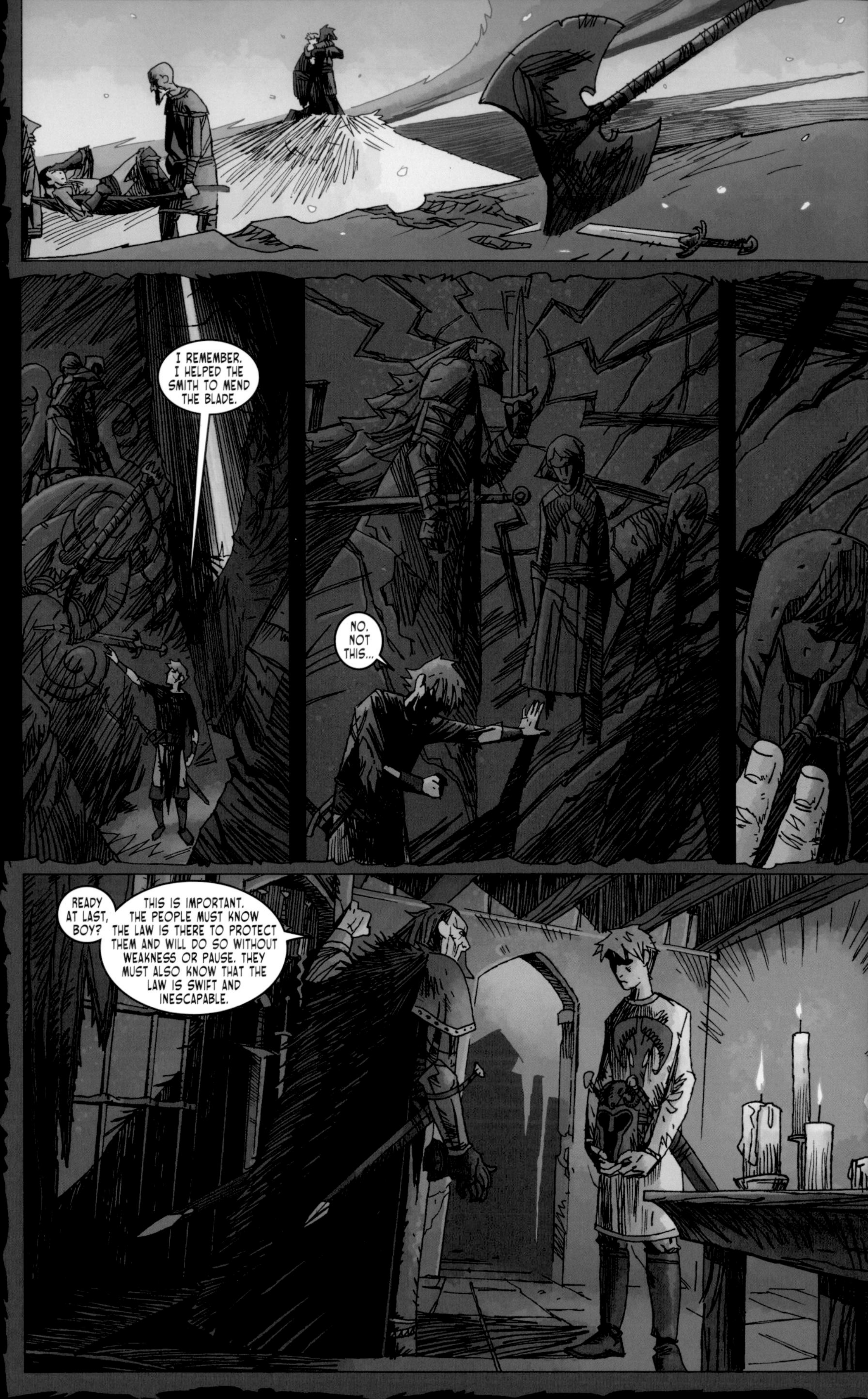
I REMEMBER. I HELPED THE SMITH TO MEND THE BLADE.
NO. NOT THIS...
READY AT LAST, BOY?
THIS IS IMPORTANT. THE PEOPLE MUST KNOW THE LAW IS THERE TO PROTECT THEM AND WILL DO SO WITHOUT WEAKNESS OR PAUSE. THEY MUST ALSO KNOW THAT THE LAW IS SWIFT AND INESCAPABLE.

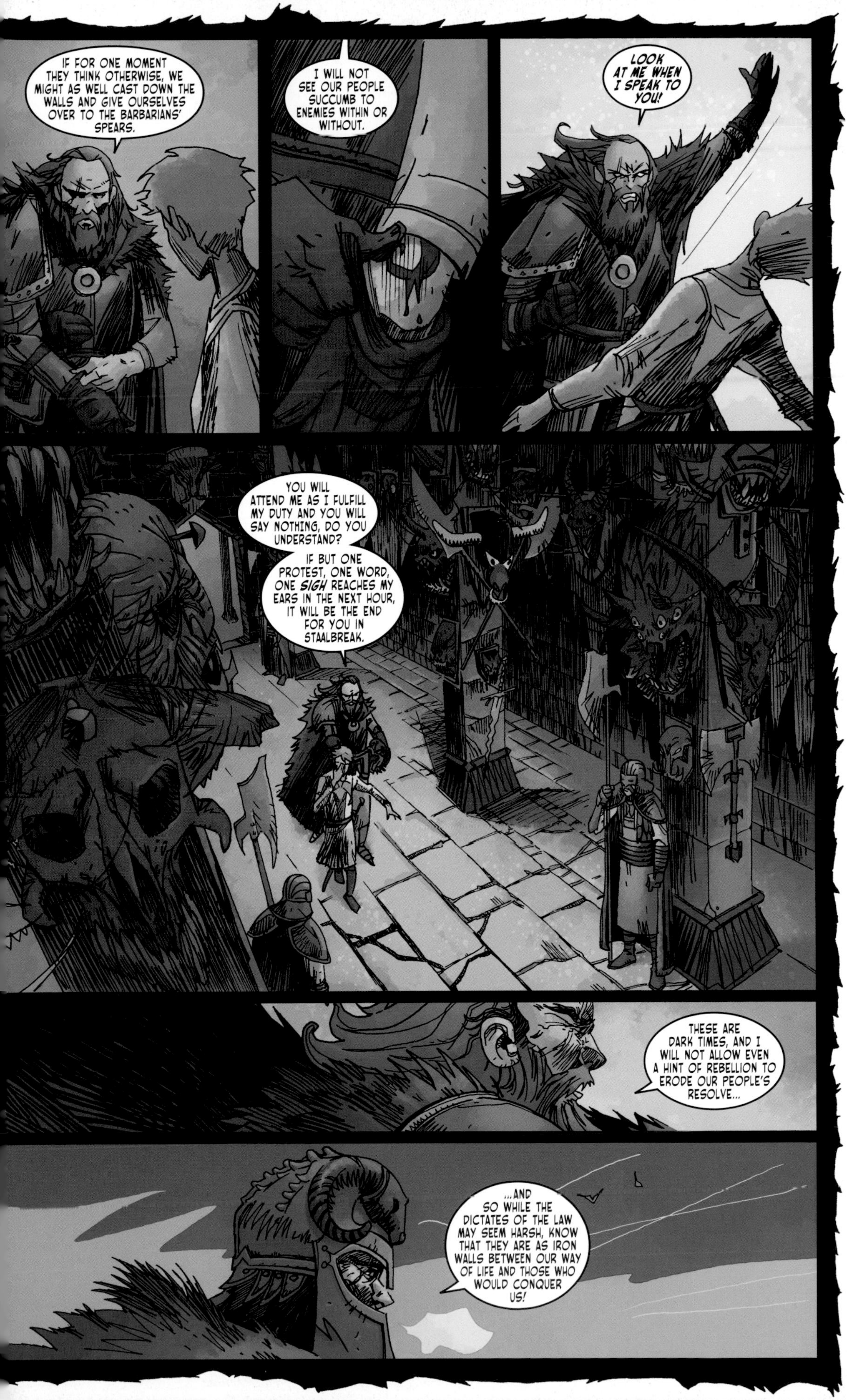
IF FOR ONE MOMENT THEY THINK OTHERWISE, WE MIGHT AS WELL CAST DOWN THE WALLS AND GIVE OURSELVES OVER TO THE BARBARIANS' SPEARS.
I WILL NOT SEE OUR PEOPLE SUCCUMB TO ENEMIES WITHIN OR WITHOUT.
LOOK AT ME WHEN I SPEAK TO YOU!
YOU WILL ATTEND ME AS I FULFILL MY DUTY AND YOU WILL SAY NOTHING, DO YOU UNDERSTAND?
IF BUT ONE PROTEST, ONE WORD, ONE SIGH REACHES MY EARS IN THE NEXT HOUR, IT WILL BE THE END FOR YOU IN STAALBREAK.
THESE ARE DARK TIMES, AND I WILL NOT ALLOW EVEN A HINT OF REBELLION TO ERODE OUR PEOPLE'S RESOLVE...
...AND SO WHILE THE DICTATES OF THE LAW MAY SEEM HARSH, KNOW THAT THEY ARE AS IRON WALLS BETWEEN OUR WAY OF LIFE AND THOSE WHO WOULD CONQUER US!

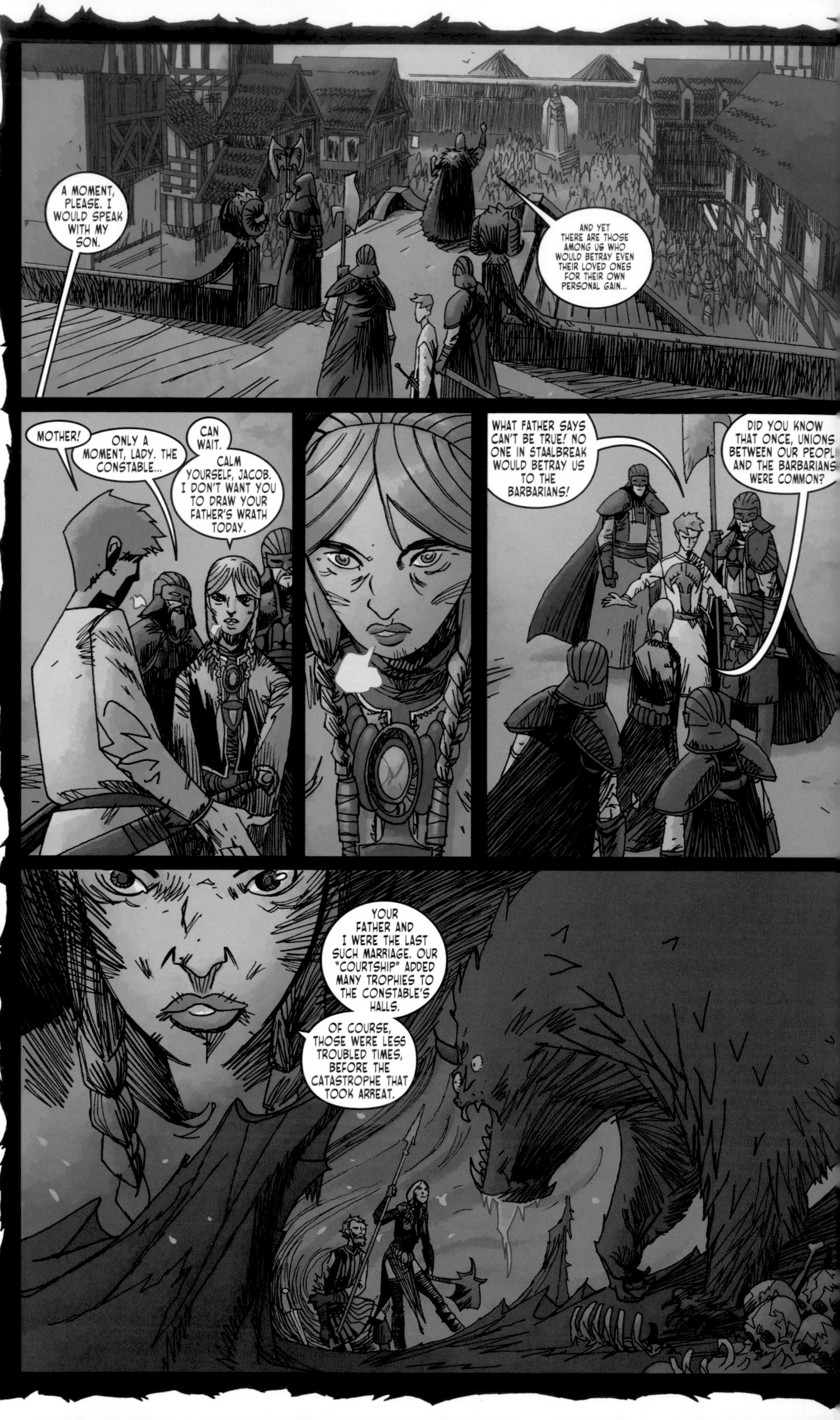
A MOMENT, PLEASE. I WOULD SPEAK WITH MY SON.
AND YET THERE ARE THOSE AMONG US WHO WOULD BETRAY EVEN THEIR LOVED ONES FOR THEIR OWN PERSONAL GAIN...
MOTHER!
ONLY A MOMENT, LADY. THE CONSTABLE...
CAN WAIT.
CALM YOURSELF, JACOB. I DON'T WANT YOU TO DRAW YOUR FATHER'S WRATH TODAY.
WHAT FATHER SAYS CAN'T BE TRUE! NO ONE IN STAALBREAK WOULD BETRAY US TO THE BARBARIANS!
DID YOU KNOW THAT ONCE, UNIONS BETWEEN OUR PEOPL AND THE BARBARIANS WERE COMMON?
YOUR FATHER AND I WERE THE LAST SUCH MARRIAGE. OUR "COURTSHIP" ADDED MANY TROPHIES TO THE CONSTABLE'S HALLS.
OF COURSE, THOSE WERE LESS TROUBLED TIMES, BEFORE THE CATASTROPHE THAT TOOK ARREAT.

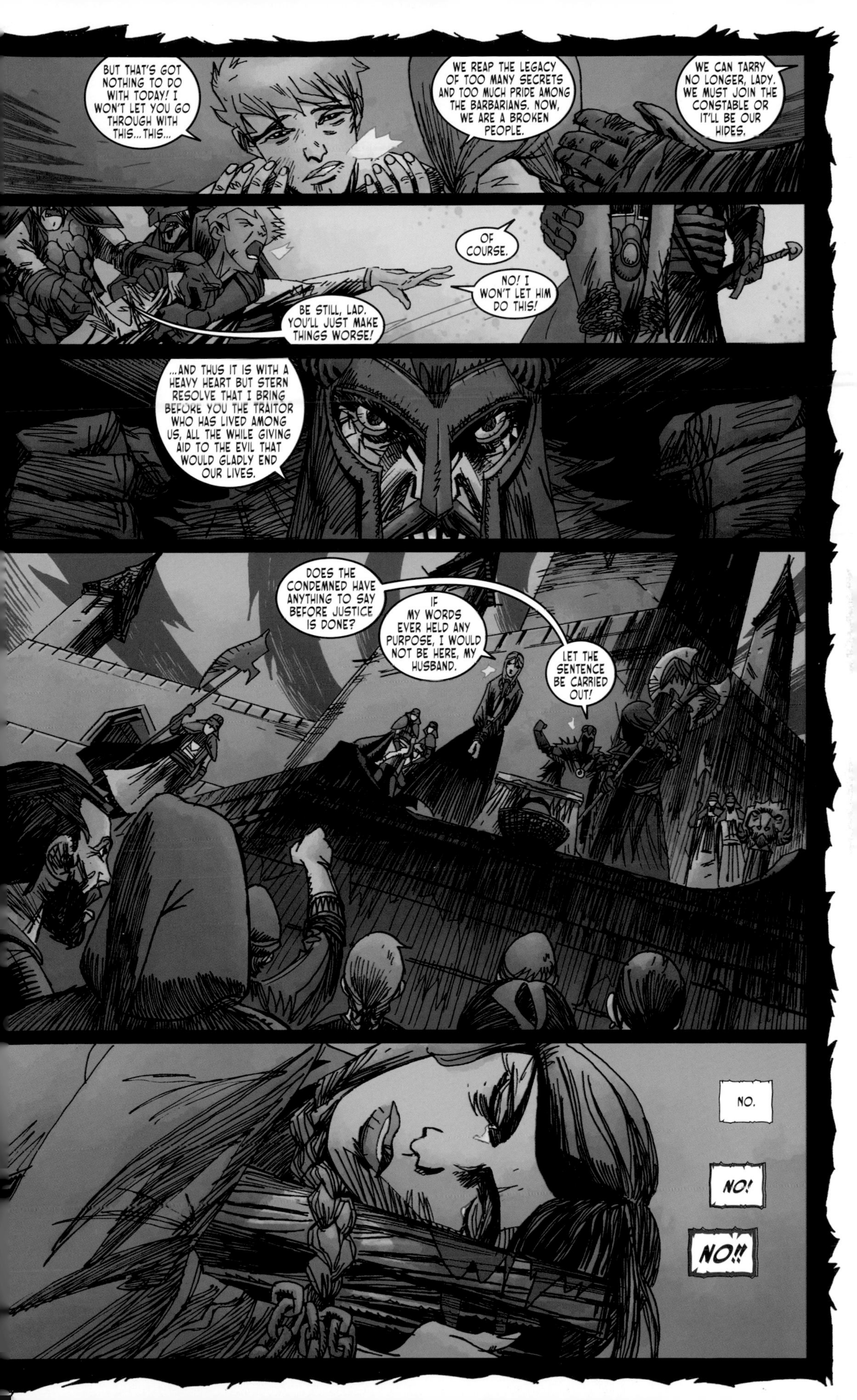
BUT THAT'S GOT NOTHING TO DO WITH TODAY! I WON'T LET YOU GO THROUGH WITH THIS... THIS...
WE REAP THE LEGACY OF TOO MANY SECRETS AND TOO MUCH PRIDE AMONG THE BARBARIANS. NOW, WE ARE A BROKEN PEOPLE.
WE CAN TARRY NO LONGER, LADY. WE MUST JOIN THE CONSTABLE OR IT'LL BE OUR HIDES.
OF COURSE.
NO! I WON'T LET HIM DO THIS!
BE STILL, LAD. YOU'LL JUST MAKE THINGS WORSE!
...AND THUS IT IS WITH A HEAVY HEART BUT STERN RESOLVE THAT I BRING BEFORE YOU THE TRAITOR WHO HAS LIVED AMONG US, ALL THE WHILE GIVING AID TO THE EVIL THAT WOULD GLADLY END OUR LIVES.
DOES THE CONDEMNED HAVE ANYTHING TO SAY BEFORE JUSTICE IS DONE?
IF MY WORDS EVER HELD ANY PURPOSE, I WOULD NOT BE HERE, MY HUSBAND.
LET THE SENTENCE BE CARRIED OUT!
NO.
NO!
NO!!

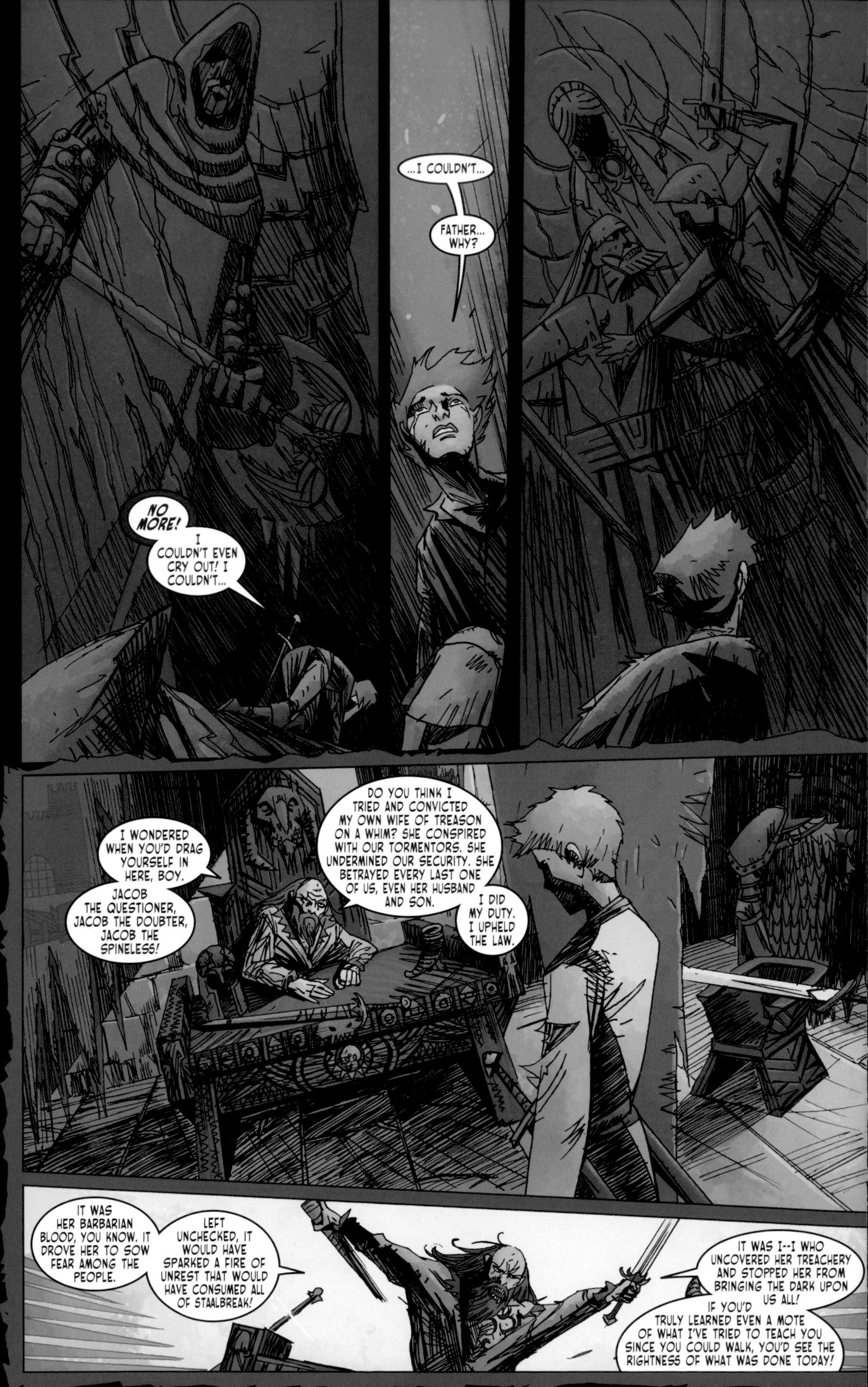

NO MORE!
I COULDN'T EVEN CRY OUT! I COULDN'T...
...I COULDN'T...
FATHER... WHY?
I WONDERED WHEN YOU'D DRAG YOURSELF IN HERE, BOY.
JACOB THE QUESTIONER, JACOB THE DOUBTER, JACOB THE SPINELESS!
DO YOU THINK I TRIED AND CONVICTED MY OWN WIFE OF TREASON ON A WHIM? SHE CONSPIRED WITH OUR TORMENTORS. SHE UNDERMINED OUR SECURITY. SHE BETRAYED EVERY LAST ONE OF US, EVEN HER HUSBAND AND SON.
I DID MY DUTY. I UPHELD THE LAW.
IT WAS HER BARBARIAN BLOOD, YOU KNOW. IT DROVE HER TO SOW FEAR AMONG THE PEOPLE.
LEFT UNCHECKED, IT WOULD HAVE SPARKED A FIRE OF UNREST THAT WOULD HAVE CONSUMED ALL OF STAALBREAK!
IT WAS I--I WHO UNCOVERED HER TREACHERY AND STOPPED HER FROM BRINGING THE DARK UPON US ALL!
IF YOU'D TRULY LEARNED EVEN A MOTE OF WHAT I'VE TRIED TO TEACH YOU SINCE YOU COULD WALK, YOU'D SEE THE RIGHTNESS OF WHAT WAS DONE TODAY!

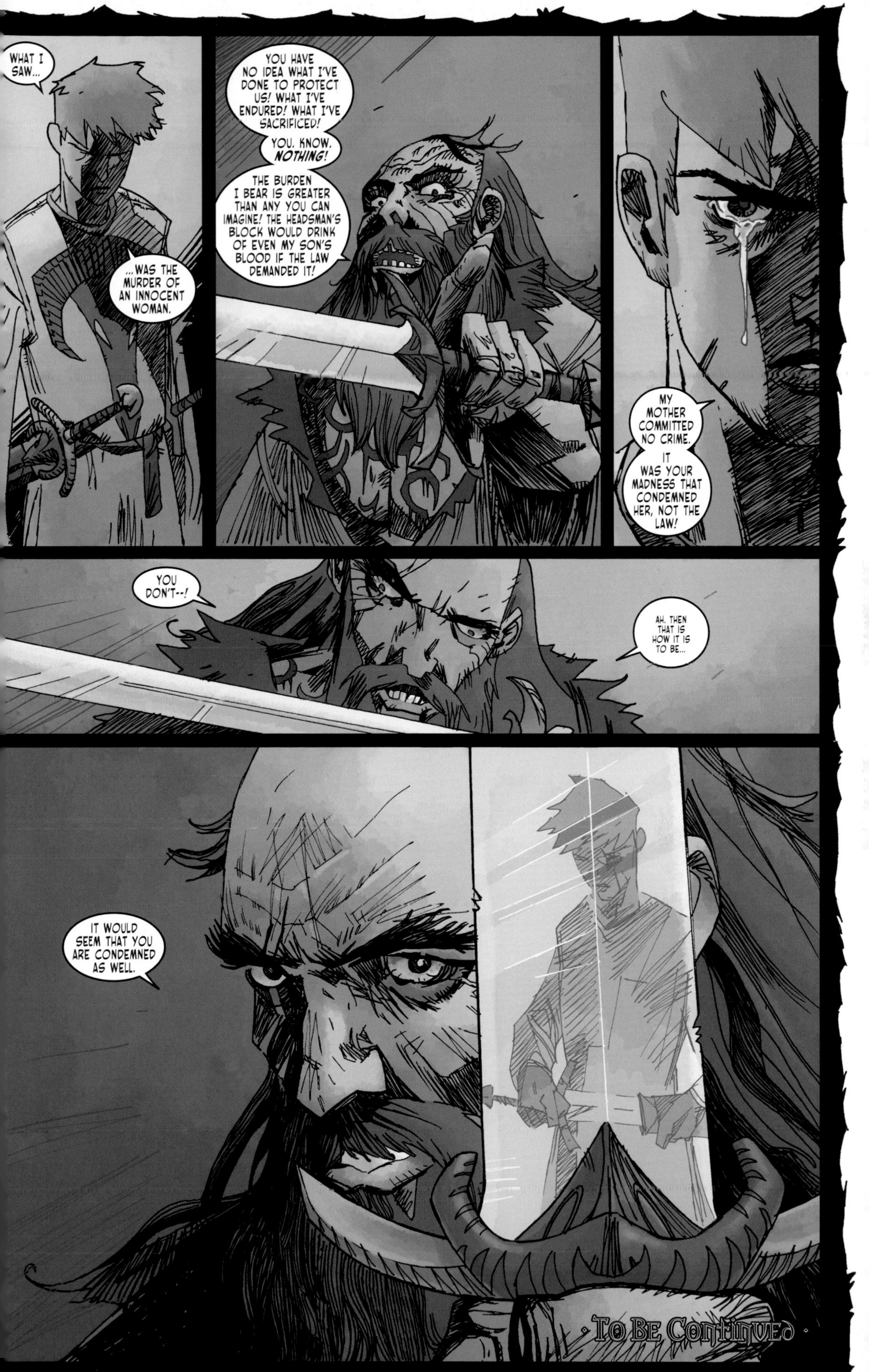
WHAT I SAW...
...WAS THE MURDER OF AN INNOCENT WOMAN.
YOU HAVE NO IDEA WHAT I'VE DONE TO PROTECT US! WHAT I'VE ENDURED! WHAT I'VE SACRIFICED!
YOU. KNOW. NOTHING!
THE BURDEN I BEAR IS GREATER THAN ANY YOU CAN IMAGINE! THE HEADSMAN'S BLOCK WOULD DRINK OF EVEN MY SON'S BLOOD IF THE LAW DEMANDED IT!
MY MOTHER COMMITTED NO CRIME.
IT WAS YOUR MADNESS THAT CONDEMNED HER, NOT THE LAW!
YOU DON'T--!
AH. THEN THAT IS HOW IT IS TO BE...
IT WOULD SEEM THAT YOU ARE CONDEMNED AS WELL.
TO BE CONTINUED

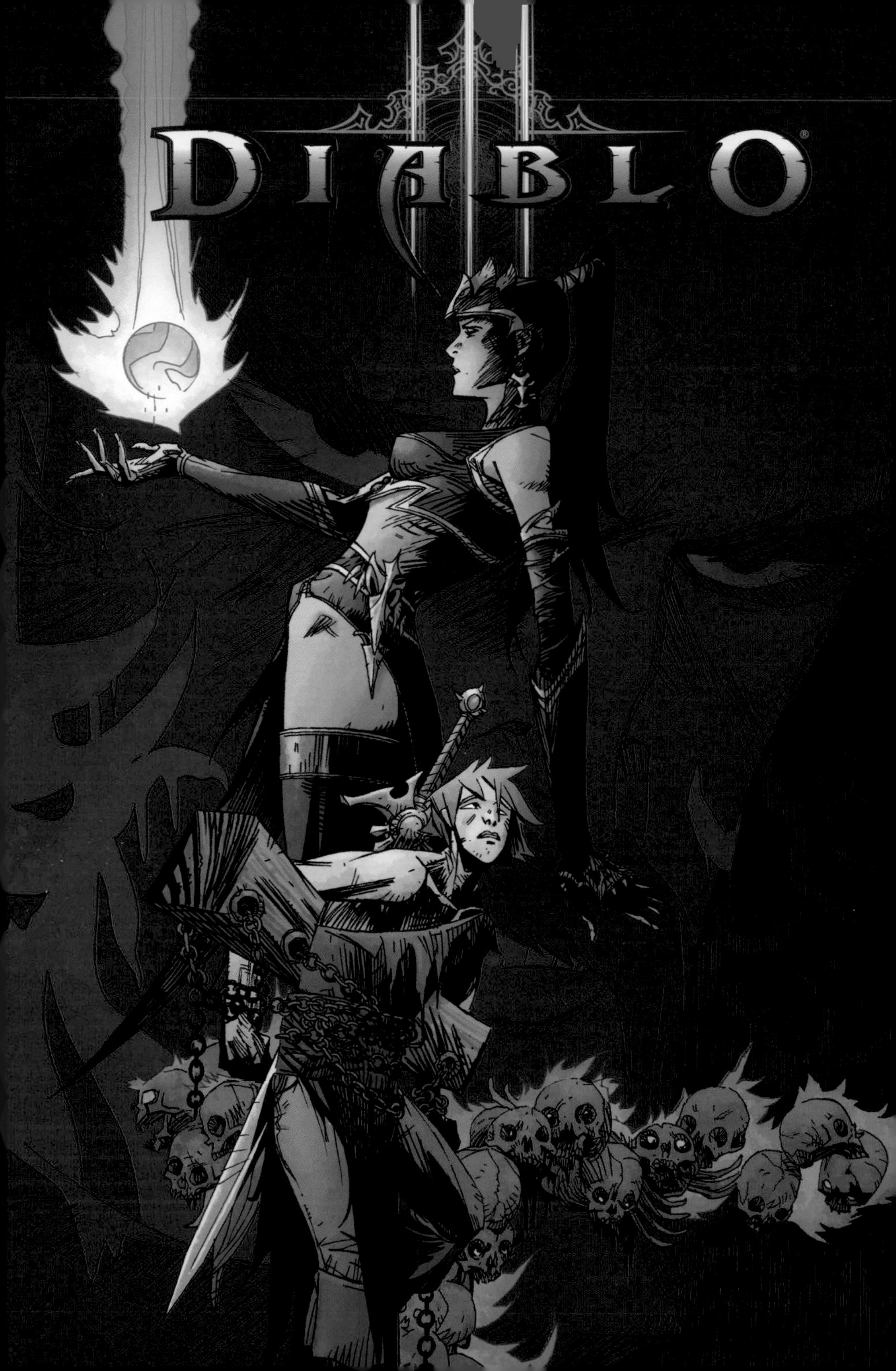
DIABLO

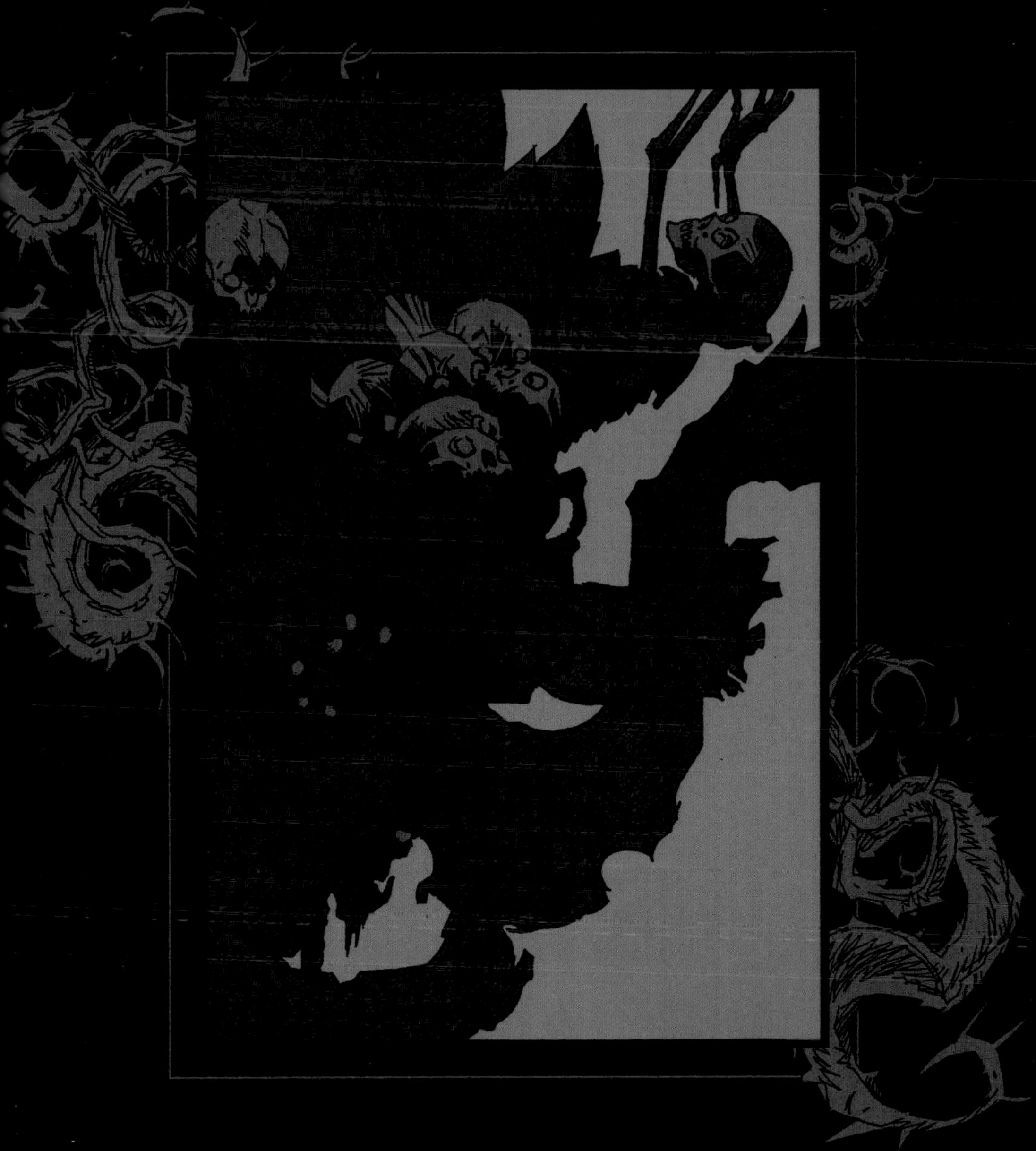

ACT II

AARON WILLIAMS
JOSEPH LACROIX
DAVE STEWART

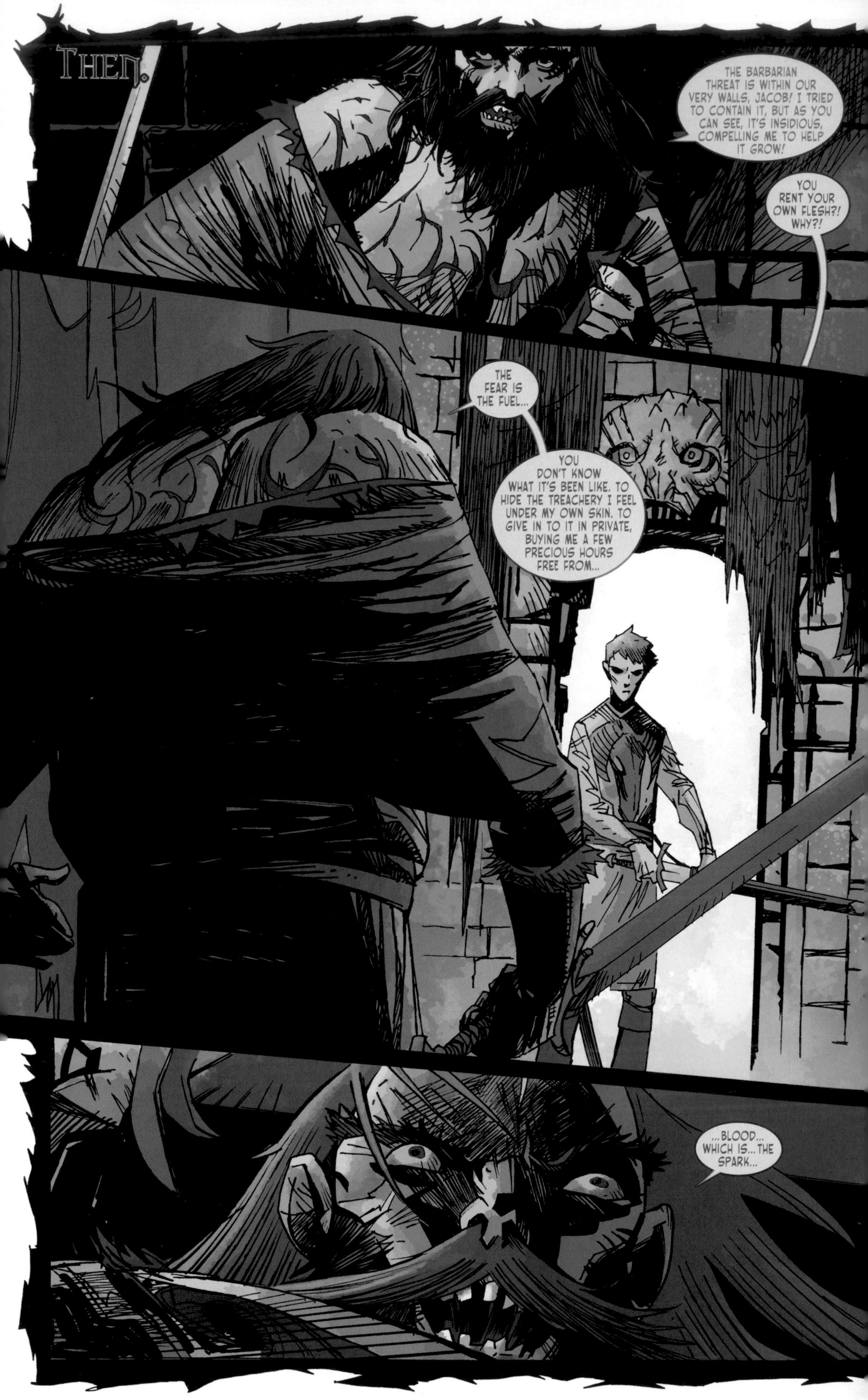
THEN.
THE BARBARIAN THREAT IS WITHIN OUR VERY WALLS, JACOB! I TRIED TO CONTAIN IT, BUT AS YOU CAN SEE, IT'S INSIDIOUS, COMPELLING ME TO HELP IT GROW!
YOU RENT YOUR OWN FLESH?! WHY?!
THE FEAR IS THE FUEL...
YOU DON'T KNOW WHAT IT'S BEEN LIKE. TO HIDE THE TREACHERY I FEEL UNDER MY OWN SKIN. TO GIVE IN TO IT IN PRIVATE, BUYING ME A FEW PRECIOUS HOURS FREE FROM...
...BLOOD... WHICH IS... THE SPARK...

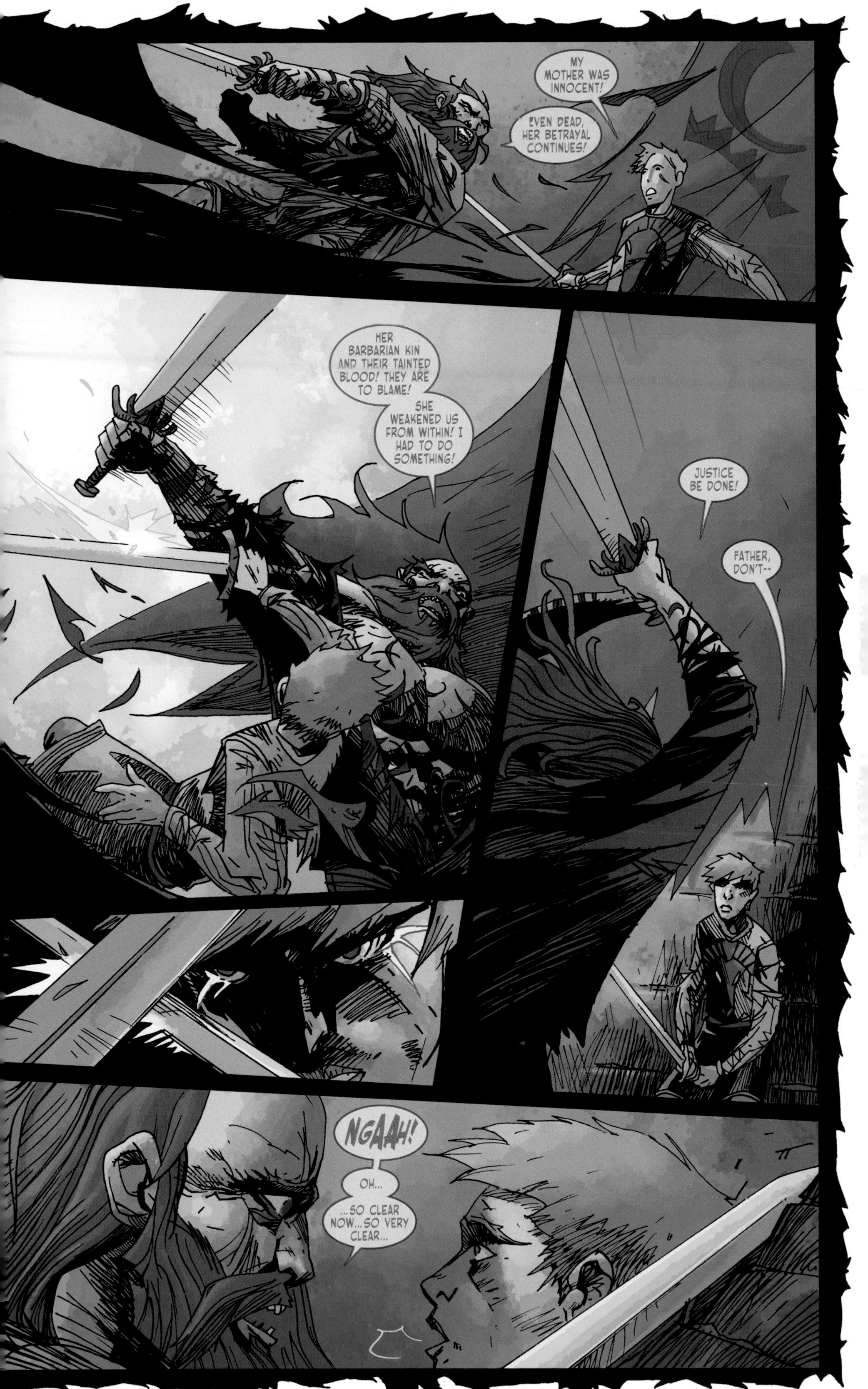

MY MOTHER WAS INNOCENT!
EVEN DEAD, HER BETRAYAL CONTINUES!
HER BARBARIAN KIN AND THEIR TAINTED BLOOD! THEY ARE TO BLAME!
SHE WEAKENED US FROM WITHIN! I HAD TO DO SOMETHING!
JUSTICE BE DONE!
FATHER, DON'T--
NGAAH!
OH...
...SO CLEAR NOW...SO VERY CLEAR...

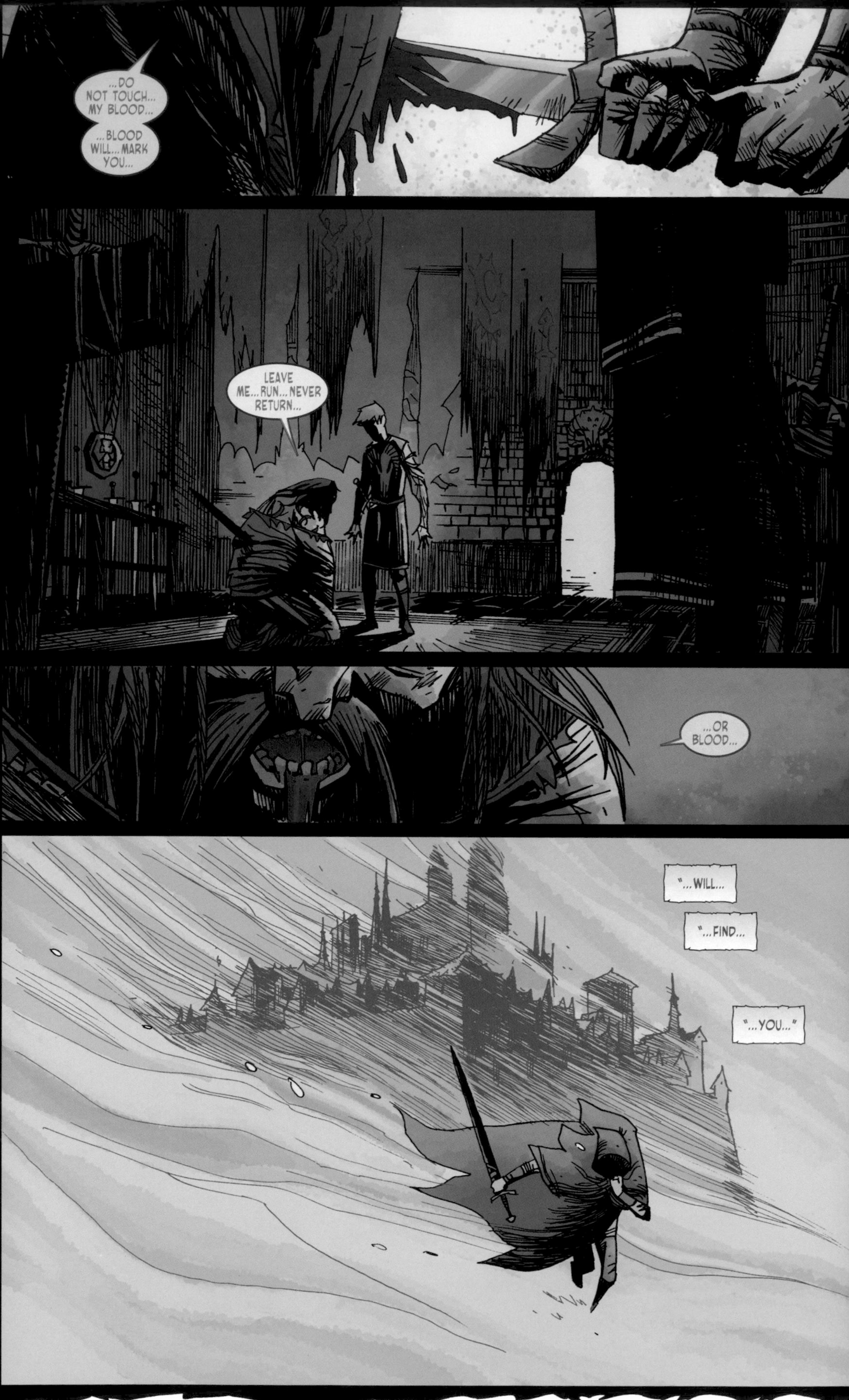
...DO NOT TOUCH... MY BLOOD...
...BLOOD WILL... MARK YOU...
LEAVE ME... RUN... NEVER RETURN...
...OR BLOOD...
"...WILL...
"...FIND...
"...YOU..."

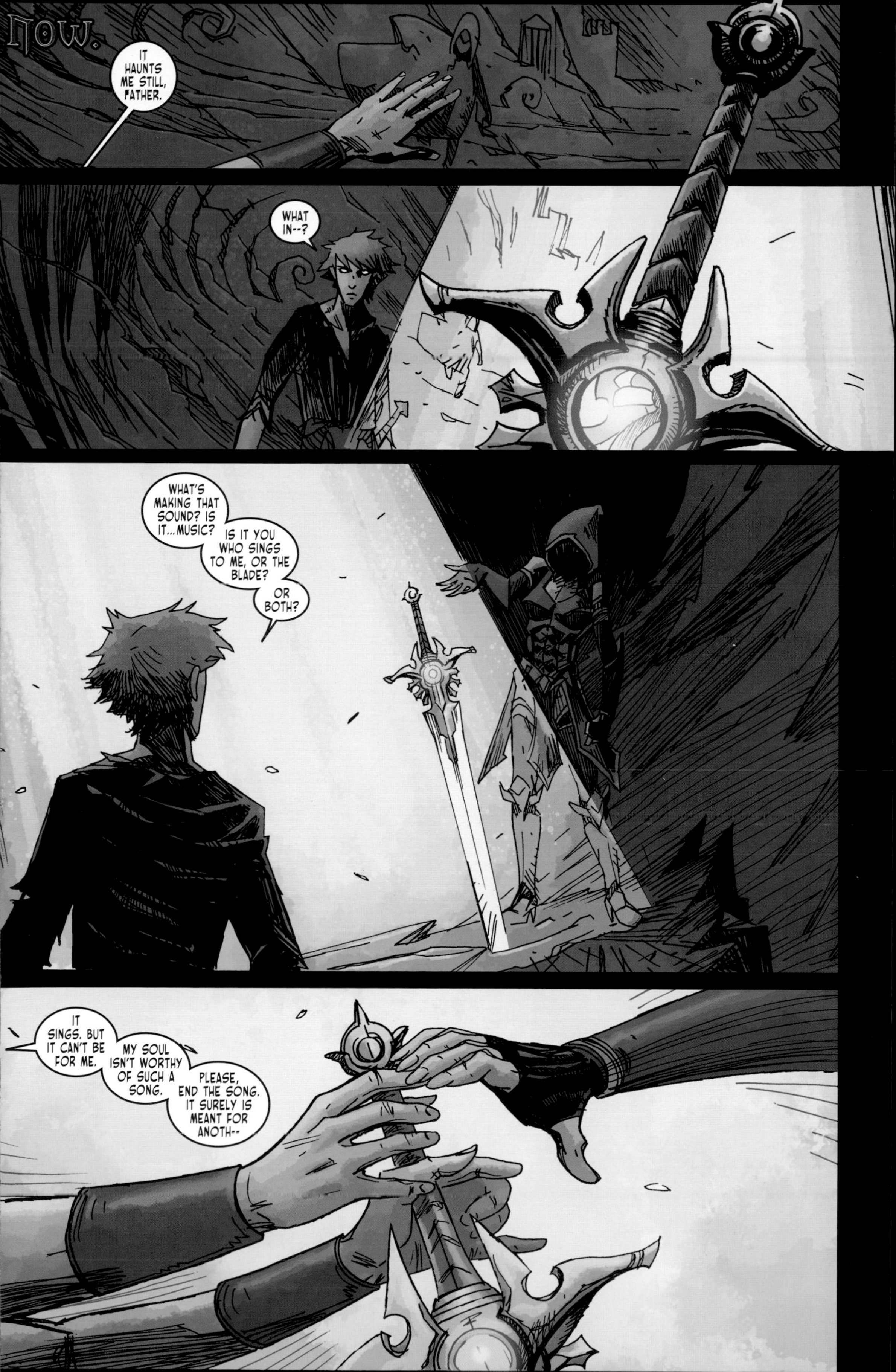
Now.
IT HAUNTS ME STILL, FATHER.
WHAT IN--?
WHAT'S MAKING THAT SOUND? IS IT...MUSIC?
IS IT YOU WHO SINGS TO ME, OR THE BLADE?
OR BOTH?
IT SINGS. BUT IT CAN'T BE FOR ME.
MY SOUL ISN'T WORTHY OF SUCH A SONG.
PLEASE, END THE SONG. IT SURELY IS MEANT FOR ANOTH--

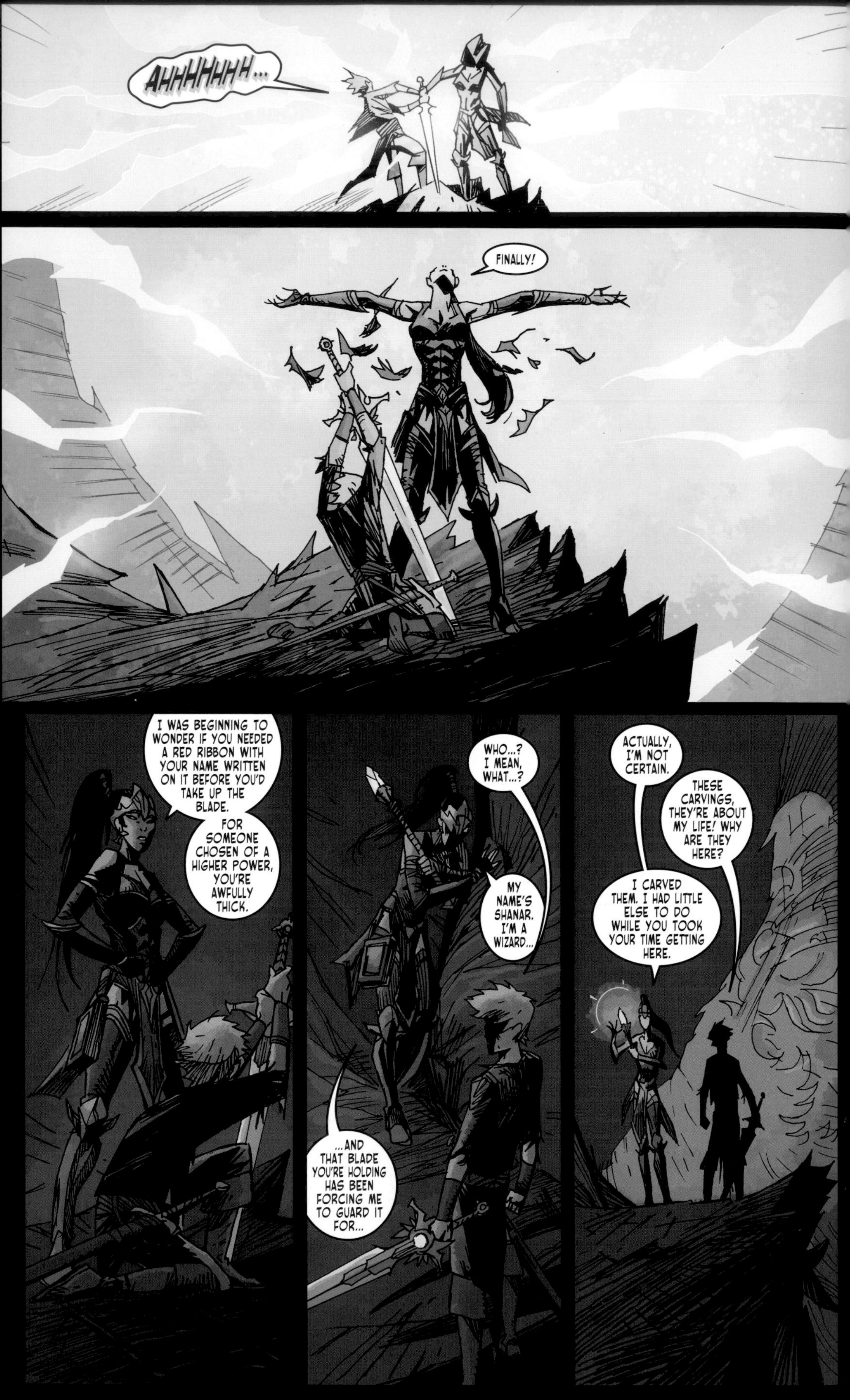
AHHHHHHH...
FINALLY!
I WAS BEGINNING TO WONDER IF YOU NEEDED A RED RIBBON WITH YOUR NAME WRITTEN ON IT BEFORE YOU'D TAKE UP THE BLADE.
FOR SOMEONE CHOSEN OF A HIGHER POWER, YOU'RE AWFULLY THICK.
WHO...? I MEAN, WHAT...?
MY NAME'S SHANAR. I'M A WIZARD...
...AND THAT BLADE YOU'RE HOLDING HAS BEEN FORCING ME TO GUARD IT FOR...
ACTUALLY, I'M NOT CERTAIN.
THESE CARVINGS, THEY'RE ABOUT MY LIFE! WHY ARE THEY HERE?
I CARVED THEM. I HAD LITTLE ELSE TO DO WHILE YOU TOOK YOUR TIME GETTING HERE.

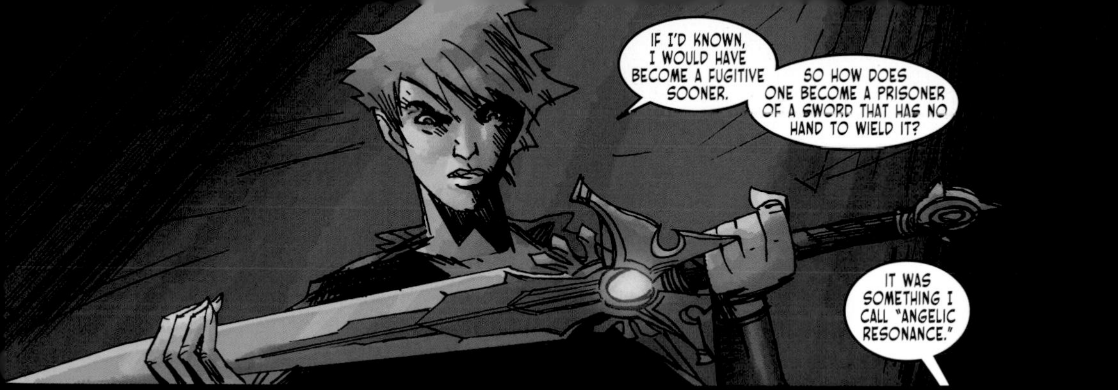
IF I'D KNOWN, I WOULD HAVE BECOME A FUGITIVE SOONER.
SO HOW DOES ONE BECOME A PRISONER OF A SWORD THAT HAS NO HAND TO WIELD IT?
IT WAS SOMETHING I CALL "ANGELIC RESONANCE."

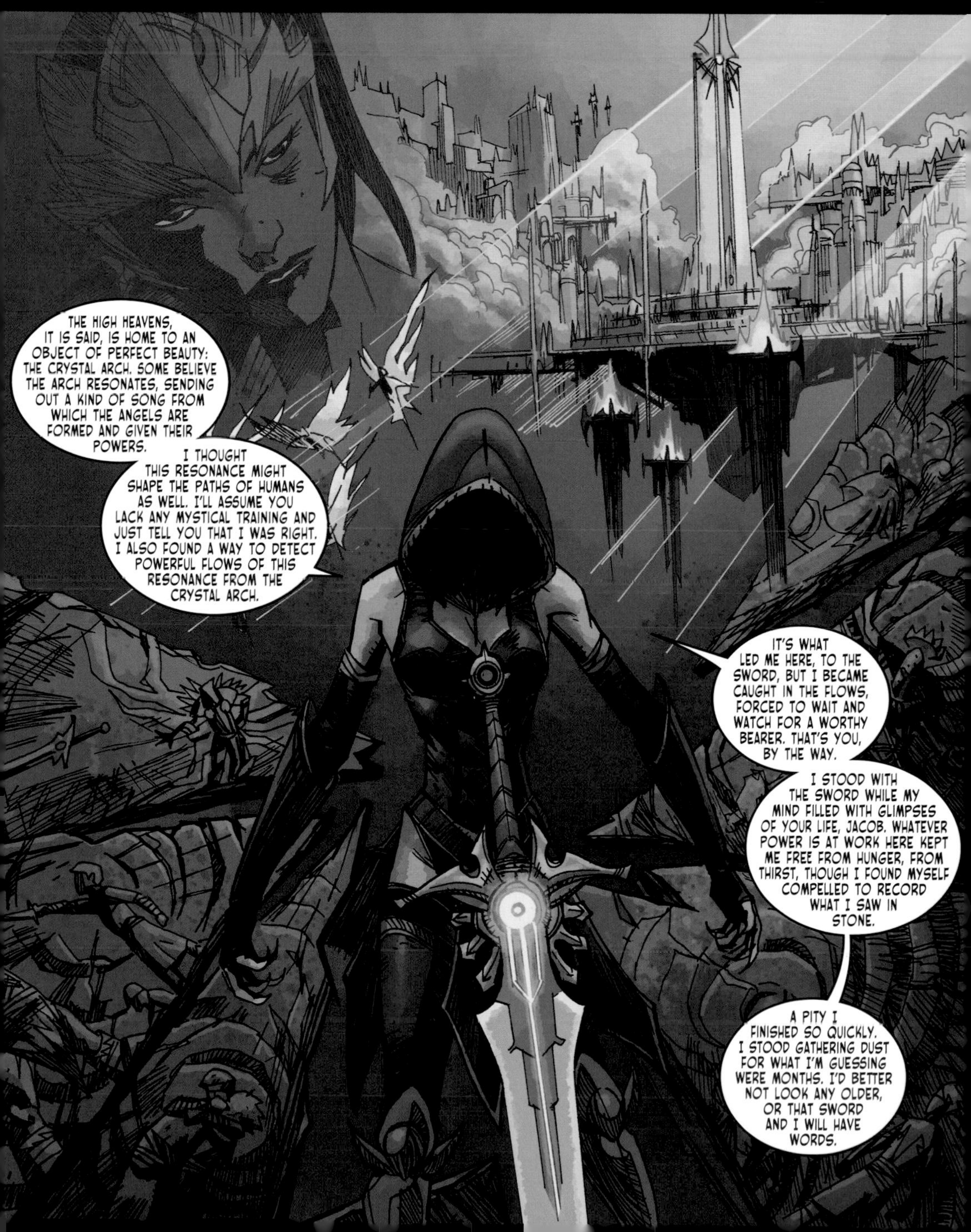
THE HIGH HEAVENS, IT IS SAID, IS HOME TO AN OBJECT OF PERFECT BEAUTY: THE CRYSTAL ARCH. SOME BELIEVE THE ARCH RESONATES, SENDING OUT A KIND OF SONG FROM WHICH THE ANGELS ARE FORMED AND GIVEN THEIR POWERS.
I THOUGHT THIS RESONANCE MIGHT SHAPE THE PATHS OF HUMANS AS WELL. I'LL ASSUME YOU LACK ANY MYSTICAL TRAINING AND JUST TELL YOU THAT I WAS RIGHT. I ALSO FOUND A WAY TO DETECT POWERFUL FLOWS OF THIS RESONANCE FROM THE CRYSTAL ARCH.
IT'S WHAT LED ME HERE, TO THE SWORD, BUT I BECAME CAUGHT IN THE FLOWS, FORCED TO WAIT AND WATCH FOR A WORTHY BEARER. THAT'S YOU, BY THE WAY.
I STOOD WITH THE SWORD WHILE MY MIND FILLED WITH GLIMPSES OF YOUR LIFE, JACOB. WHATEVER POWER IS AT WORK HERE KEPT ME FREE FROM HUNGER, FROM THIRST, THOUGH I FOUND MYSELF COMPELLED TO RECORD WHAT I SAW IN STONE.
A PITY I FINISHED SO QUICKLY. I STOOD GATHERING DUST FOR WHAT I'M GUESSING WERE MONTHS. I'D BETTER NOT LOOK ANY OLDER, OR THAT SWORD AND I WILL HAVE WORDS.

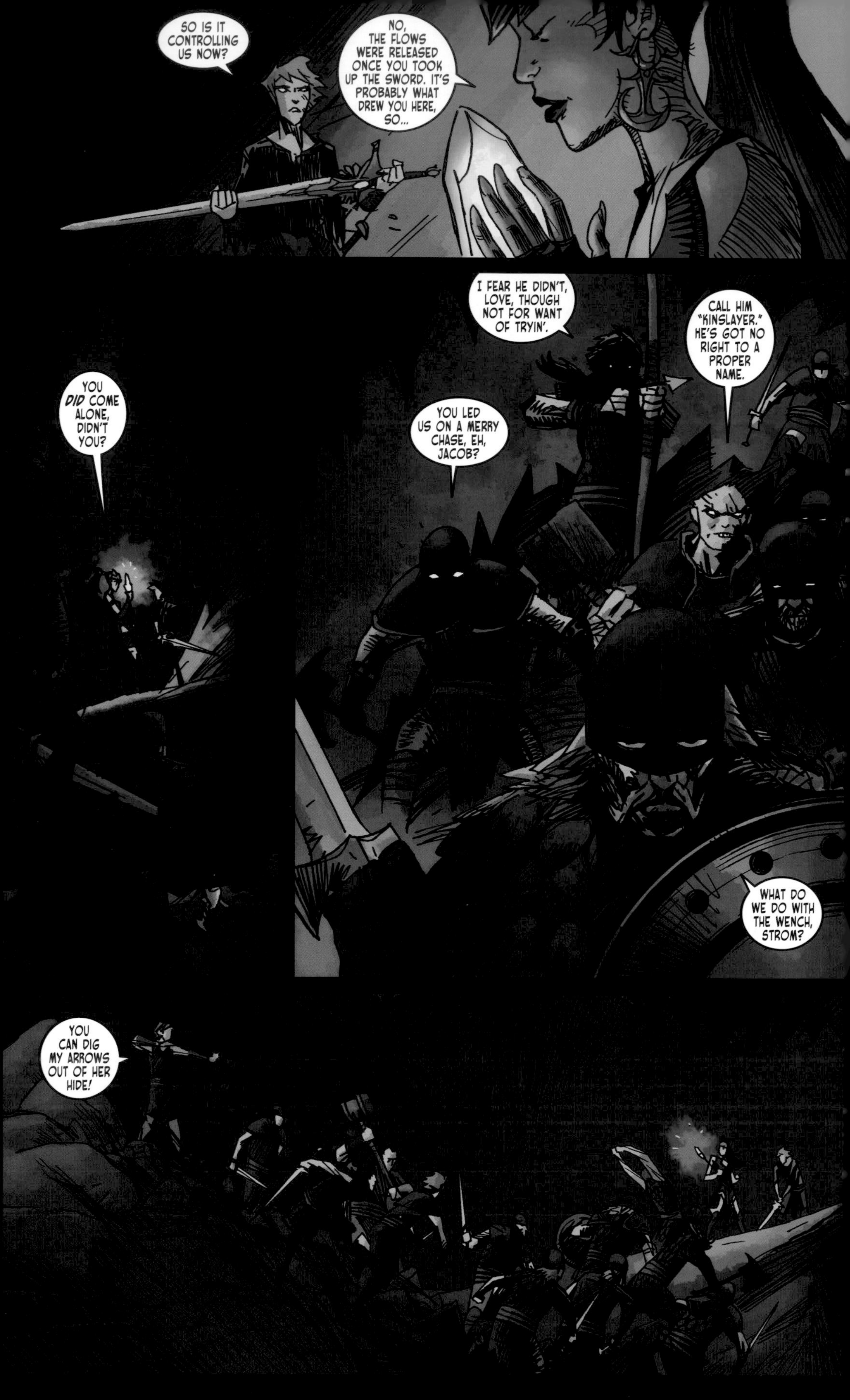
SO IS IT CONTROLLING US NOW?
NO, THE FLOWS WERE RELEASED ONCE YOU TOOK UP THE SWORD. IT'S PROBABLY WHAT DREW YOU HERE, SO...
YOU *DID* COME ALONE, DIDN'T YOU?
I FEAR HE DIDN'T, LOVE, THOUGH NOT FOR WANT OF TRYIN'.
YOU LED US ON A MERRY CHASE, EH, JACOB?
CALL HIM "KINSLAYER." HE'S GOT NO RIGHT TO A PROPER NAME.
WHAT DO WE DO WITH THE WENCH, STROM?
YOU CAN DIG MY ARROWS OUT OF HER HIDE!

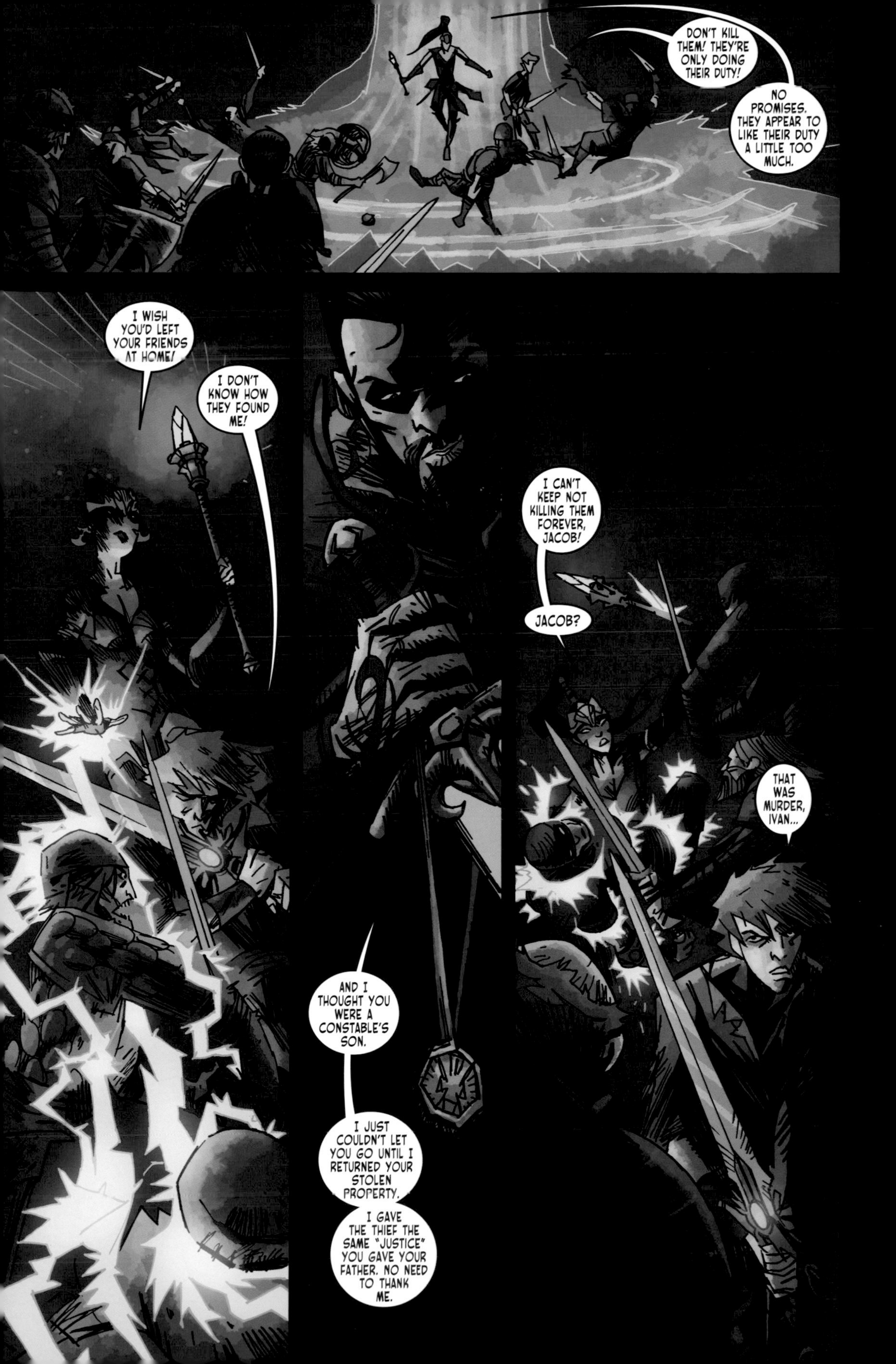
DON'T KILL THEM! THEY'RE ONLY DOING THEIR DUTY!
NO PROMISES. THEY APPEAR TO LIKE THEIR DUTY A LITTLE TOO MUCH.
I WISH YOU'D LEFT YOUR FRIENDS AT HOME!
I DON'T KNOW HOW THEY FOUND ME!
AND I THOUGHT YOU WERE A CONSTABLE'S SON.
I JUST COULDN'T LET YOU GO UNTIL I RETURNED YOUR STOLEN PROPERTY.
I GAVE THE THIEF THE SAME "JUSTICE" YOU GAVE YOUR FATHER. NO NEED TO THANK ME.
I CAN'T KEEP NOT KILLING THEM FOREVER, JACOB!
JACOB?
THAT WAS MURDER, IVAN...

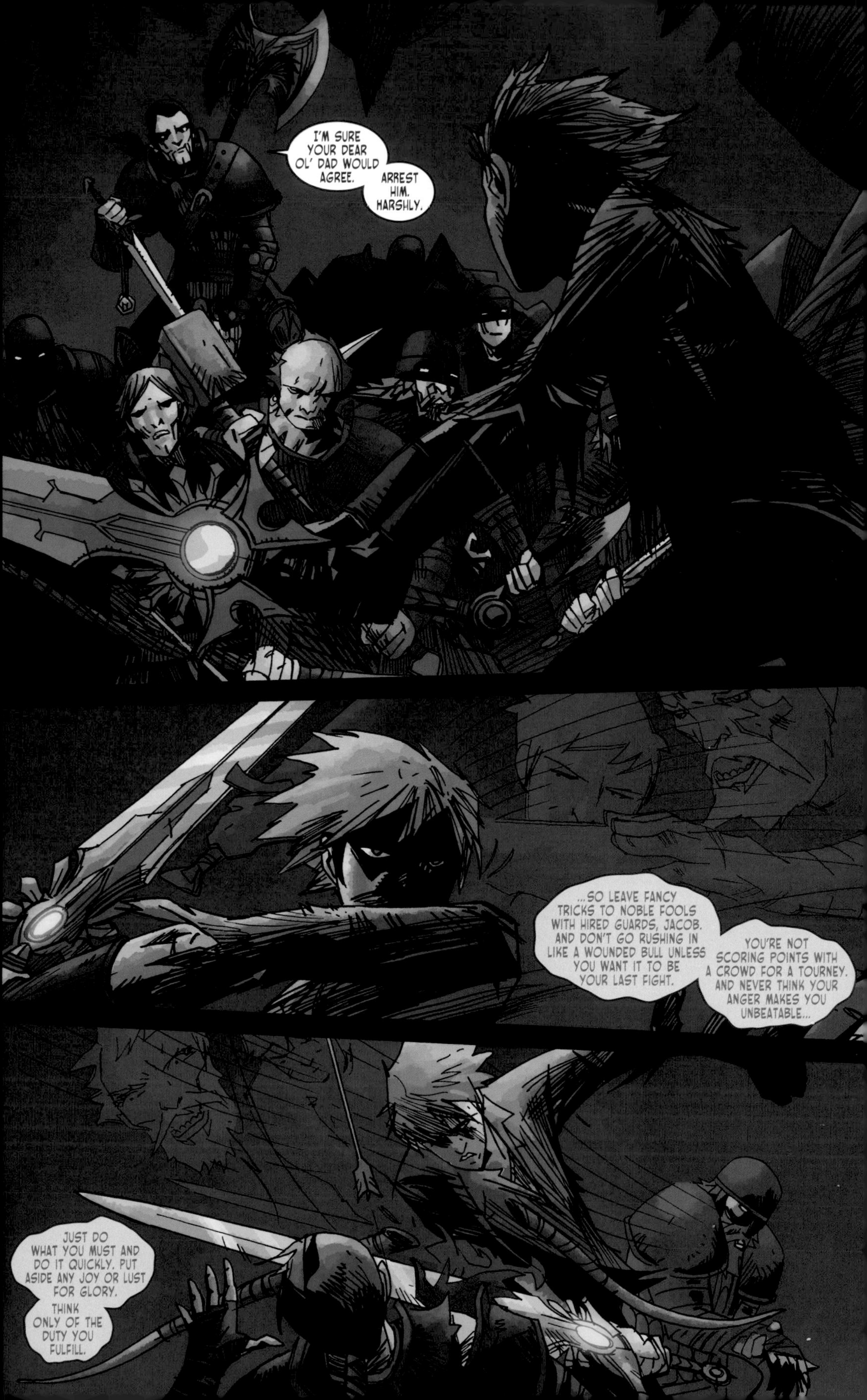
I'M SURE YOUR DEAR OL' DAD WOULD AGREE.
ARREST HIM. HARSHLY.
...SO LEAVE FANCY TRICKS TO NOBLE FOOLS WITH HIRED GUARDS, JACOB. AND DON'T GO RUSHING IN LIKE A WOUNDED BULL UNLESS YOU WANT IT TO BE YOUR LAST FIGHT.
YOU'RE NOT SCORING POINTS WITH A CROWD FOR A TOURNEY. AND NEVER THINK YOUR ANGER MAKES YOU UNBEATABLE...
JUST DO WHAT YOU MUST AND DO IT QUICKLY. PUT ASIDE ANY JOY OR LUST FOR GLORY.
THINK ONLY OF THE DUTY YOU FULFILL.

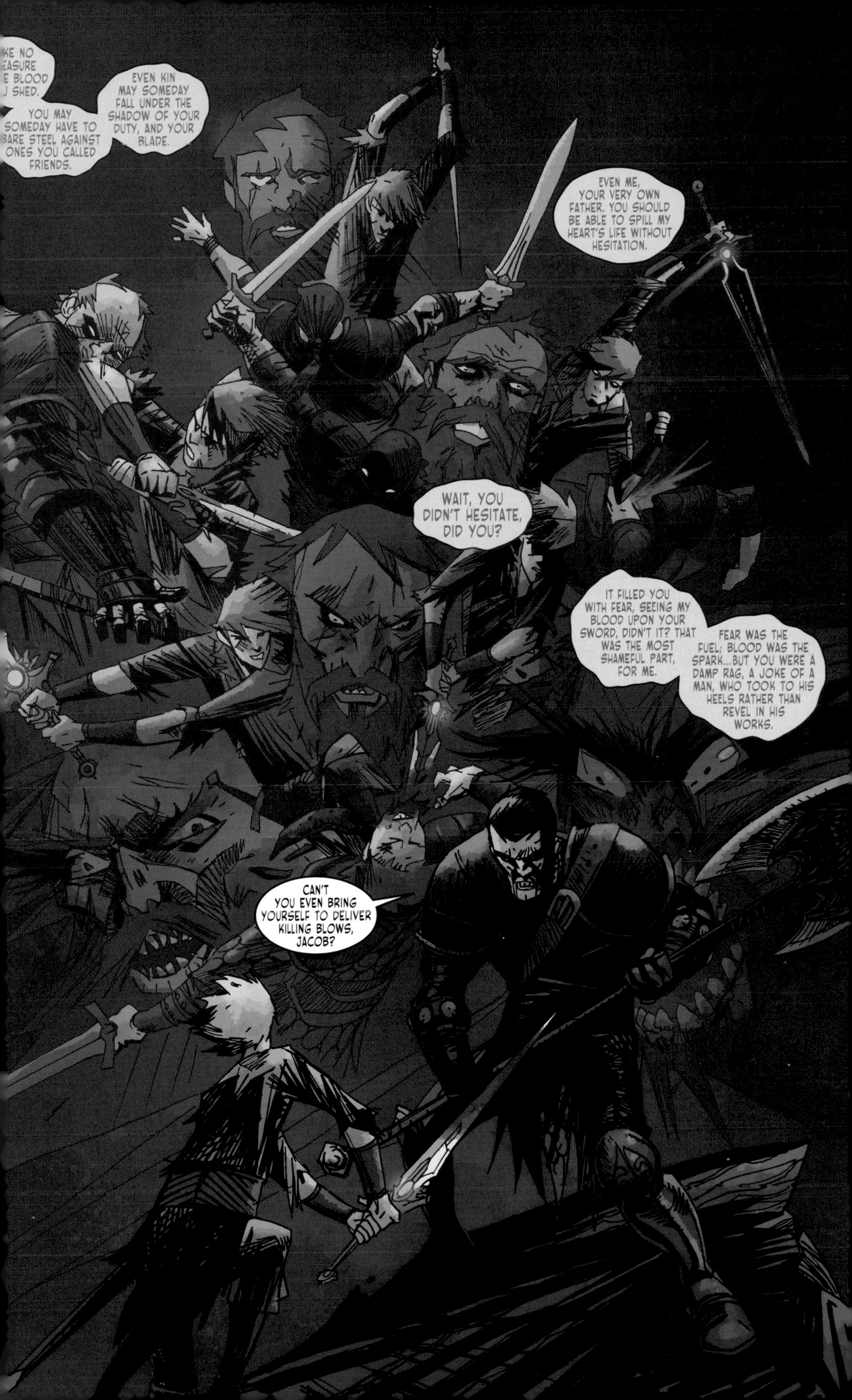
KE NO EASURE E BLOOD J SHED.
YOU MAY SOMEDAY HAVE TO BARE STEEL AGAINST ONES YOU CALLED FRIENDS.
EVEN KIN MAY SOMEDAY FALL UNDER THE SHADOW OF YOUR DUTY, AND YOUR BLADE.
EVEN ME, YOUR VERY OWN FATHER. YOU SHOULD BE ABLE TO SPILL MY HEART'S LIFE WITHOUT HESITATION.
WAIT, YOU DIDN'T HESITATE, DID YOU?
IT FILLED YOU WITH FEAR, SEEING MY BLOOD UPON YOUR SWORD, DIDN'T IT? THAT WAS THE MOST SHAMEFUL PART, FOR ME.
FEAR WAS THE FUEL; BLOOD WAS THE SPARK...BUT YOU WERE A DAMP RAG, A JOKE OF A MAN, WHO TOOK TO HIS HEELS RATHER THAN REVEL IN HIS WORKS.
CAN'T YOU EVEN BRING YOURSELF TO DELIVER KILLING BLOWS, JACOB?

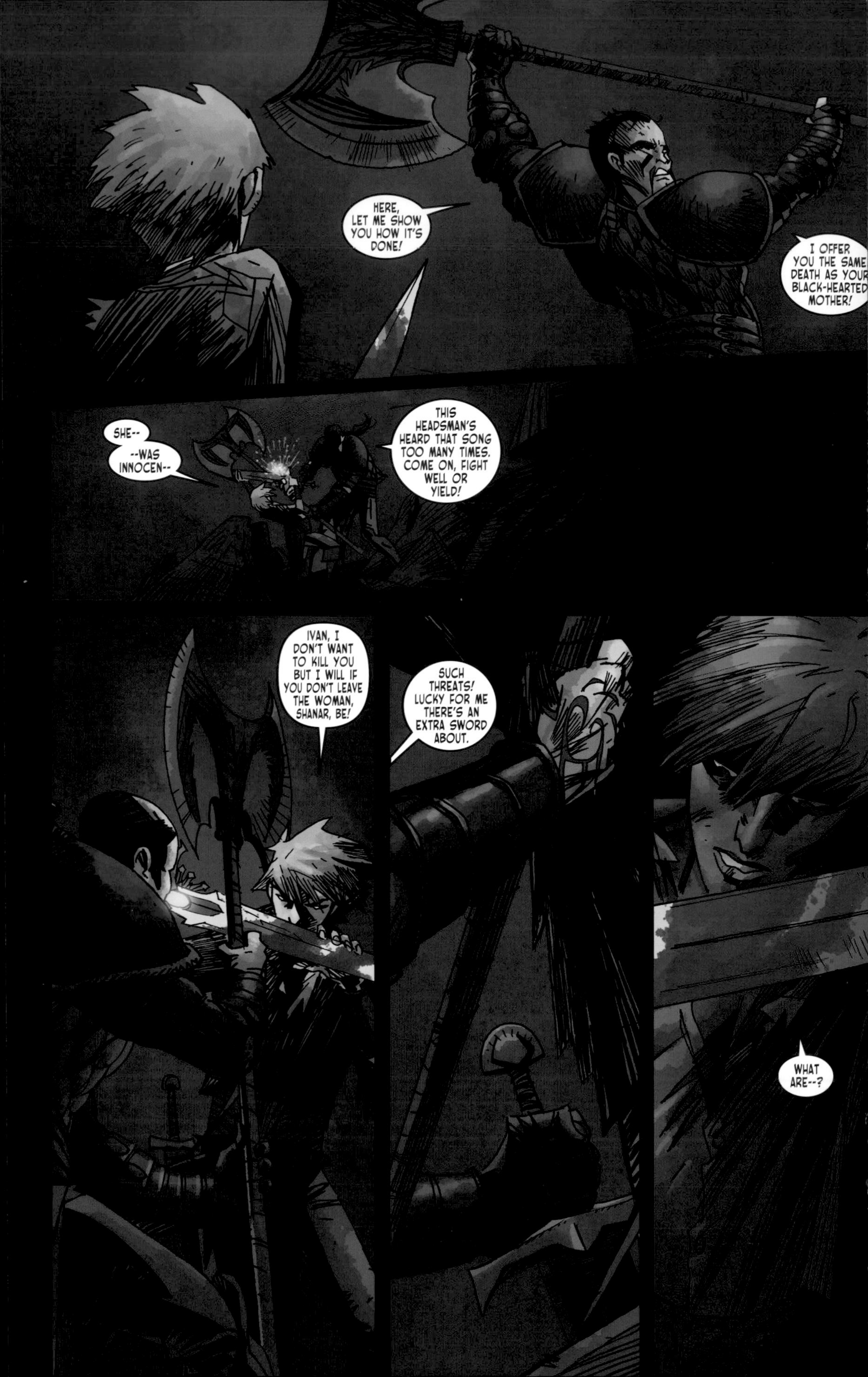
HERE, LET ME SHOW YOU HOW IT'S DONE!
I OFFER YOU THE SAME DEATH AS YOUR BLACK-HEARTED MOTHER!
SHE--
--WAS INNOCEN--
THIS HEADSMAN'S HEARD THAT SONG TOO MANY TIMES. COME ON, FIGHT WELL OR YIELD!
IVAN, I DON'T WANT TO KILL YOU BUT I WILL IF YOU DON'T LEAVE THE WOMAN, SHANAR, BE!
SUCH THREATS! LUCKY FOR ME THERE'S AN EXTRA SWORD ABOUT.
WHAT ARE--?

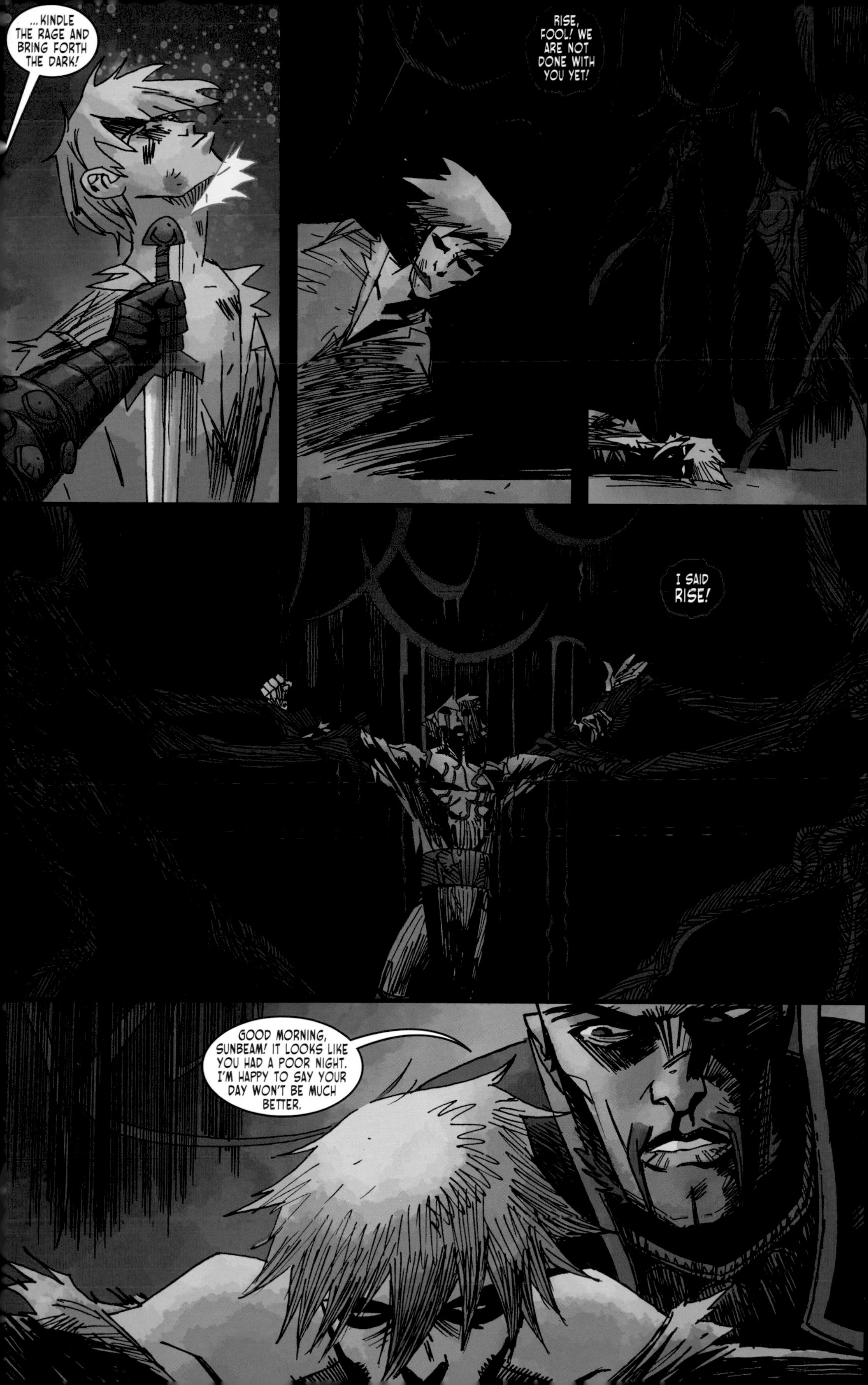
...KINDLE THE RAGE AND BRING FORTH THE DARK!
RISE, FOOL! WE ARE NOT DONE WITH YOU YET!
I SAID RISE!
GOOD MORNING, SUNBEAM! IT LOOKS LIKE YOU HAD A POOR NIGHT. I'M HAPPY TO SAY YOUR DAY WON'T BE MUCH BETTER.

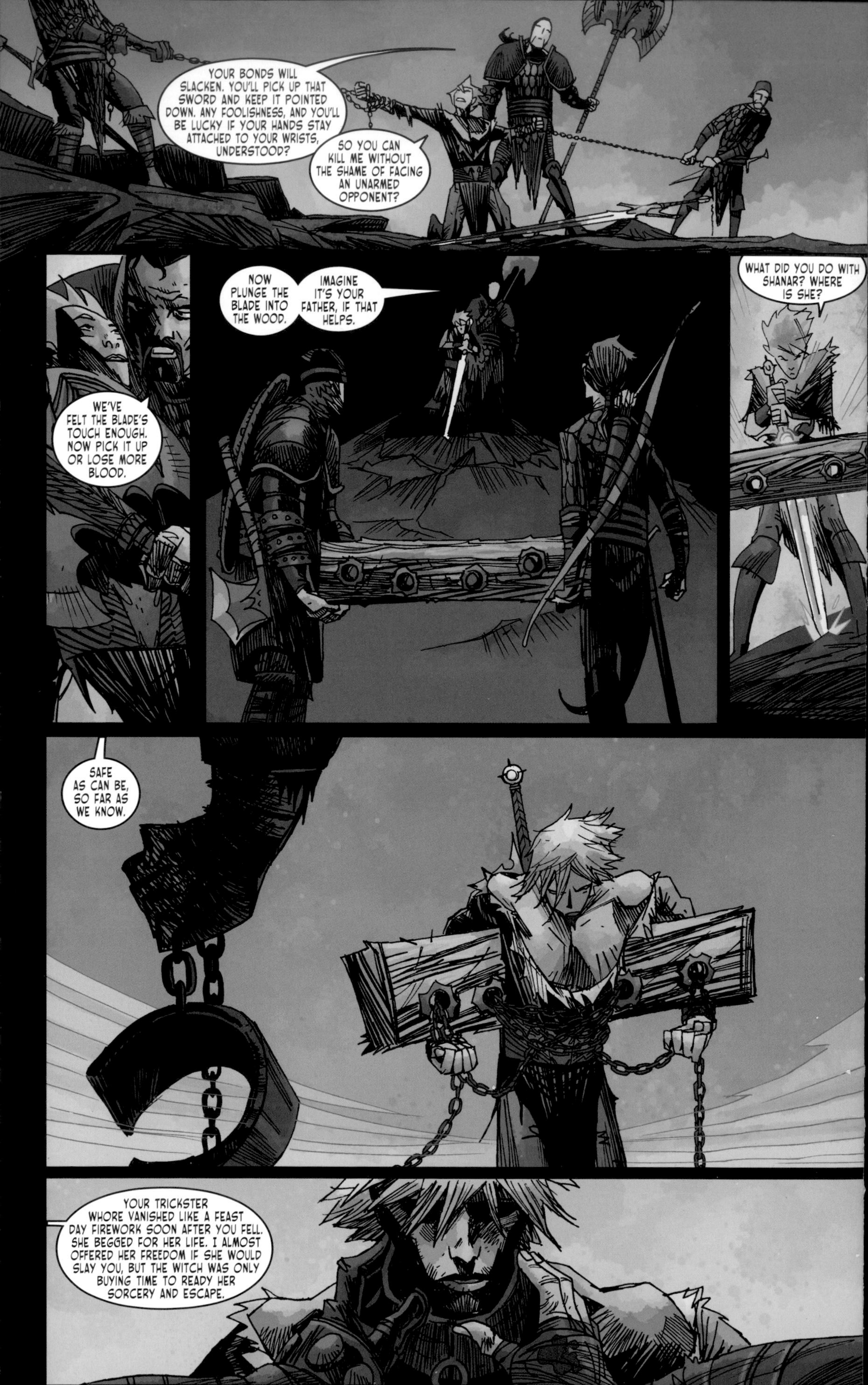
YOUR BONDS WILL SLACKEN. YOU'LL PICK UP THAT SWORD AND KEEP IT POINTED DOWN. ANY FOOLISHNESS, AND YOU'LL BE LUCKY IF YOUR HANDS STAY ATTACHED TO YOUR WRISTS, UNDERSTOOD?
SO YOU CAN KILL ME WITHOUT THE SHAME OF FACING AN UNARMED OPPONENT?
WE'VE FELT THE BLADE'S TOUCH ENOUGH. NOW PICK IT UP OR LOSE MORE BLOOD.
NOW PLUNGE THE BLADE INTO THE WOOD.
IMAGINE IT'S YOUR FATHER, IF THAT HELPS.
WHAT DID YOU DO WITH SHANAR? WHERE IS SHE?
SAFE AS CAN BE, SO FAR AS WE KNOW.
YOUR TRICKSTER WHORE VANISHED LIKE A FEAST DAY FIREWORK SOON AFTER YOU FELL. SHE BEGGED FOR HER LIFE. I ALMOST OFFERED HER FREEDOM IF SHE WOULD SLAY YOU, BUT THE WITCH WAS ONLY BUYING TIME TO READY HER SORCERY AND ESCAPE.

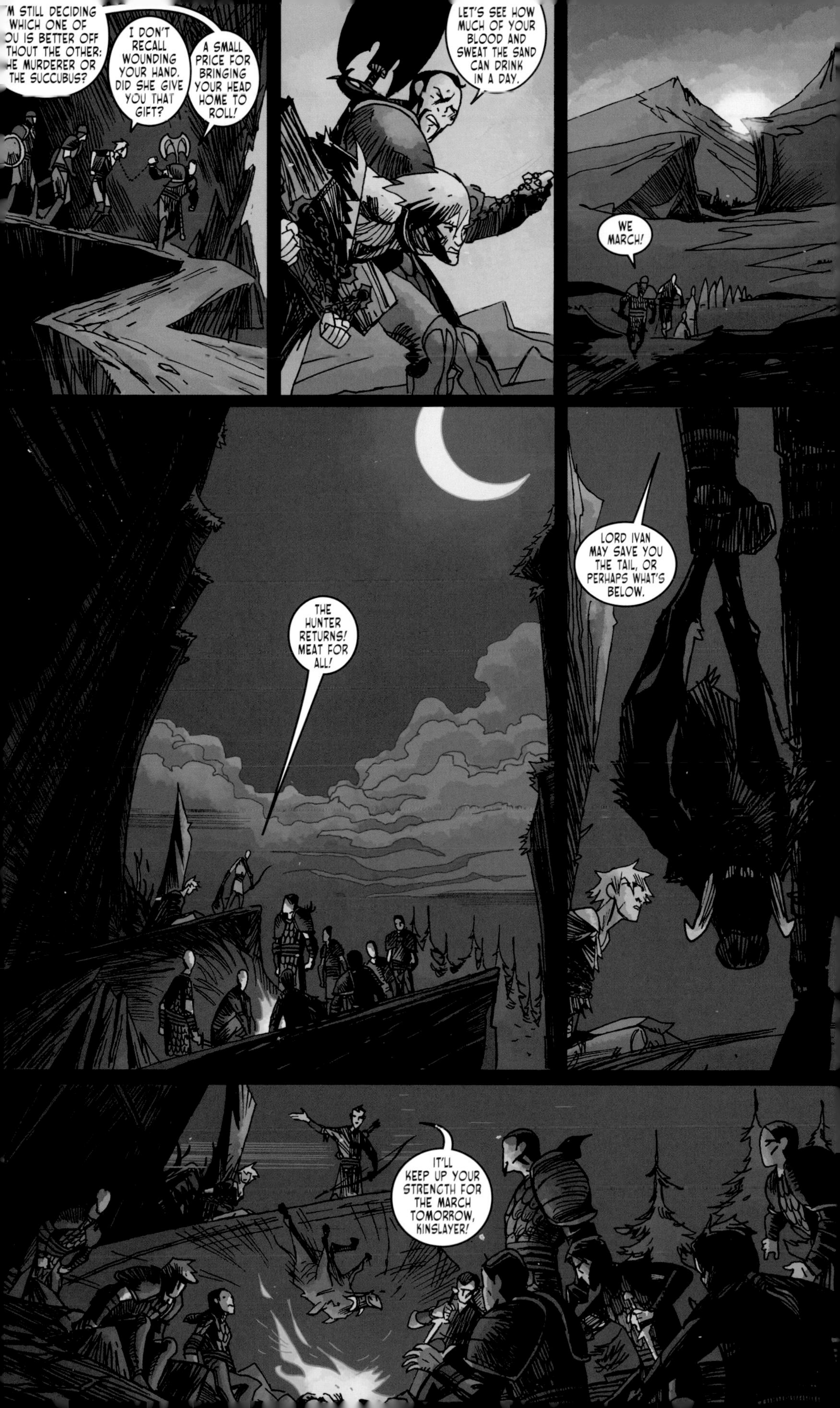
'M STILL DECIDING WHICH ONE OF OU IS BETTER OFF THOUT THE OTHER: HE MURDERER OR THE SUCCUBUS?
I DON'T RECALL WOUNDING YOUR HAND. DID SHE GIVE YOU THAT GIFT?
A SMALL PRICE FOR BRINGING YOUR HEAD HOME TO ROLL!
LET'S SEE HOW MUCH OF YOUR BLOOD AND SWEAT THE SAND CAN DRINK IN A DAY.
WE MARCH!
THE HUNTER RETURNS! MEAT FOR ALL!
LORD IVAN MAY SAVE YOU THE TAIL, OR PERHAPS WHAT'S BELOW.
IT'LL KEEP UP YOUR STRENGTH FOR THE MARCH TOMORROW, KINSLAYER!

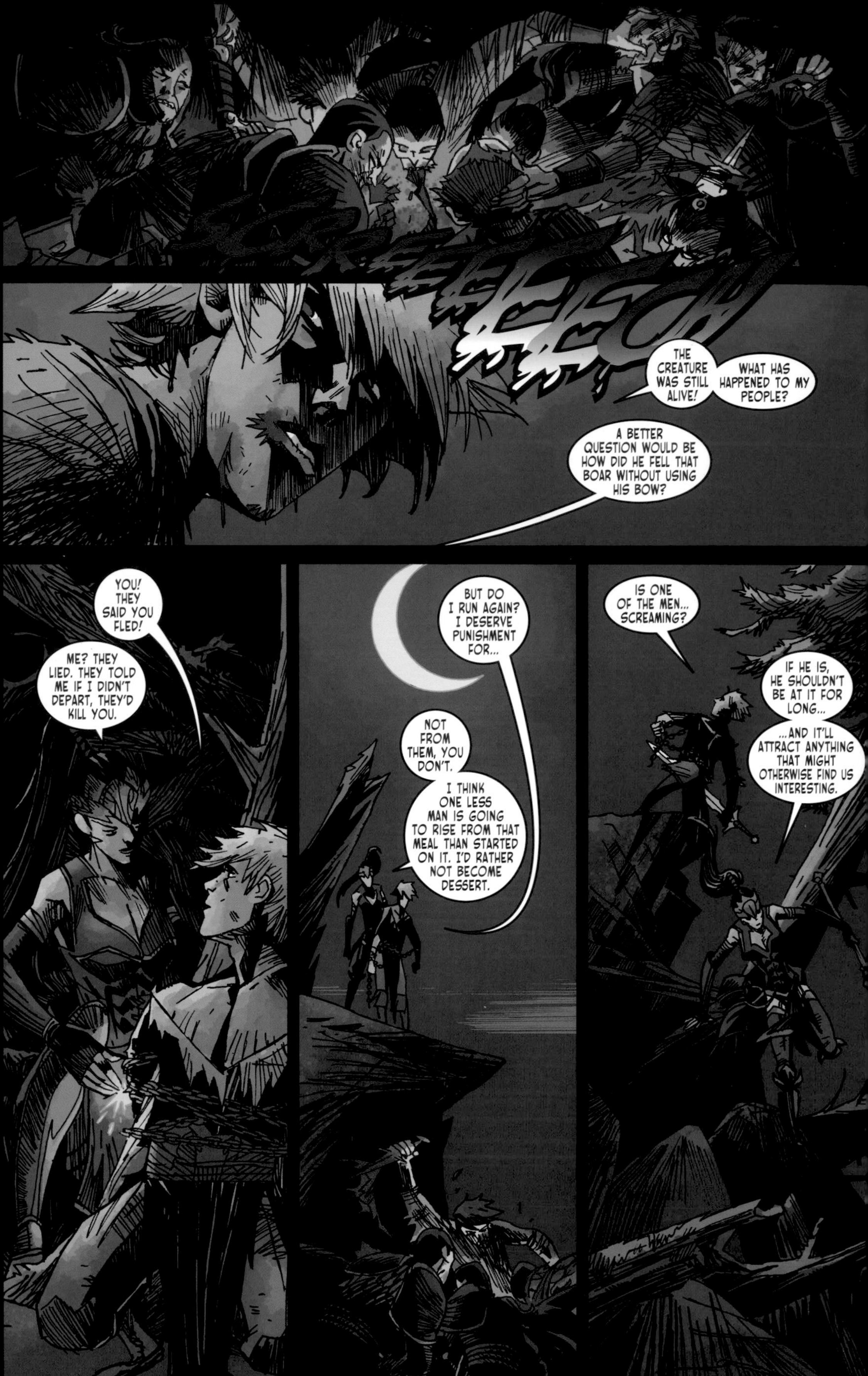
THE CREATURE WAS STILL ALIVE!
WHAT HAS HAPPENED TO MY PEOPLE?
A BETTER QUESTION WOULD BE HOW DID HE FELL THAT BOAR WITHOUT USING HIS BOW?
YOU! THEY SAID YOU FLED!
ME? THEY LIED. THEY TOLD ME IF I DIDN'T DEPART, THEY'D KILL YOU.
BUT DO I RUN AGAIN? I DESERVE PUNISHMENT FOR...
NOT FROM THEM, YOU DON'T.
I THINK ONE LESS MAN IS GOING TO RISE FROM THAT MEAL THAN STARTED ON IT. I'D RATHER NOT BECOME DESSERT.
IS ONE OF THE MEN... SCREAMING?
IF HE IS, HE SHOULDN'T BE AT IT FOR LONG...
...AND IT'LL ATTRACT ANYTHING THAT MIGHT OTHERWISE FIND US INTERESTING.

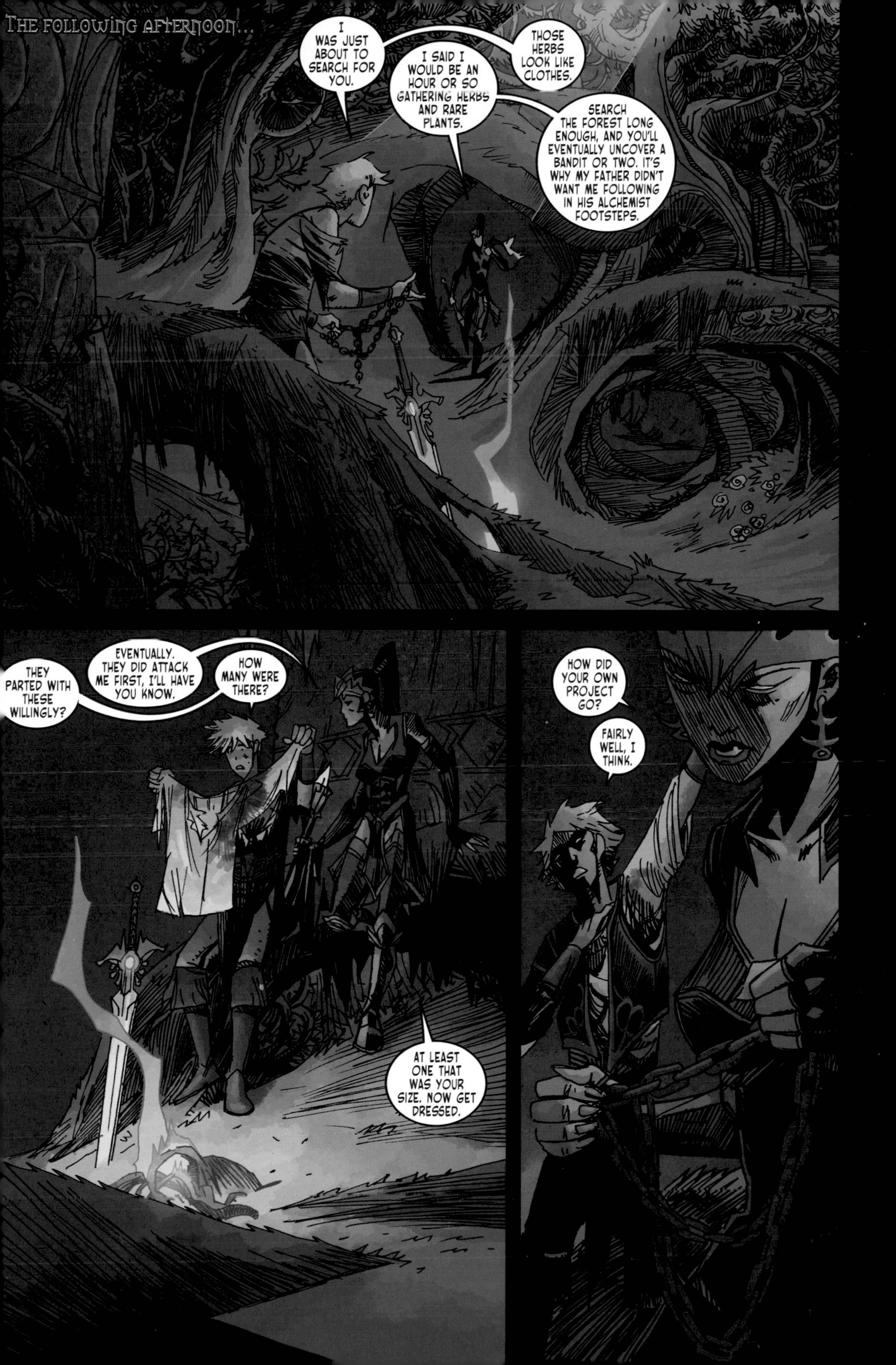
The following afternoon...
I was just about to search for you.
I said I would be an hour or so gathering herbs and rare plants.
Those herbs look like clothes.
Search the forest long enough, and you'll eventually uncover a bandit or two. It's why my father didn't want me following in his alchemist footsteps.
They parted with these willingly?
Eventually. They did attack me first, I'll have you know.
How many were there?
At least one that was your size. Now get dressed.
How did your own project go?
Fairly well, I think.

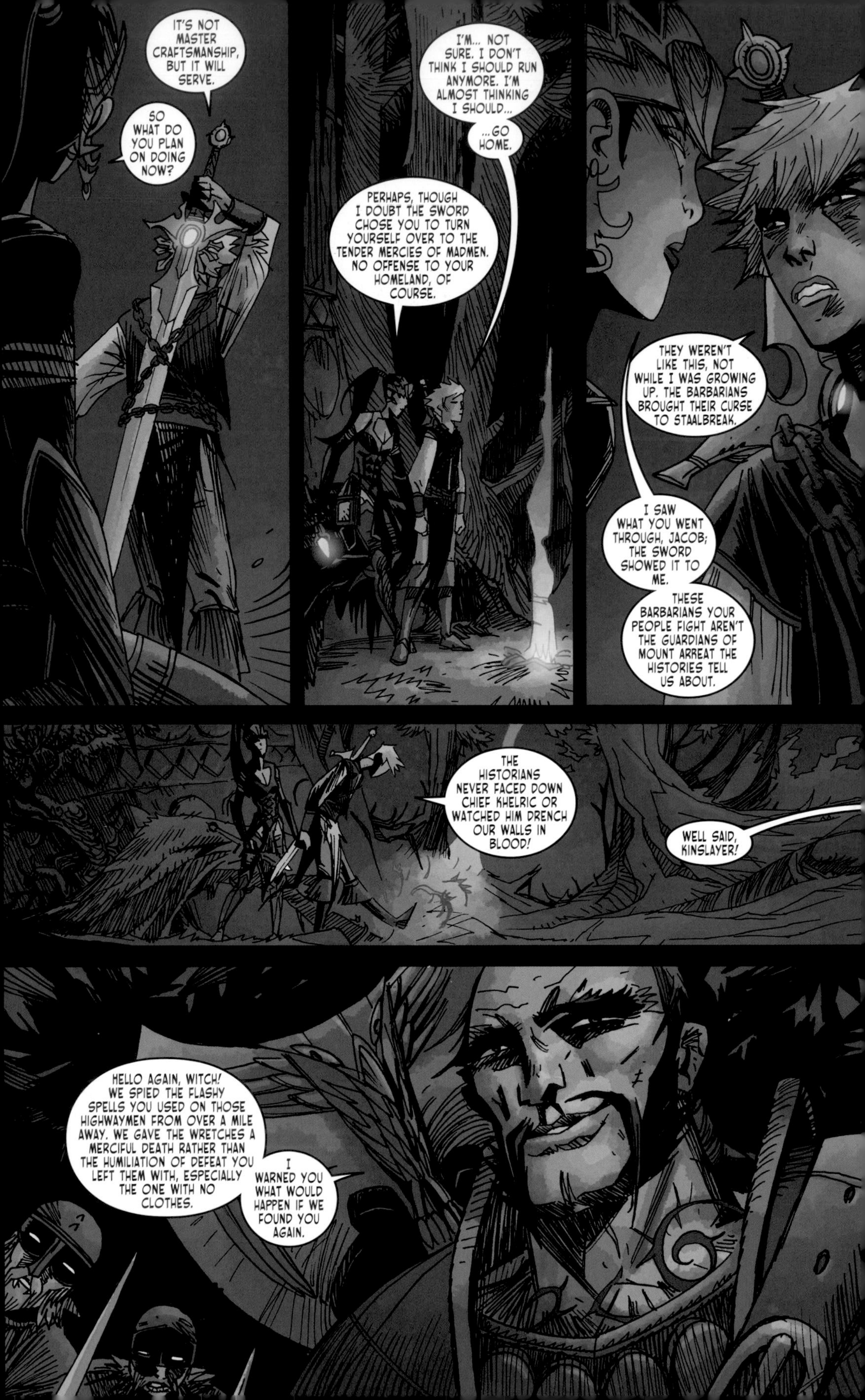
IT'S NOT MASTER CRAFTSMANSHIP, BUT IT WILL SERVE.
SO WHAT DO YOU PLAN ON DOING NOW?
I'M... NOT SURE. I DON'T THINK I SHOULD RUN ANYMORE. I'M ALMOST THINKING I SHOULD...
...GO HOME.
PERHAPS, THOUGH I DOUBT THE SWORD CHOSE YOU TO TURN YOURSELF OVER TO THE TENDER MERCIES OF MADMEN. NO OFFENSE TO YOUR HOMELAND, OF COURSE.
THEY WEREN'T LIKE THIS, NOT WHILE I WAS GROWING UP. THE BARBARIANS BROUGHT THEIR CURSE TO STAALBREAK.
I SAW WHAT YOU WENT THROUGH, JACOB; THE SWORD SHOWED IT TO ME.
THESE BARBARIANS YOUR PEOPLE FIGHT AREN'T THE GUARDIANS OF MOUNT ARREAT THE HISTORIES TELL US ABOUT.
THE HISTORIANS NEVER FACED DOWN CHIEF KHELRIC OR WATCHED HIM DRENCH OUR WALLS IN BLOOD!
WELL SAID, KINSLAYER!
HELLO AGAIN, WITCH! WE SPIED THE FLASHY SPELLS YOU USED ON THOSE HIGHWAYMEN FROM OVER A MILE AWAY. WE GAVE THE WRETCHES A MERCIFUL DEATH RATHER THAN THE HUMILIATION OF DEFEAT YOU LEFT THEM WITH, ESPECIALLY THE ONE WITH NO CLOTHES.
I WARNED YOU WHAT WOULD HAPPEN IF WE FOUND YOU AGAIN.

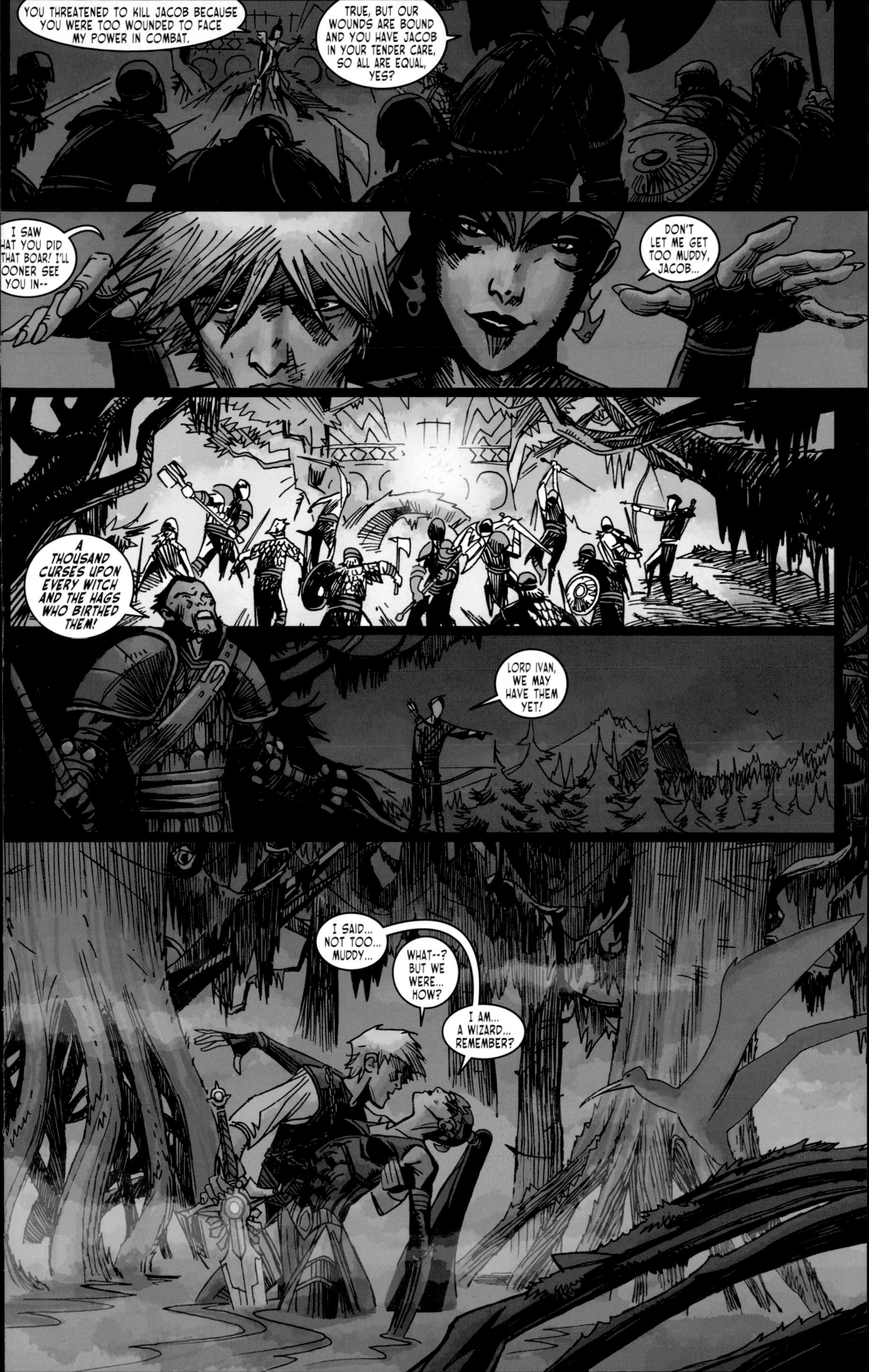
YOU THREATENED TO KILL JACOB BECAUSE YOU WERE TOO WOUNDED TO FACE MY POWER IN COMBAT.
TRUE, BUT OUR WOUNDS ARE BOUND AND YOU HAVE JACOB IN YOUR TENDER CARE, SO ALL ARE EQUAL, YES?
I SAW HAT YOU DID THAT BOAR! I'LL OONER SEE YOU IN--
DON'T LET ME GET TOO MUDDY, JACOB...
A THOUSAND CURSES UPON EVERY WITCH AND THE HAGS WHO BIRTHED THEM!
LORD IVAN, WE MAY HAVE THEM YET!
I SAID... NOT TOO... MUDDY...
WHAT--? BUT WE WERE... HOW?
I AM... A WIZARD... REMEMBER?

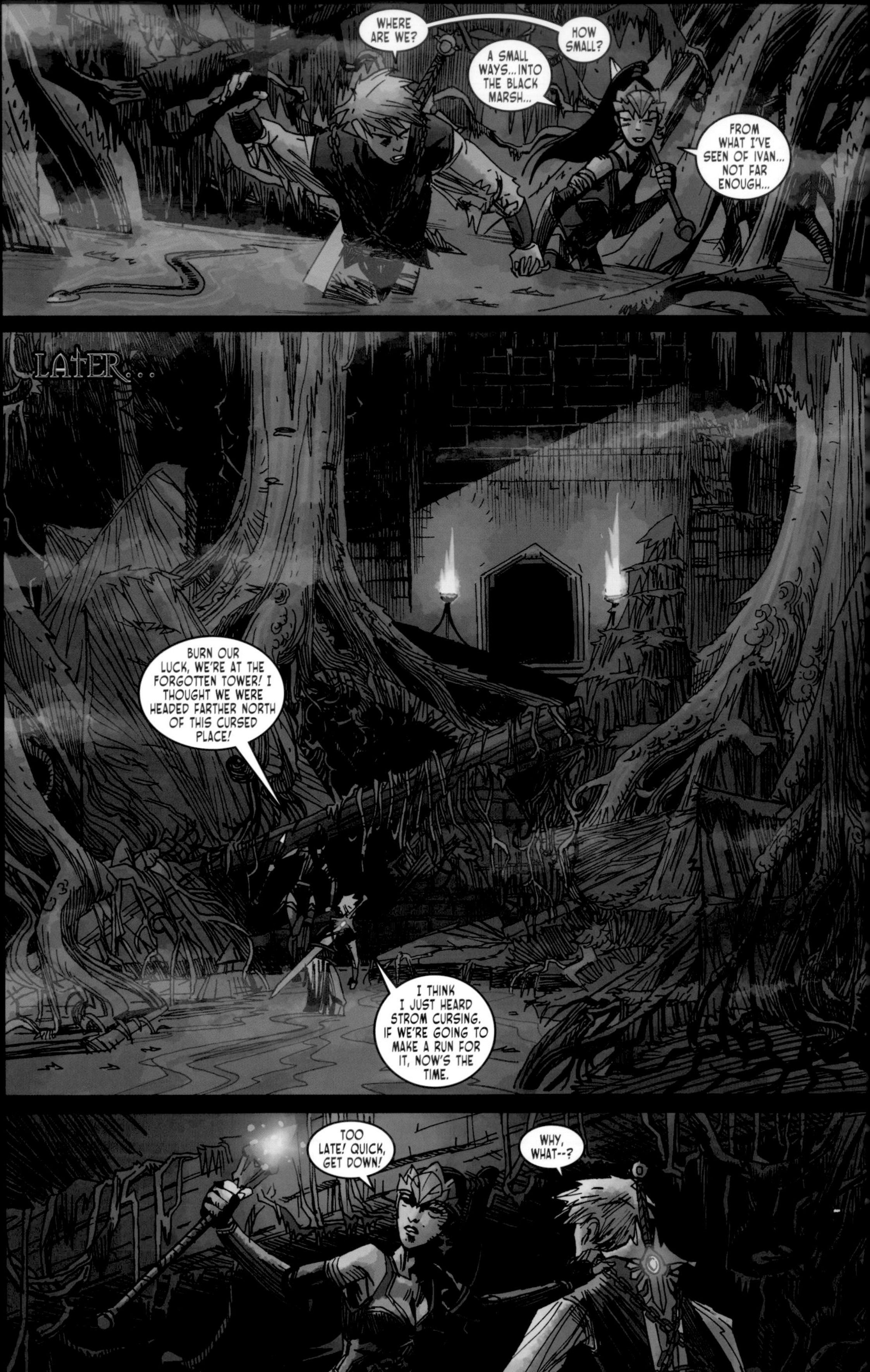
WHERE ARE WE?
HOW SMALL?
A SMALL WAYS...INTO THE BLACK MARSH...
FROM WHAT I'VE SEEN OF IVAN... NOT FAR ENOUGH...
LATER...
BURN OUR LUCK, WE'RE AT THE FORGOTTEN TOWER! I THOUGHT WE WERE HEADED FARTHER NORTH OF THIS CURSED PLACE!
I THINK I JUST HEARD STROM CURSING. IF WE'RE GOING TO MAKE A RUN FOR IT, NOW'S THE TIME.
TOO LATE! QUICK, GET DOWN!
WHY, WHAT--?

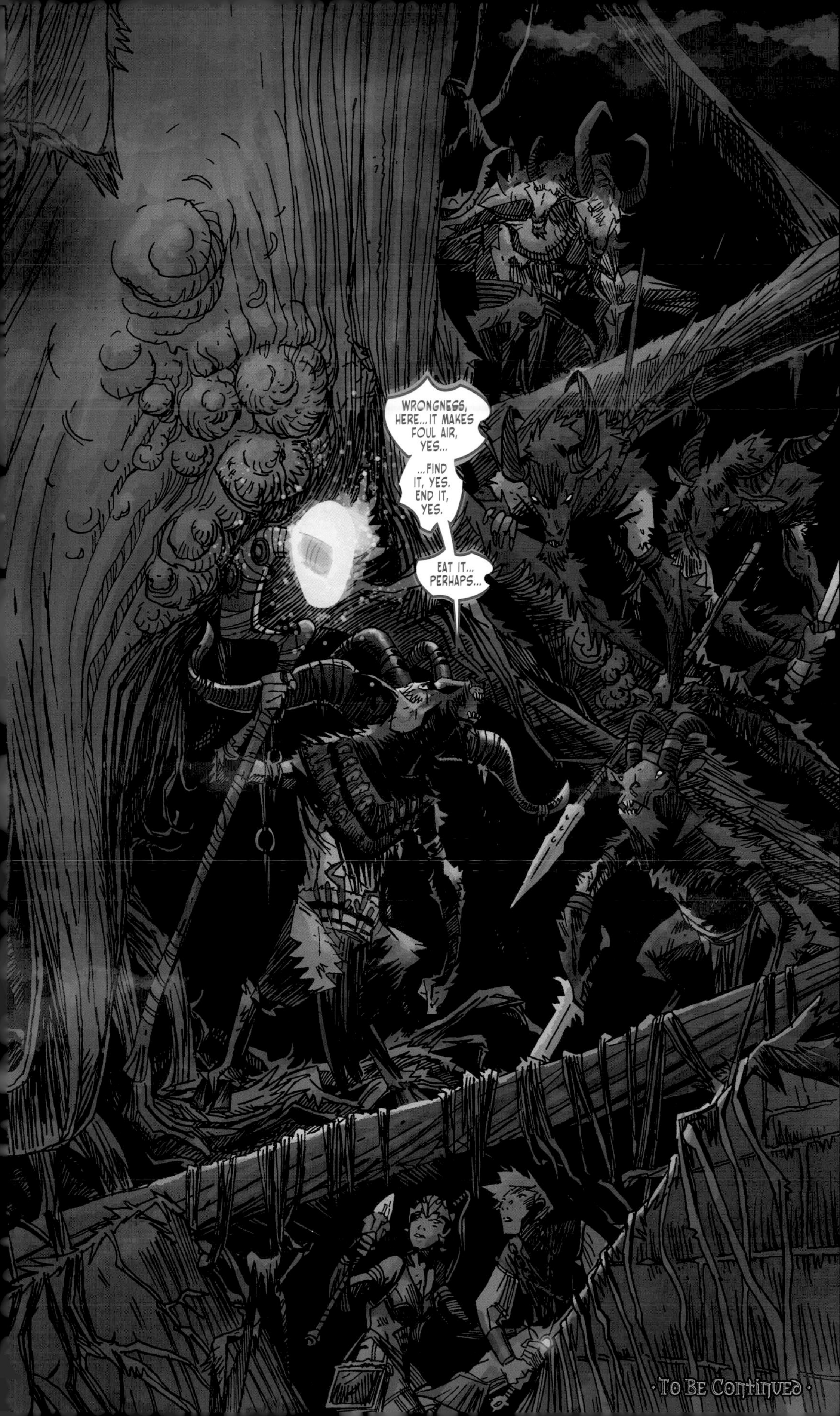
WRONGNESS, HERE...IT MAKES FOUL AIR, YES...
...FIND IT, YES. END IT, YES.
EAT IT... PERHAPS...
·TO BE CONTINUED·

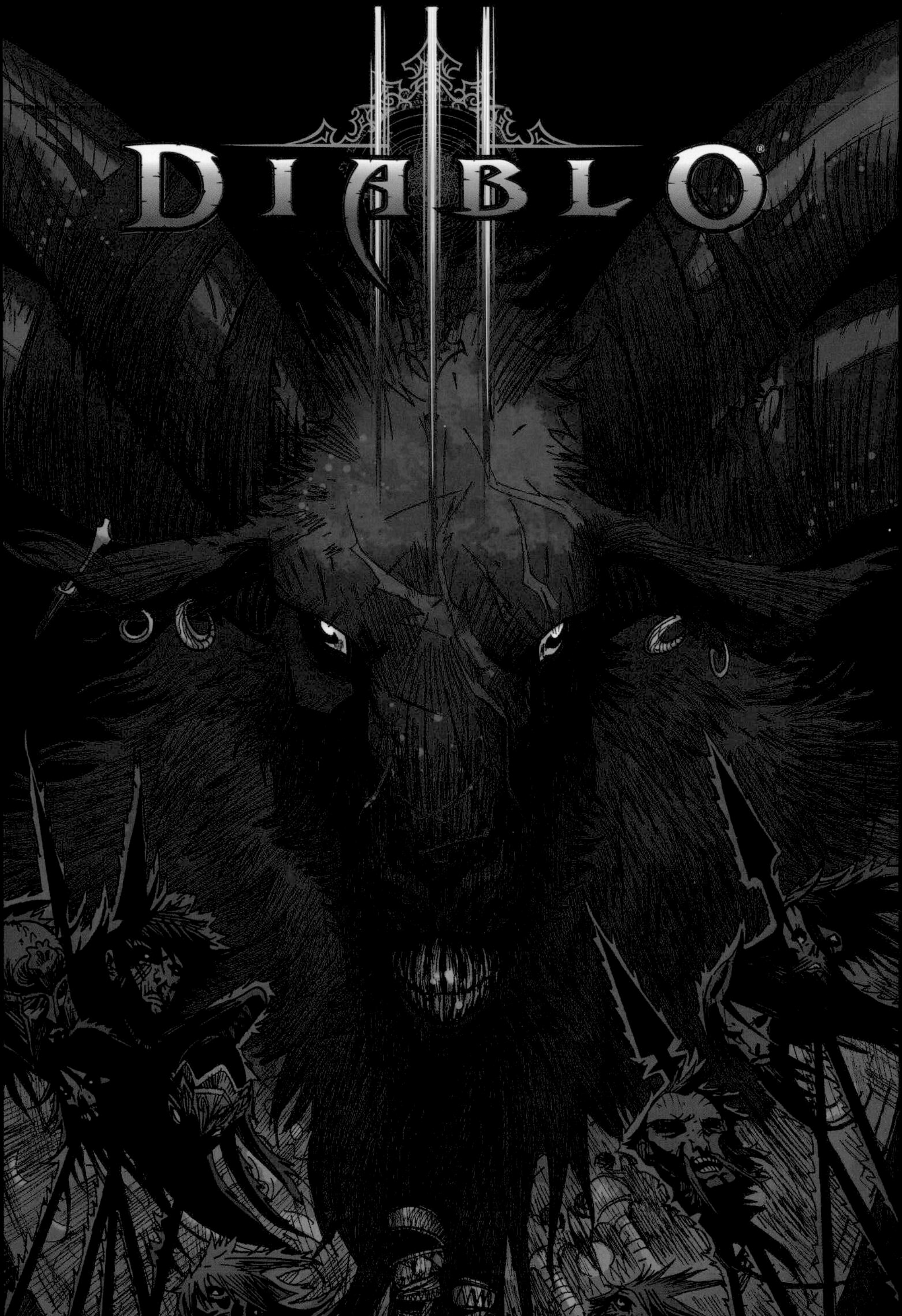
DIABLO III

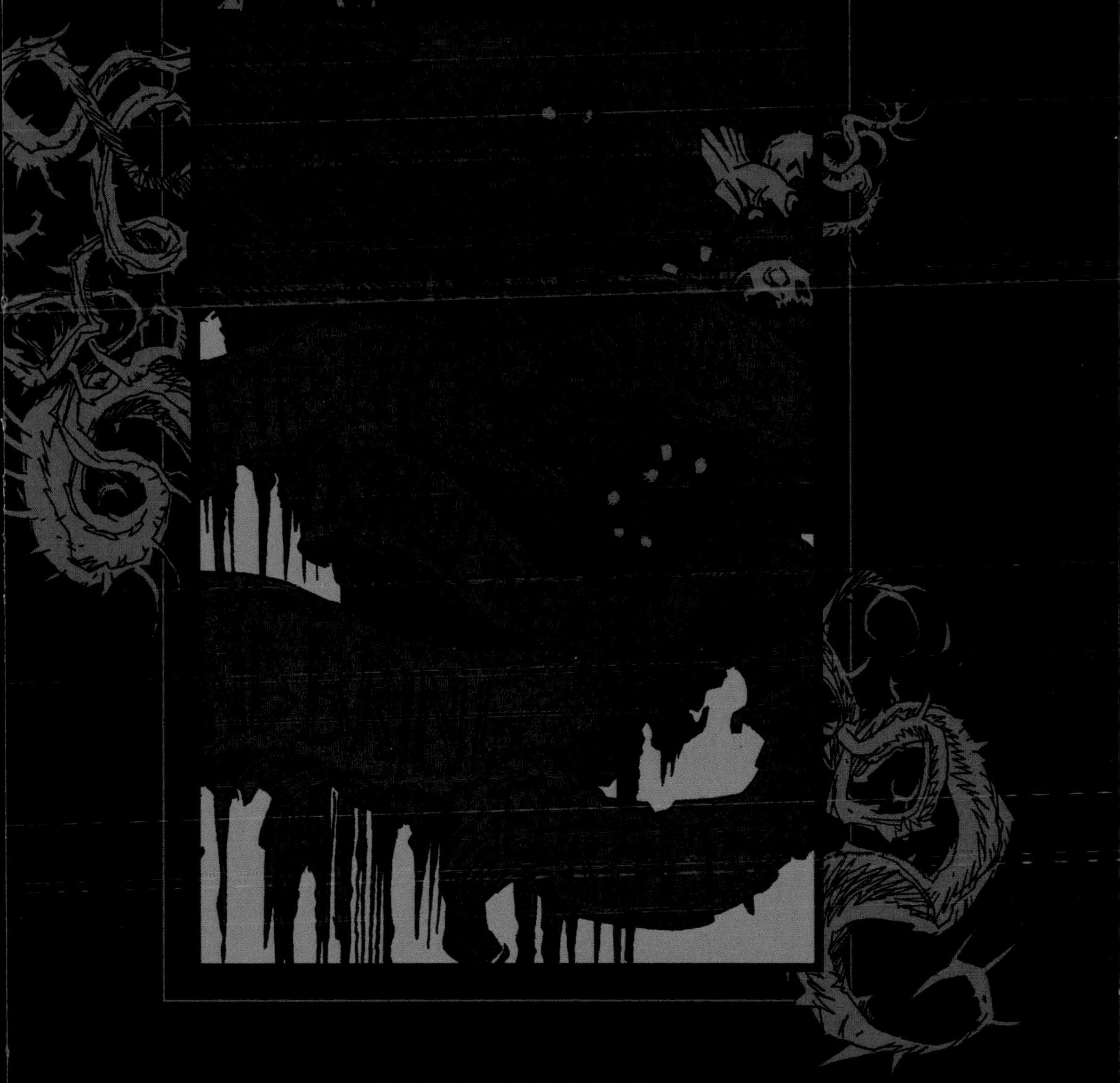

ACT III

AARON WILLIAMS
JOSEPH LACROIX
LEE LOUGHRIDGE

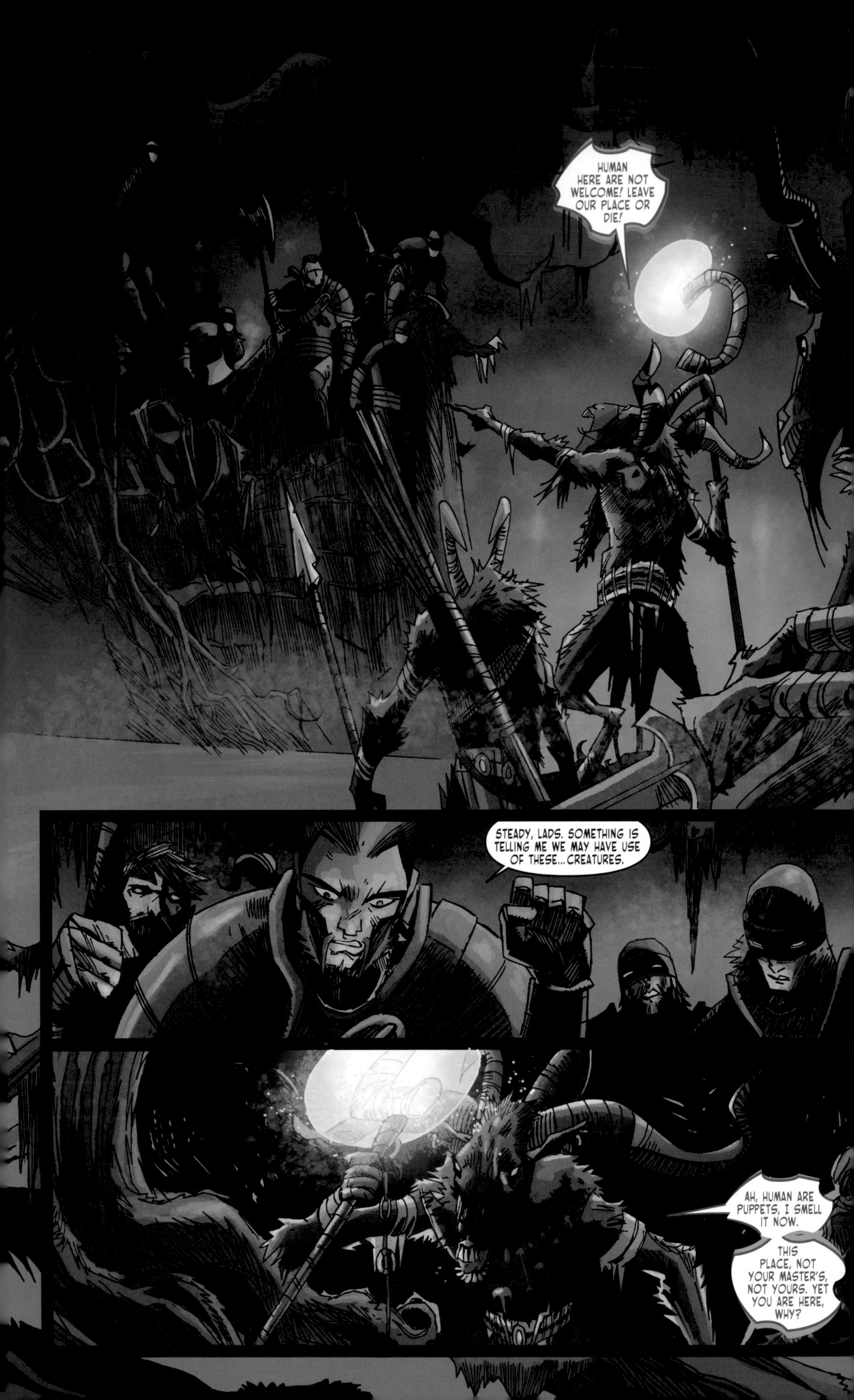
HUMAN HERE ARE NOT WELCOME! LEAVE OUR PLACE OR DIE!
STEADY, LADS. SOMETHING IS TELLING ME WE MAY HAVE USE OF THESE...CREATURES.
AH, HUMAN ARE PUPPETS, I SMELL IT NOW.
THIS PLACE, NOT YOUR MASTER'S, NOT YOURS. YET YOU ARE HERE, WHY?

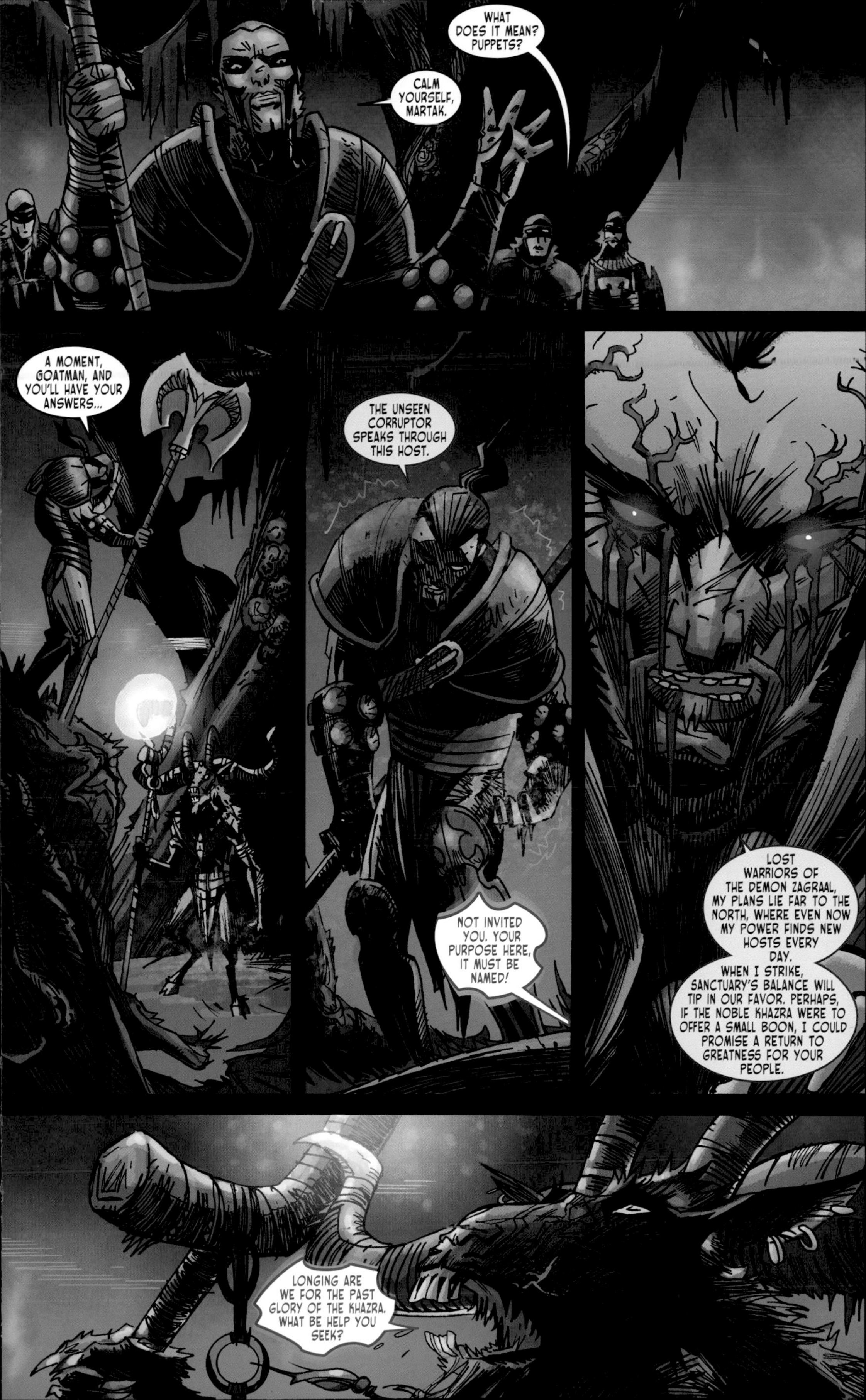
WHAT DOES IT MEAN? PUPPETS?
CALM YOURSELF, MARTAK.
A MOMENT, GOATMAN, AND YOU'LL HAVE YOUR ANSWERS...
THE UNSEEN CORRUPTOR SPEAKS THROUGH THIS HOST.
NOT INVITED YOU. YOUR PURPOSE HERE, IT MUST BE NAMED!
LOST WARRIORS OF THE DEMON ZAGRAAL, MY PLANS LIE FAR TO THE NORTH, WHERE EVEN NOW MY POWER FINDS NEW HOSTS EVERY DAY.
WHEN I STRIKE, SANCTUARY'S BALANCE WILL TIP IN OUR FAVOR. PERHAPS, IF THE NOBLE KHAZRA WERE TO OFFER A SMALL BOON, I COULD PROMISE A RETURN TO GREATNESS FOR YOUR PEOPLE.
LONGING ARE WE FOR THE PAST GLORY OF THE KHAZRA. WHAT BE HELP YOU SEEK?

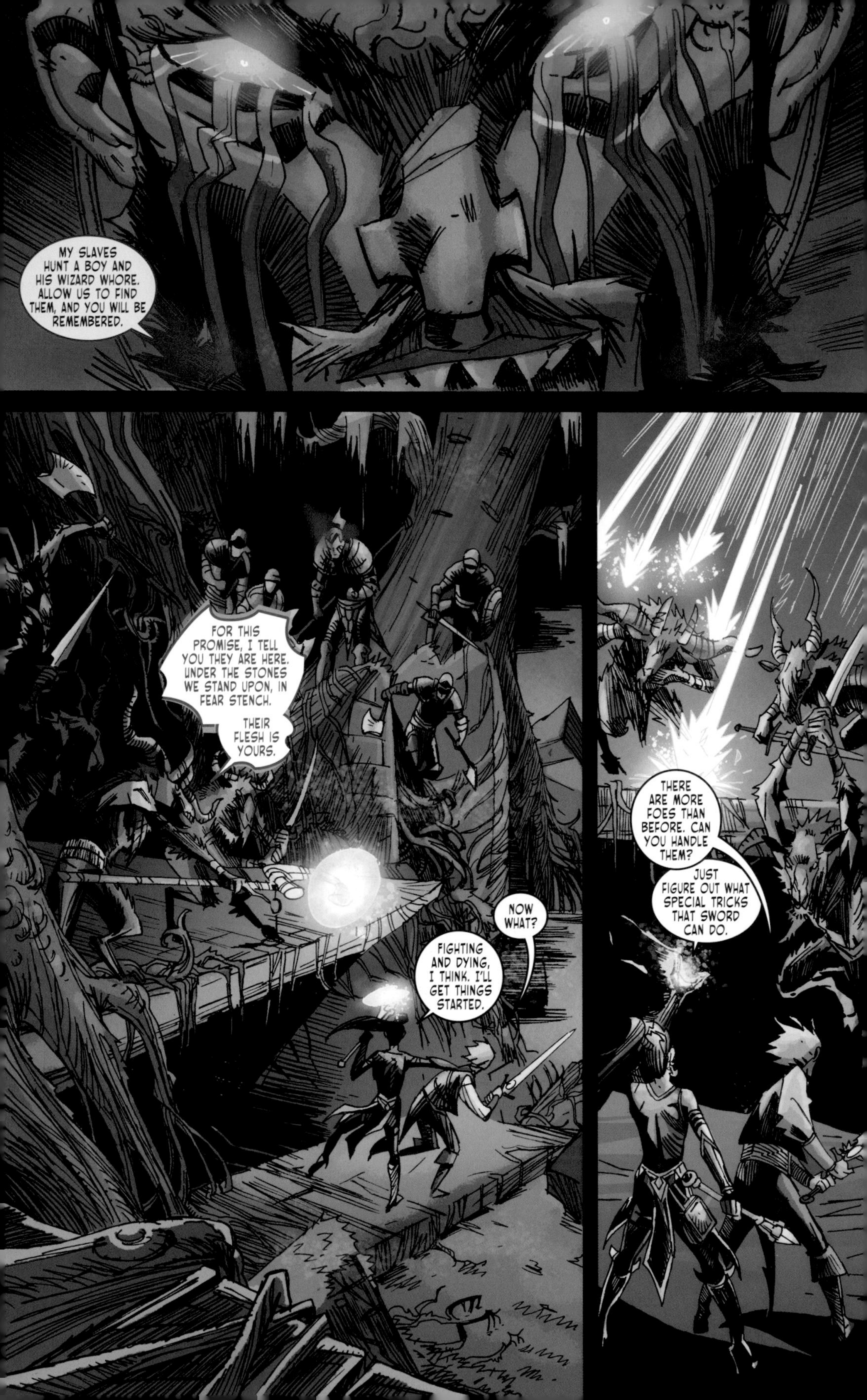

MY SLAVES HUNT A BOY AND HIS WIZARD WHORE. ALLOW US TO FIND THEM, AND YOU WILL BE REMEMBERED.
FOR THIS PROMISE, I TELL YOU THEY ARE HERE. UNDER THE STONES WE STAND UPON, IN FEAR STENCH.
THEIR FLESH IS YOURS.
NOW WHAT?
FIGHTING AND DYING, I THINK. I'LL GET THINGS STARTED.
THERE ARE MORE FOES THAN BEFORE. CAN YOU HANDLE THEM?
JUST FIGURE OUT WHAT SPECIAL TRICKS THAT SWORD CAN DO.

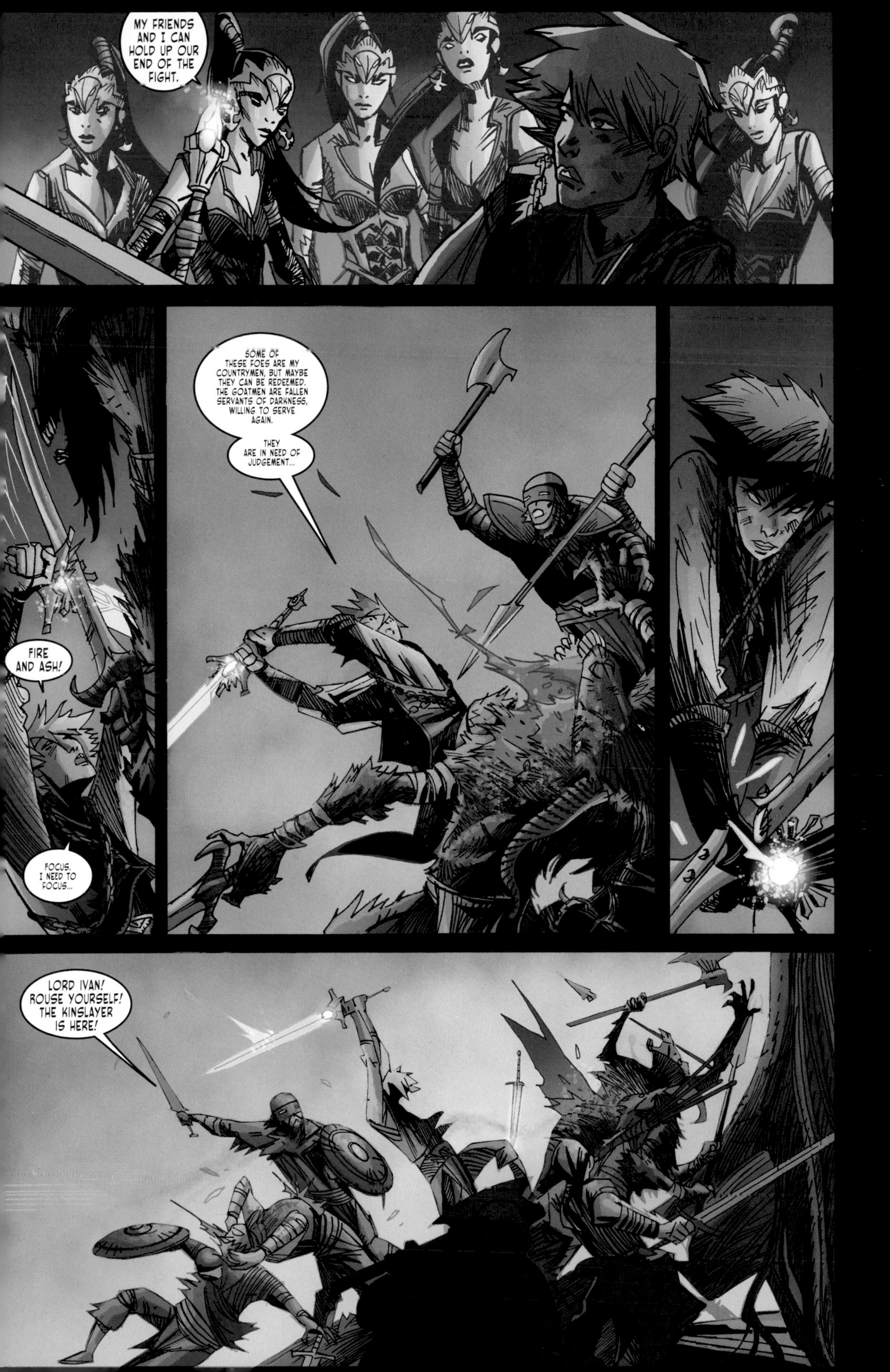
MY FRIENDS AND I CAN HOLD UP OUR END OF THE FIGHT.
SOME OF THESE FOES ARE MY COUNTRYMEN, BUT MAYBE THEY CAN BE REDEEMED. THE GOATMEN ARE FALLEN SERVANTS OF DARKNESS, WILLING TO SERVE AGAIN.
THEY ARE IN NEED OF JUDGEMENT...
FIRE AND ASH!
FOCUS. I NEED TO FOCUS...
LORD IVAN! ROUSE YOURSELF! THE KINSLAYER IS HERE!

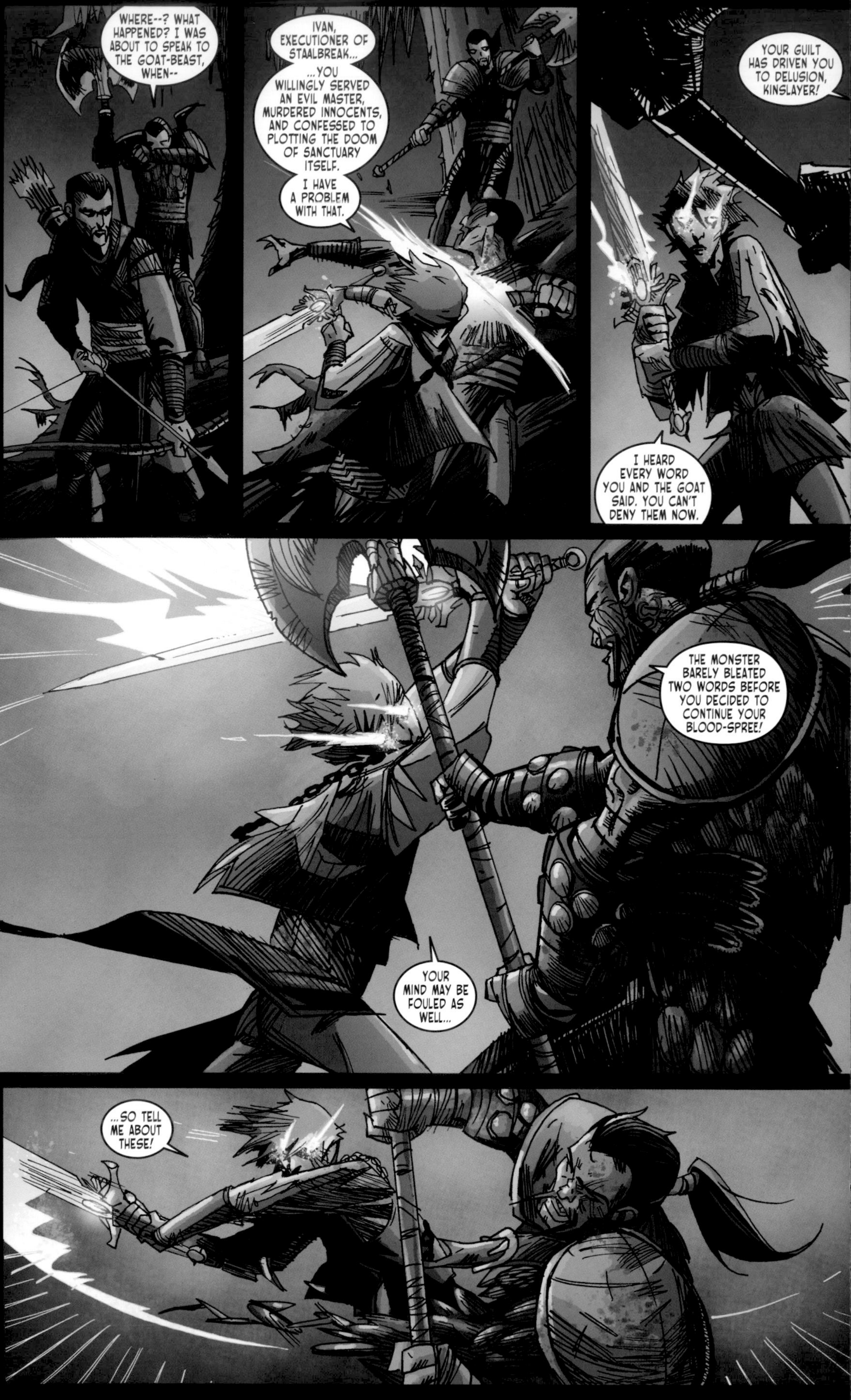
WHERE--? WHAT HAPPENED? I WAS ABOUT TO SPEAK TO THE GOAT-BEAST, WHEN--
IVAN, EXECUTIONER OF STAALBREAK...
...YOU WILLINGLY SERVED AN EVIL MASTER, MURDERED INNOCENTS, AND CONFESSED TO PLOTTING THE DOOM OF SANCTUARY ITSELF.
I HAVE A PROBLEM WITH THAT.
YOUR GUILT HAS DRIVEN YOU TO DELUSION, KINSLAYER!
I HEARD EVERY WORD YOU AND THE GOAT SAID. YOU CAN'T DENY THEM NOW.
THE MONSTER BARELY BLEATED TWO WORDS BEFORE YOU DECIDED TO CONTINUE YOUR BLOOD-SPREE!
YOUR MIND MAY BE FOULED AS WELL...
...SO TELL ME ABOUT THESE!

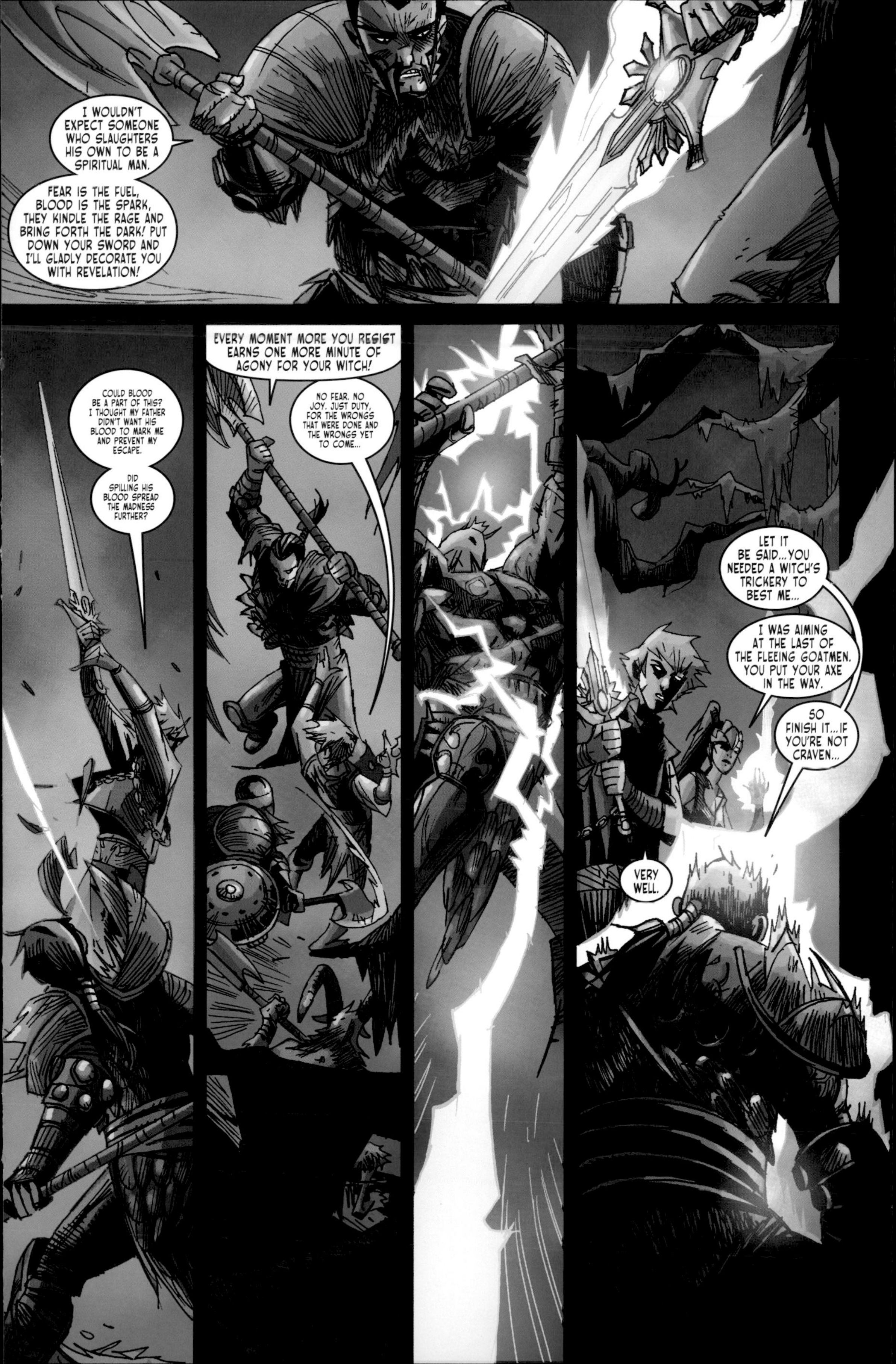
I WOULDN'T EXPECT SOMEONE WHO SLAUGHTERS HIS OWN TO BE A SPIRITUAL MAN.
FEAR IS THE FUEL, BLOOD IS THE SPARK, THEY KINDLE THE RAGE AND BRING FORTH THE DARK! PUT DOWN YOUR SWORD AND I'LL GLADLY DECORATE YOU WITH REVELATION!
COULD BLOOD BE A PART OF THIS? I THOUGHT MY FATHER DIDN'T WANT HIS BLOOD TO MARK ME AND PREVENT MY ESCAPE.
DID SPILLING HIS BLOOD SPREAD THE MADNESS FURTHER?
EVERY MOMENT MORE YOU RESIST EARNS ONE MORE MINUTE OF AGONY FOR YOUR WITCH!
NO FEAR. NO JOY. JUST DUTY, FOR THE WRONGS THAT WERE DONE AND THE WRONGS YET TO COME...
LET IT BE SAID...YOU NEEDED A WITCH'S TRICKERY TO BEST ME...
I WAS AIMING AT THE LAST OF THE FLEEING GOATMEN. YOU PUT YOUR AXE IN THE WAY.
SO FINISH IT...IF YOU'RE NOT CRAVEN...
VERY WELL.

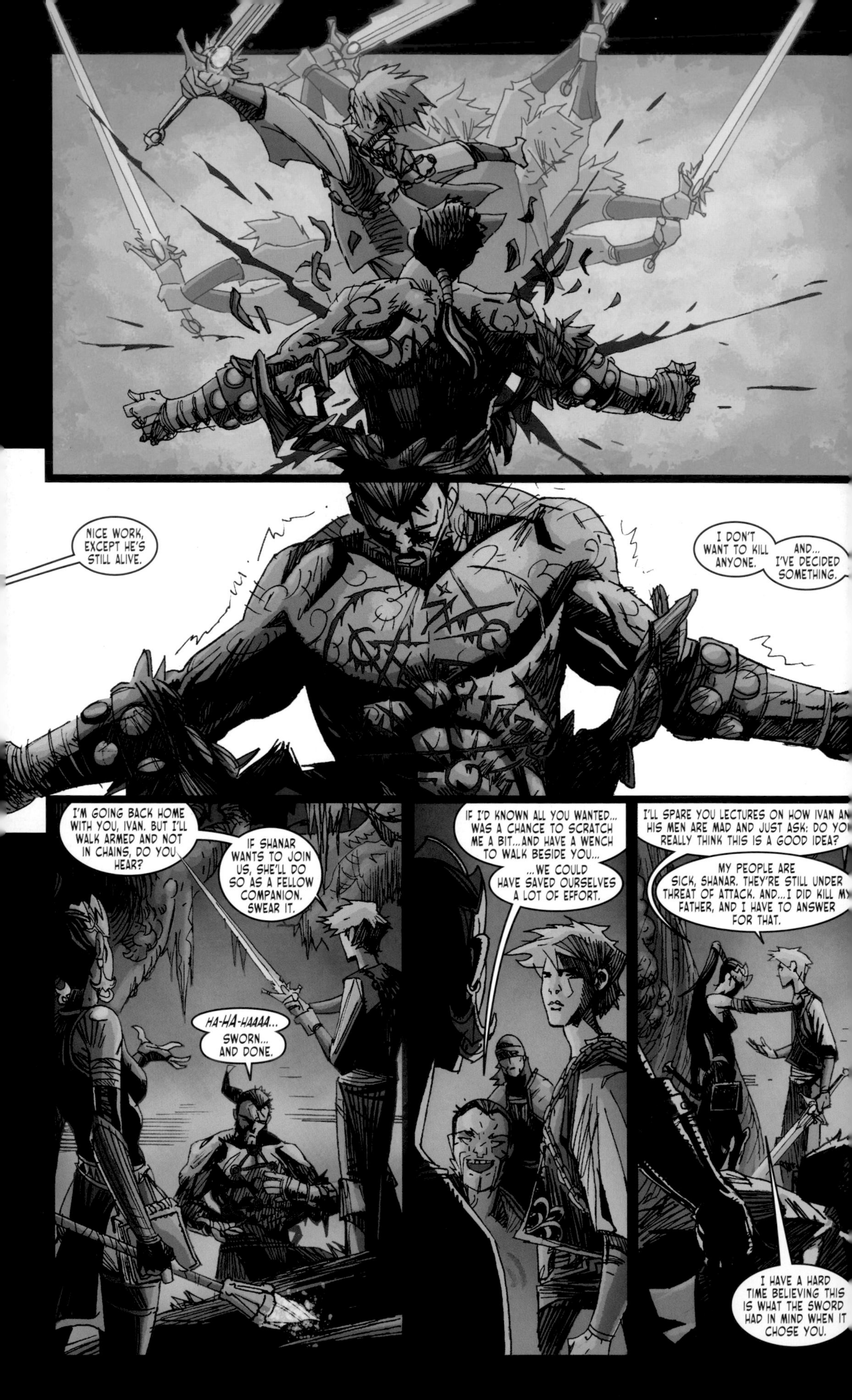

NICE WORK, EXCEPT HE'S STILL ALIVE.
I DON'T WANT TO KILL ANYONE.
AND... I'VE DECIDED SOMETHING.
I'M GOING BACK HOME WITH YOU, IVAN. BUT I'LL WALK ARMED AND NOT IN CHAINS, DO YOU HEAR?
IF SHANAR WANTS TO JOIN US, SHE'LL DO SO AS A FELLOW COMPANION. SWEAR IT.
HA-HA-HAAAA... SWORN... AND DONE.
IF I'D KNOWN ALL YOU WANTED... WAS A CHANCE TO SCRATCH ME A BIT...AND HAVE A WENCH TO WALK BESIDE YOU...
...WE COULD HAVE SAVED OURSELVES A LOT OF EFFORT.
I'LL SPARE YOU LECTURES ON HOW IVAN AN HIS MEN ARE MAD AND JUST ASK: DO YO REALLY THINK THIS IS A GOOD IDEA?
MY PEOPLE ARE SICK, SHANAR. THEY'RE STILL UNDER THREAT OF ATTACK. AND...I DID KILL M FATHER, AND I HAVE TO ANSWER FOR THAT.
I HAVE A HARD TIME BELIEVING THIS IS WHAT THE SWORD HAD IN MIND WHEN IT CHOSE YOU.

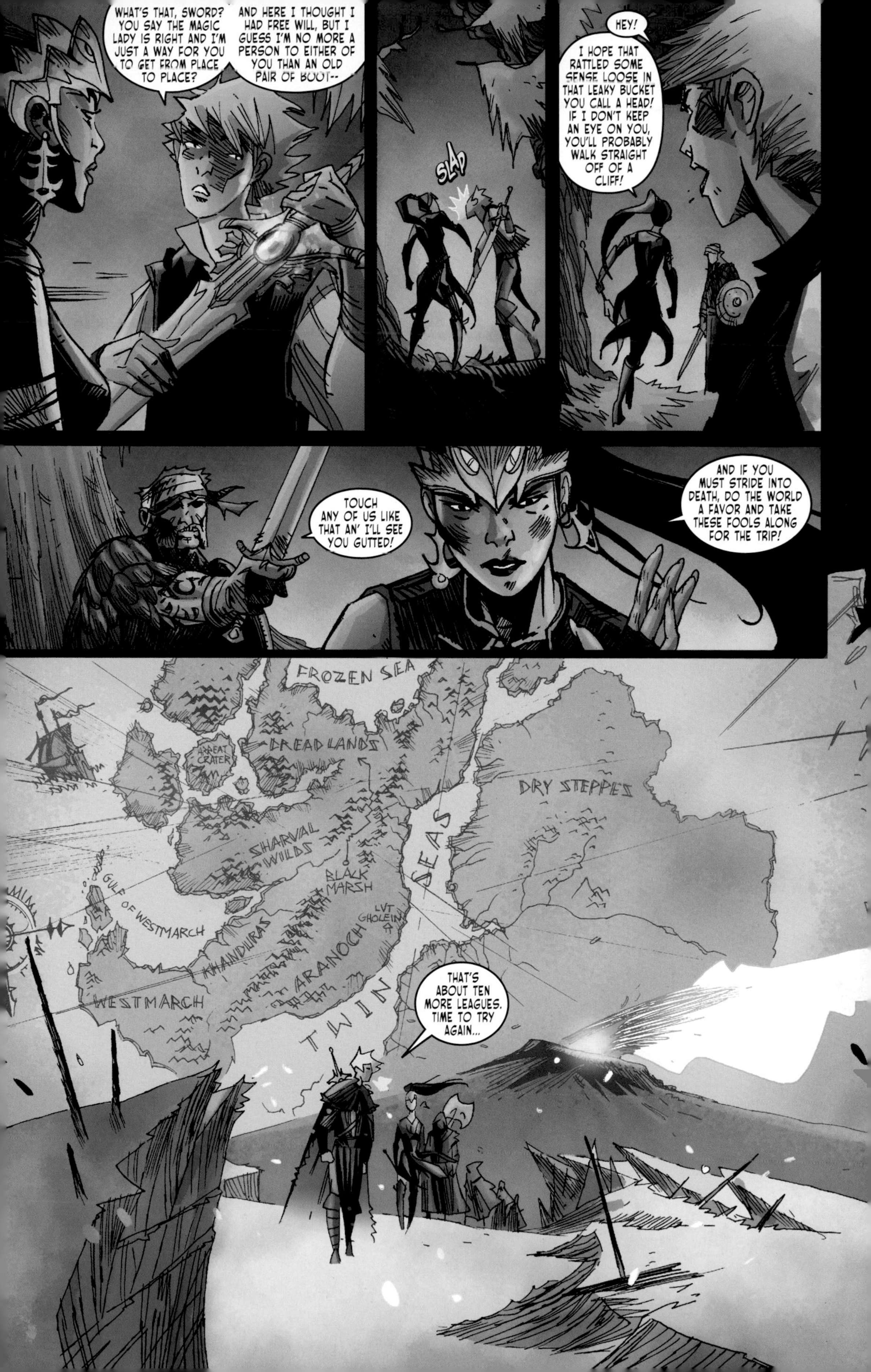
WHAT'S THAT, SWORD? YOU SAY THE MAGIC LADY IS RIGHT AND I'M JUST A WAY FOR YOU TO GET FROM PLACE TO PLACE?
AND HERE I THOUGHT I HAD FREE WILL, BUT I GUESS I'M NO MORE A PERSON TO EITHER OF YOU THAN AN OLD PAIR OF BOOT--
SLAP
HEY!
I HOPE THAT RATTLED SOME SENSE LOOSE IN THAT LEAKY BUCKET YOU CALL A HEAD! IF I DON'T KEEP AN EYE ON YOU, YOU'LL PROBABLY WALK STRAIGHT OFF OF A CLIFF!
TOUCH ANY OF US LIKE THAT AN' I'LL SEE YOU GUTTED!
AND IF YOU MUST STRIDE INTO DEATH, DO THE WORLD A FAVOR AND TAKE THESE FOOLS ALONG FOR THE TRIP!
FROZEN SEA
ARREAT CRATER
DREADLANDS
DRY STEPPES
SHARVAL WILDS
BLACK MARSH
GULF OF WESTMARCH
LUT GHOLEIN
KHANDURAS
ARANOCH
WESTMARCH
TWIN SEAS
THAT'S ABOUT TEN MORE LEAGUES. TIME TO TRY AGAIN...

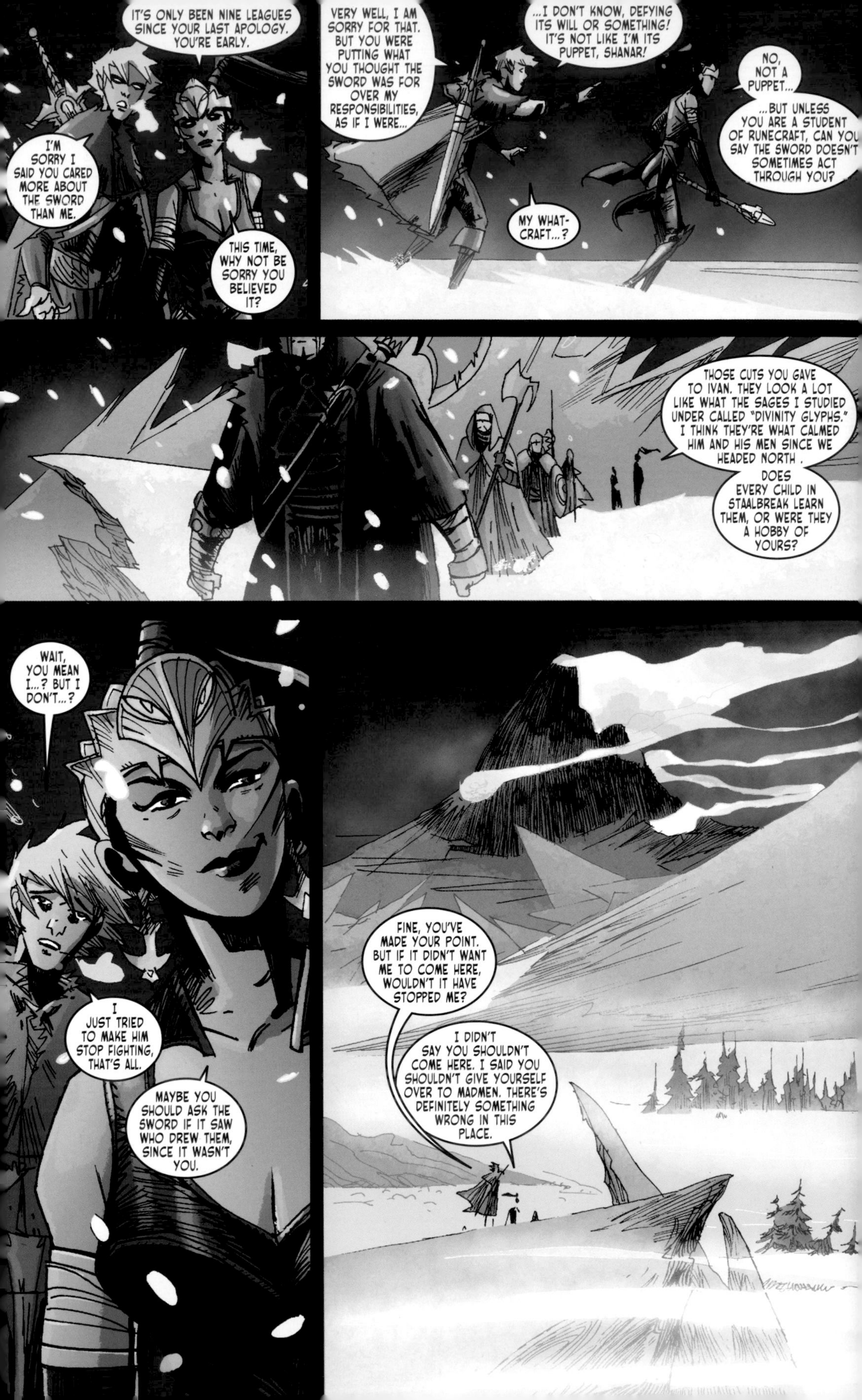
I'M SORRY I SAID YOU CARED MORE ABOUT THE SWORD THAN ME.
IT'S ONLY BEEN NINE LEAGUES SINCE YOUR LAST APOLOGY. YOU'RE EARLY.
THIS TIME, WHY NOT BE SORRY YOU BELIEVED IT?
VERY WELL, I AM SORRY FOR THAT. BUT YOU WERE PUTTING WHAT YOU THOUGHT THE SWORD WAS FOR OVER MY RESPONSIBILITIES, AS IF I WERE...
...I DON'T KNOW, DEFYING ITS WILL OR SOMETHING! IT'S NOT LIKE I'M ITS PUPPET, SHANAR!
NO, NOT A PUPPET...
...BUT UNLESS YOU ARE A STUDENT OF RUNECRAFT, CAN YOU SAY THE SWORD DOESN'T SOMETIMES ACT THROUGH YOU?
MY WHAT-CRAFT...?
THOSE CUTS YOU GAVE TO IVAN. THEY LOOK A LOT LIKE WHAT THE SAGES I STUDIED UNDER CALLED "DIVINITY GLYPHS." I THINK THEY'RE WHAT CALMED HIM AND HIS MEN SINCE WE HEADED NORTH .
DOES EVERY CHILD IN STAALBREAK LEARN THEM, OR WERE THEY A HOBBY OF YOURS?
WAIT, YOU MEAN I...? BUT I DON'T...?
I JUST TRIED TO MAKE HIM STOP FIGHTING, THAT'S ALL.
MAYBE YOU SHOULD ASK THE SWORD IF IT SAW WHO DREW THEM, SINCE IT WASN'T YOU.
FINE, YOU'VE MADE YOUR POINT. BUT IF IT DIDN'T WANT ME TO COME HERE, WOULDN'T IT HAVE STOPPED ME?
I DIDN'T SAY YOU SHOULDN'T COME HERE. I SAID YOU SHOULDN'T GIVE YOURSELF OVER TO MADMEN. THERE'S DEFINITELY SOMETHING WRONG IN THIS PLACE.

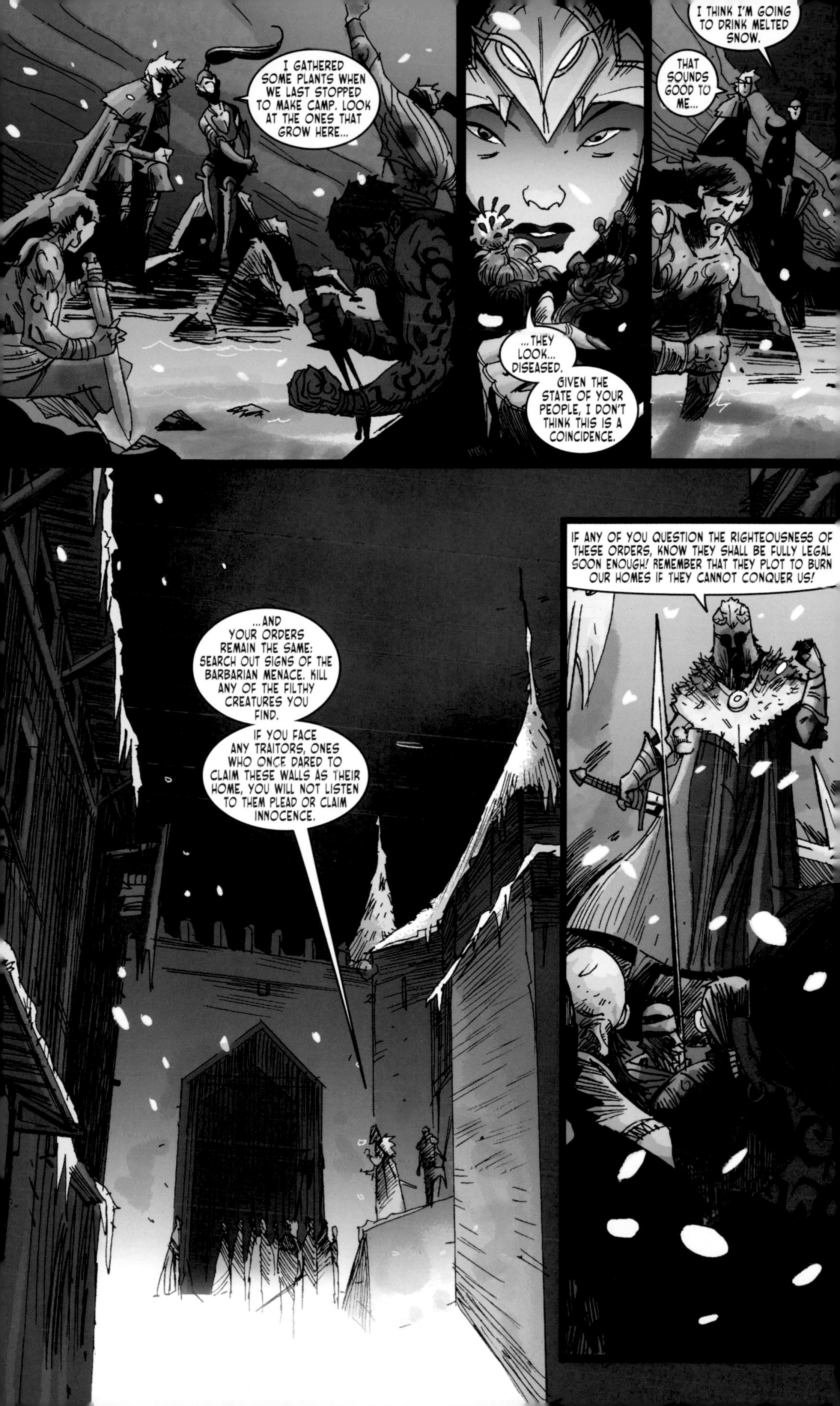
I GATHERED SOME PLANTS WHEN WE LAST STOPPED TO MAKE CAMP. LOOK AT THE ONES THAT GROW HERE...
...THEY LOOK... DISEASED.
GIVEN THE STATE OF YOUR PEOPLE, I DON'T THINK THIS IS A COINCIDENCE.
I THINK I'M GOING TO DRINK MELTED SNOW.
THAT SOUNDS GOOD TO ME...
...AND YOUR ORDERS REMAIN THE SAME: SEARCH OUT SIGNS OF THE BARBARIAN MENACE. KILL ANY OF THE FILTHY CREATURES YOU FIND.
IF YOU FACE ANY TRAITORS, ONES WHO ONCE DARED TO CLAIM THESE WALLS AS THEIR HOME, YOU WILL NOT LISTEN TO THEM PLEAD OR CLAIM INNOCENCE.
IF ANY OF YOU QUESTION THE RIGHTEOUSNESS OF THESE ORDERS, KNOW THEY SHALL BE FULLY LEGAL SOON ENOUGH! REMEMBER THAT THEY PLOT TO BURN OUR HOMES IF THEY CANNOT CONQUER US!

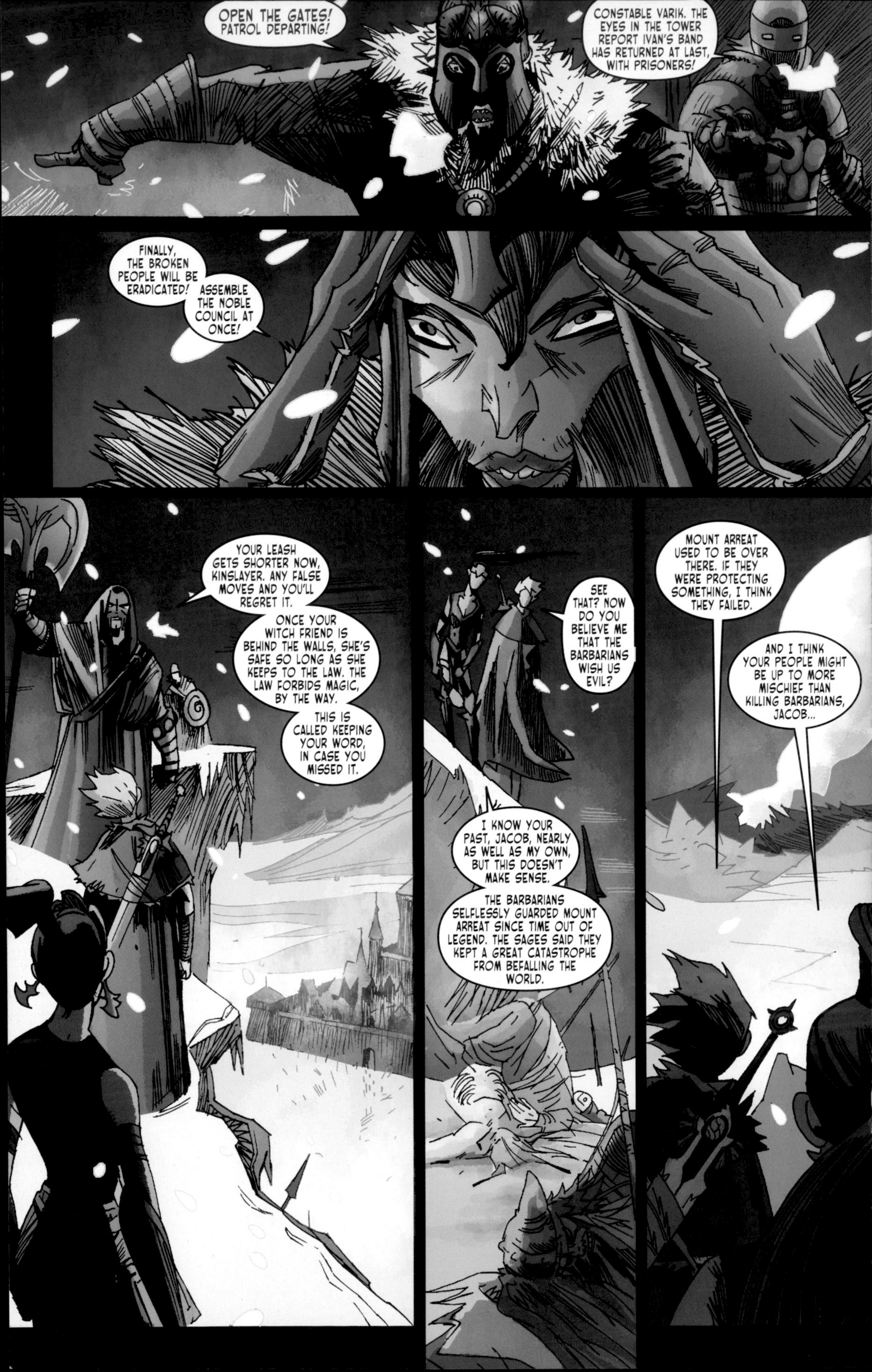
OPEN THE GATES! PATROL DEPARTING!
CONSTABLE VARIK. THE EYES IN THE TOWER REPORT IVAN'S BAND HAS RETURNED AT LAST, WITH PRISONERS!
FINALLY, THE BROKEN PEOPLE WILL BE ERADICATED!
ASSEMBLE THE NOBLE COUNCIL AT ONCE!
YOUR LEASH GETS SHORTER NOW, KINSLAYER. ANY FALSE MOVES AND YOU'LL REGRET IT.
ONCE YOUR WITCH FRIEND IS BEHIND THE WALLS, SHE'S SAFE SO LONG AS SHE KEEPS TO THE LAW. THE LAW FORBIDS MAGIC, BY THE WAY.
THIS IS CALLED KEEPING YOUR WORD, IN CASE YOU MISSED IT.
SEE THAT? NOW DO YOU BELIEVE ME THAT THE BARBARIANS WISH US EVIL?
I KNOW YOUR PAST, JACOB, NEARLY AS WELL AS MY OWN, BUT THIS DOESN'T MAKE SENSE.
THE BARBARIANS SELFLESSLY GUARDED MOUNT ARREAT SINCE TIME OUT OF LEGEND. THE SAGES SAID THEY KEPT A GREAT CATASTROPHE FROM BEFALLING THE WORLD.
MOUNT ARREAT USED TO BE OVER THERE. IF THEY WERE PROTECTING SOMETHING, I THINK THEY FAILED.
AND I THINK YOUR PEOPLE MIGHT BE UP TO MORE MISCHIEF THAN KILLING BARBARIANS, JACOB...

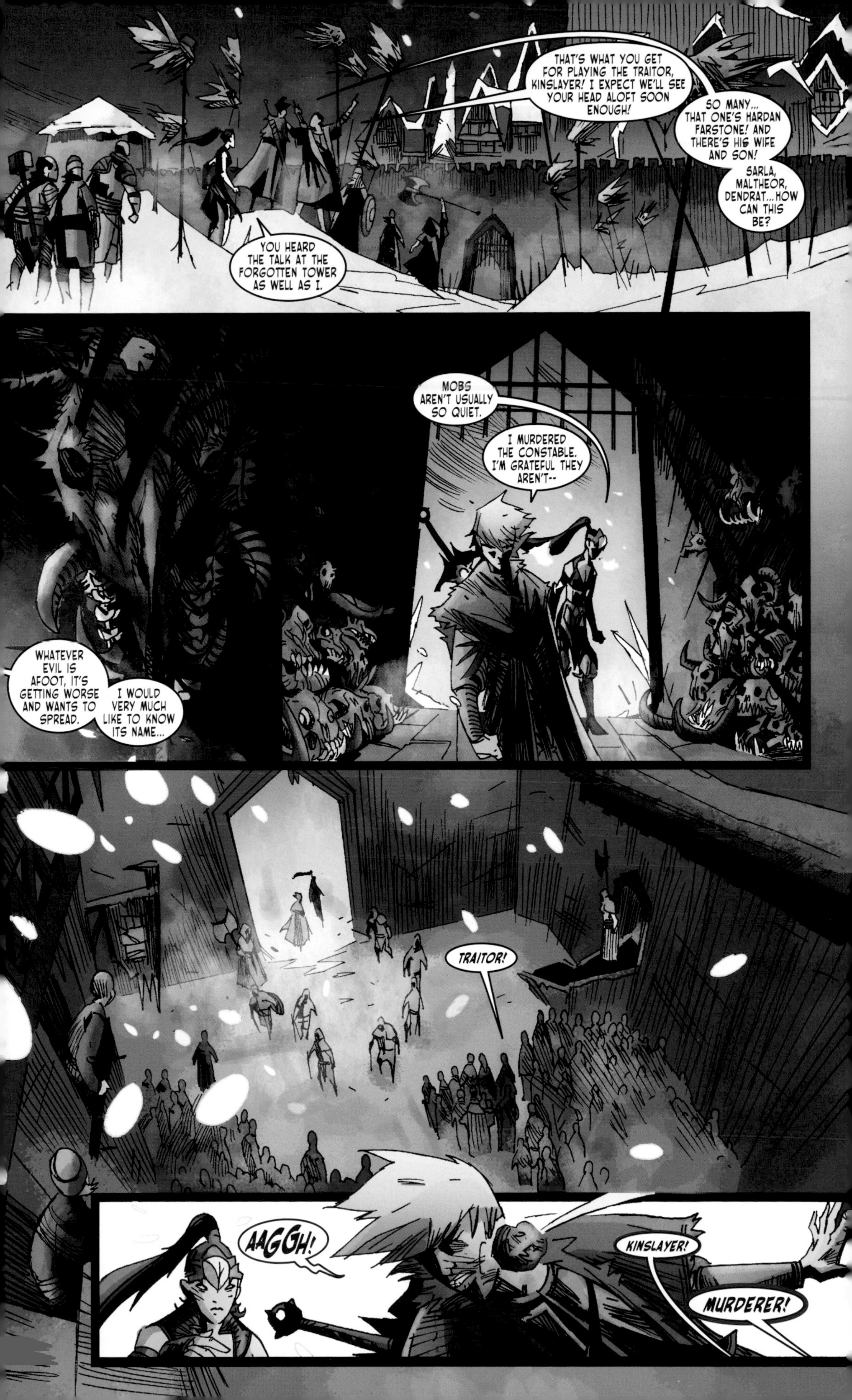
THAT'S WHAT YOU GET FOR PLAYING THE TRAITOR, KINSLAYER! I EXPECT WE'LL SEE YOUR HEAD ALOFT SOON ENOUGH!
SO MANY... THAT ONE'S HARDAN FARSTONE! AND THERE'S HIS WIFE AND SON!
SARLA, MALTHEOR, DENDRAT...HOW CAN THIS BE?
YOU HEARD THE TALK AT THE FORGOTTEN TOWER AS WELL AS I.
MOBS AREN'T USUALLY SO QUIET.
I MURDERED THE CONSTABLE. I'M GRATEFUL THEY AREN'T--
WHATEVER EVIL IS AFOOT, IT'S GETTING WORSE AND WANTS TO SPREAD.
I WOULD VERY MUCH LIKE TO KNOW ITS NAME...
TRAITOR!
AAGGH!
KINSLAYER!
MURDERER!

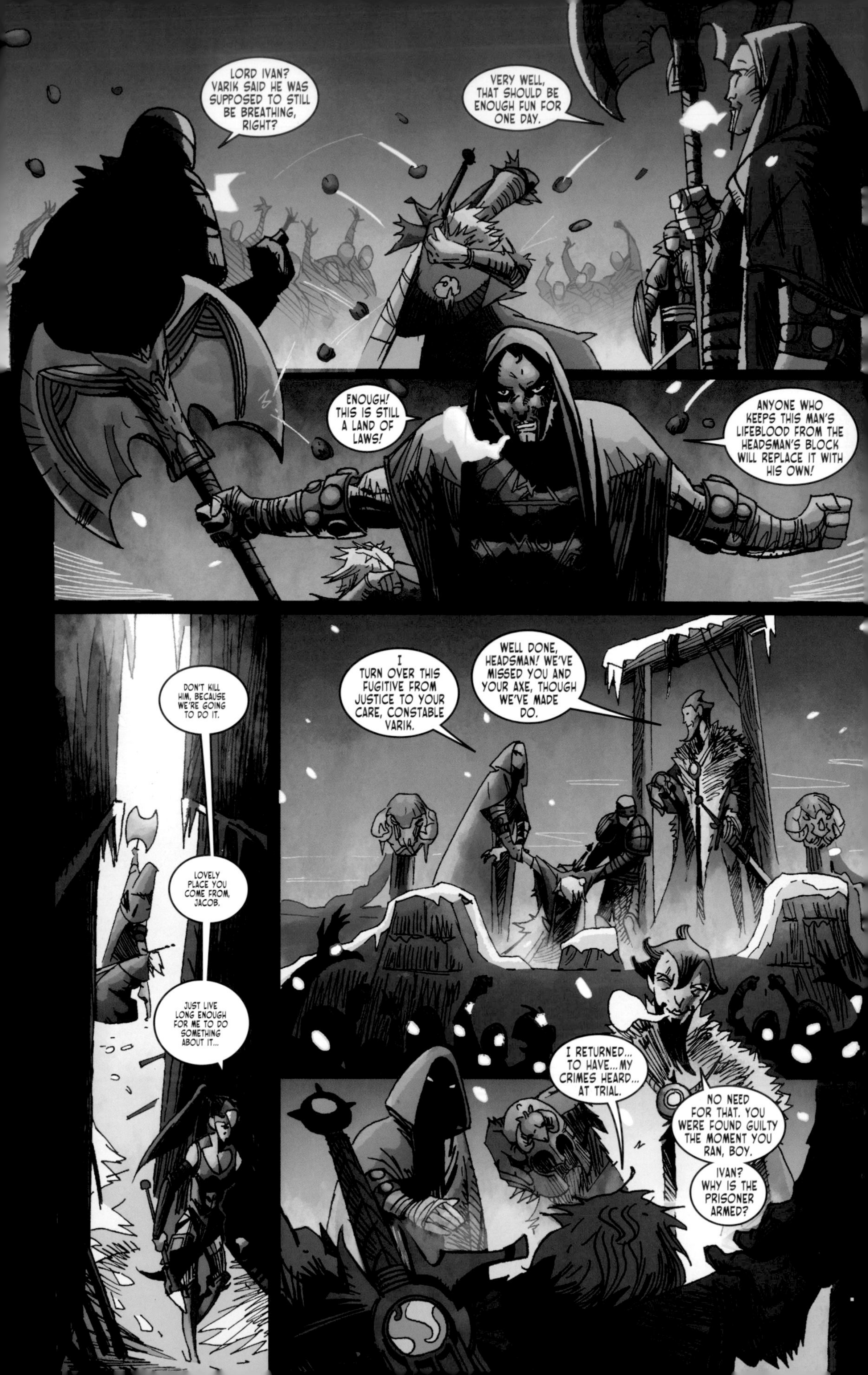
LORD IVAN? VARIK SAID HE WAS SUPPOSED TO STILL BE BREATHING, RIGHT?
VERY WELL, THAT SHOULD BE ENOUGH FUN FOR ONE DAY.
ENOUGH! THIS IS STILL A LAND OF LAWS!
ANYONE WHO KEEPS THIS MAN'S LIFEBLOOD FROM THE HEADSMAN'S BLOCK WILL REPLACE IT WITH HIS OWN!
DON'T KILL HIM, BECAUSE WE'RE GOING TO DO IT.
LOVELY PLACE YOU COME FROM, JACOB.
JUST LIVE LONG ENOUGH FOR ME TO DO SOMETHING ABOUT IT...
I TURN OVER THIS FUGITIVE FROM JUSTICE TO YOUR CARE, CONSTABLE VARIK.
WELL DONE, HEADSMAN! WE'VE MISSED YOU AND YOUR AXE, THOUGH WE'VE MADE DO.
I RETURNED... TO HAVE... MY CRIMES HEARD... AT TRIAL.
NO NEED FOR THAT. YOU WERE FOUND GUILTY THE MOMENT YOU RAN, BOY.
IVAN? WHY IS THE PRISONER ARMED?

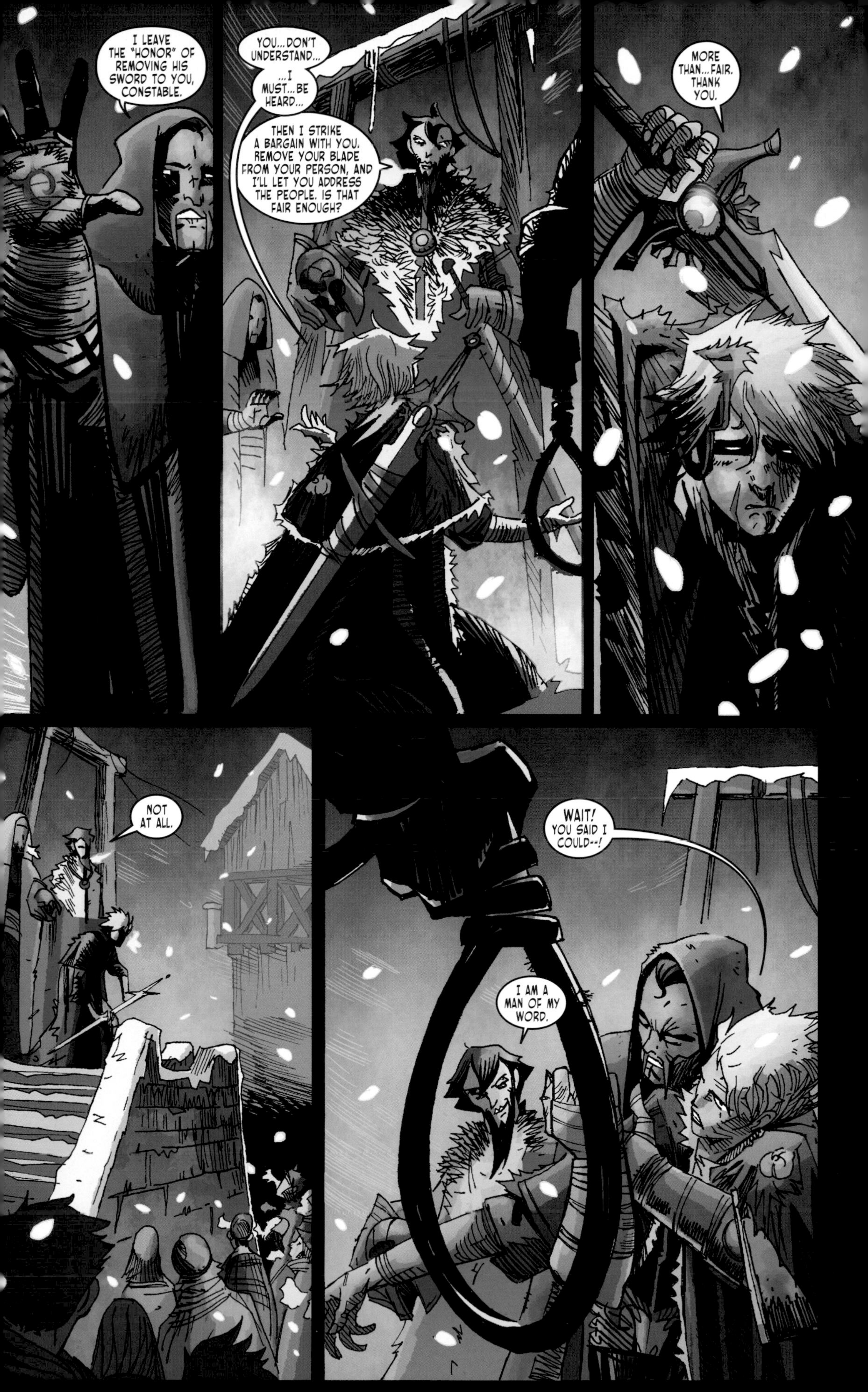
I LEAVE THE "HONOR" OF REMOVING HIS SWORD TO YOU, CONSTABLE.
YOU...DON'T UNDERSTAND...
...I MUST...BE HEARD...
THEN I STRIKE A BARGAIN WITH YOU. REMOVE YOUR BLADE FROM YOUR PERSON, AND I'LL LET YOU ADDRESS THE PEOPLE. IS THAT FAIR ENOUGH?
MORE THAN...FAIR. THANK YOU.
NOT AT ALL.
WAIT! YOU SAID I COULD--!
I AM A MAN OF MY WORD.

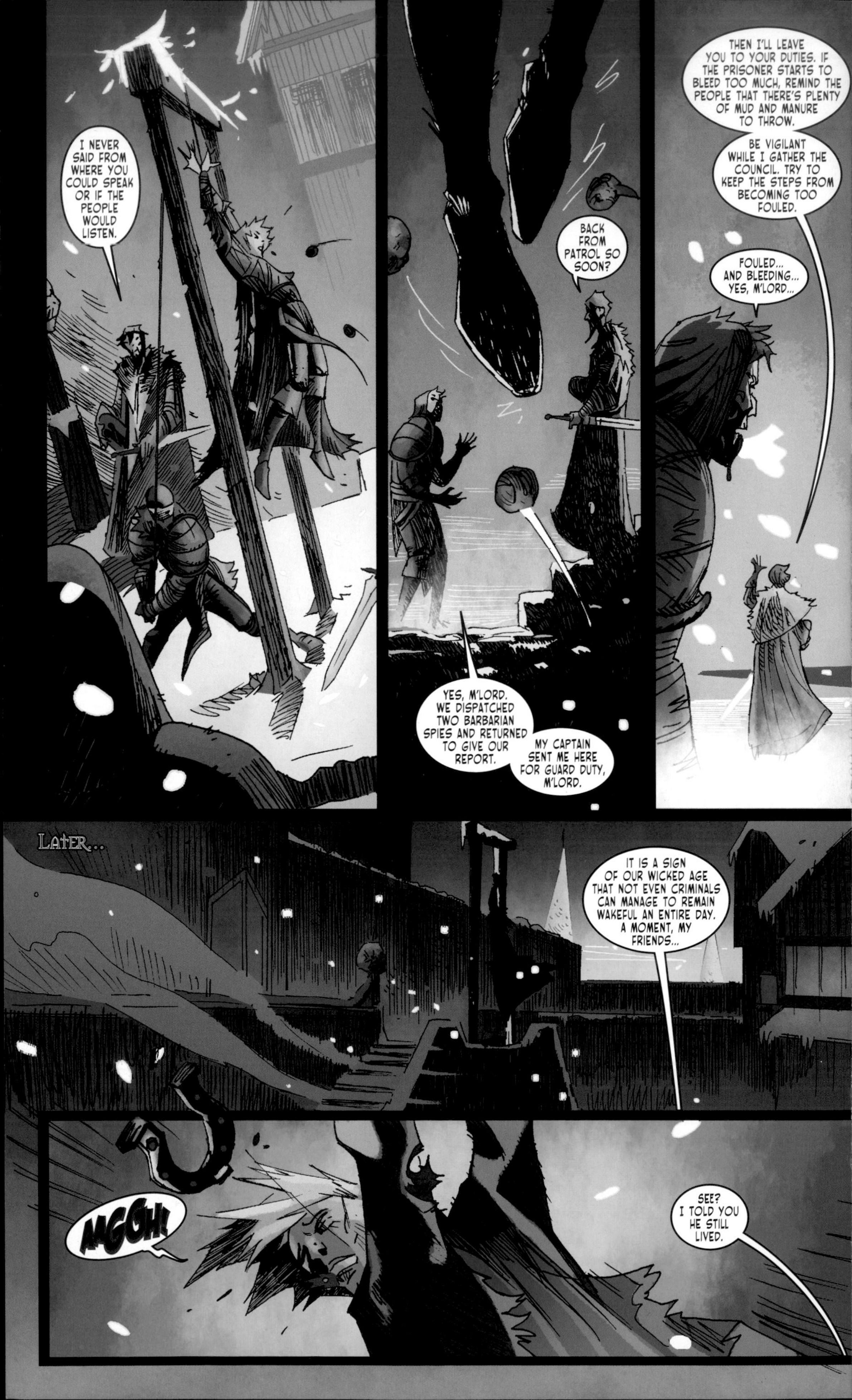
I NEVER SAID FROM WHERE YOU COULD SPEAK OR IF THE PEOPLE WOULD LISTEN.
BACK FROM PATROL SO SOON?
YES, M'LORD. WE DISPATCHED TWO BARBARIAN SPIES AND RETURNED TO GIVE OUR REPORT.
MY CAPTAIN SENT ME HERE FOR GUARD DUTY, M'LORD.
THEN I'LL LEAVE YOU TO YOUR DUTIES. IF THE PRISONER STARTS TO BLEED TOO MUCH, REMIND THE PEOPLE THAT THERE'S PLENTY OF MUD AND MANURE TO THROW.
BE VIGILANT WHILE I GATHER THE COUNCIL. TRY TO KEEP THE STEPS FROM BECOMING TOO FOULED.
FOULED... AND BLEEDING... YES, M'LORD...
LATER...
IT IS A SIGN OF OUR WICKED AGE THAT NOT EVEN CRIMINALS CAN MANAGE TO REMAIN WAKEFUL AN ENTIRE DAY. A MOMENT, MY FRIENDS...
AAGGH!
SEE? I TOLD YOU HE STILL LIVED.

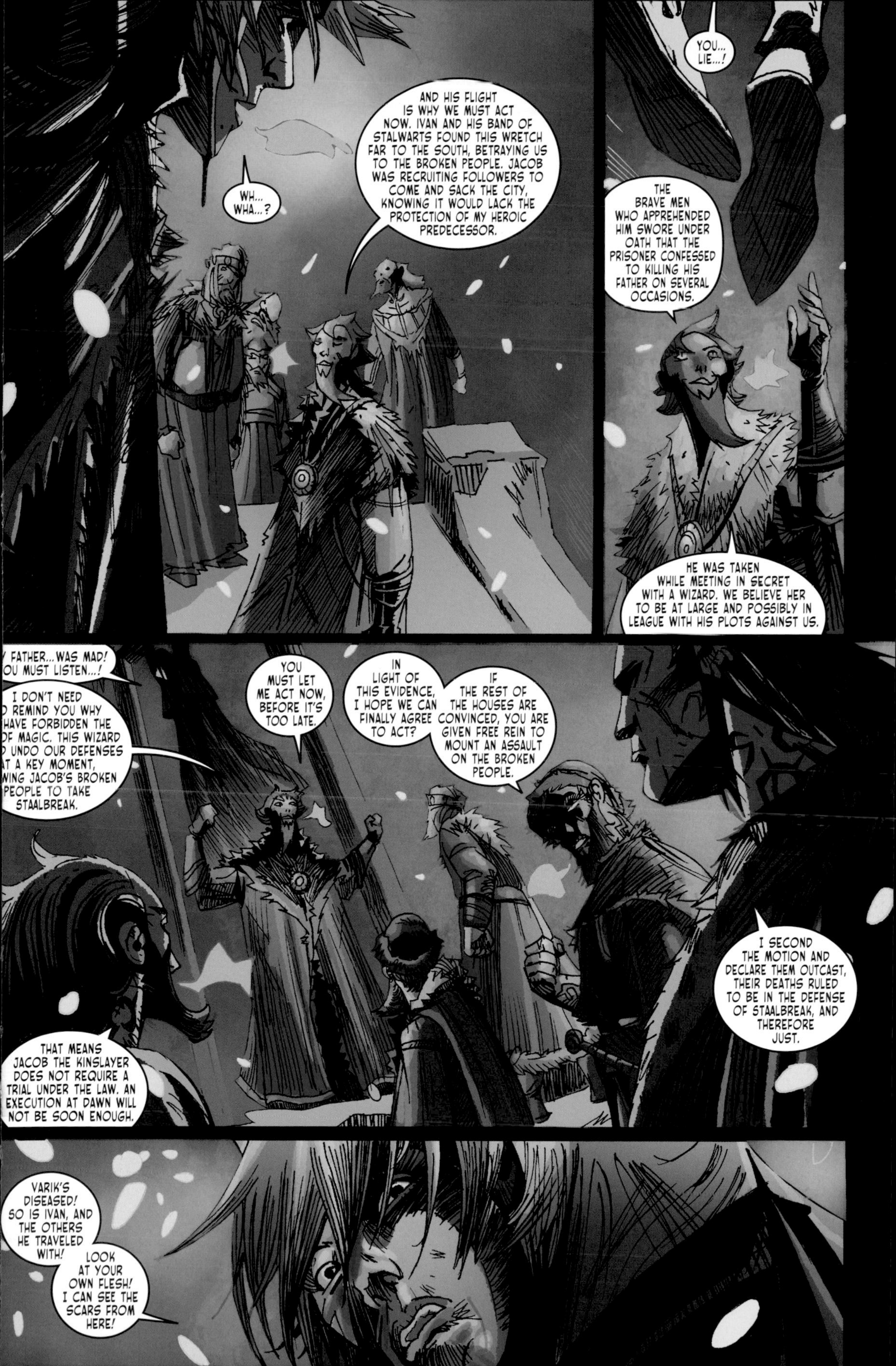
AND HIS FLIGHT IS WHY WE MUST ACT NOW. IVAN AND HIS BAND OF STALWARTS FOUND THIS WRETCH FAR TO THE SOUTH, BETRAYING US TO THE BROKEN PEOPLE. JACOB WAS RECRUITING FOLLOWERS TO COME AND SACK THE CITY, KNOWING IT WOULD LACK THE PROTECTION OF MY HEROIC PREDECESSOR.
WH... WHA...?
YOU... LIE...!
THE BRAVE MEN WHO APPREHENDED HIM SWORE UNDER OATH THAT THE PRISONER CONFESSED TO KILLING HIS FATHER ON SEVERAL OCCASIONS.
HE WAS TAKEN WHILE MEETING IN SECRET WITH A WIZARD. WE BELIEVE HER TO BE AT LARGE AND POSSIBLY IN LEAGUE WITH HIS PLOTS AGAINST US.
Y FATHER...WAS MAD! OU MUST LISTEN...!
I DON'T NEED D REMIND YOU WHY HAVE FORBIDDEN THE OF MAGIC. THIS WIZARD D UNDO OUR DEFENSES AT A KEY MOMENT, WING JACOB'S BROKEN PEOPLE TO TAKE STAALBREAK.
YOU MUST LET ME ACT NOW, BEFORE IT'S TOO LATE.
IN LIGHT OF THIS EVIDENCE, I HOPE WE CAN FINALLY AGREE TO ACT?
IF THE REST OF THE HOUSES ARE CONVINCED, YOU ARE GIVEN FREE REIN TO MOUNT AN ASSAULT ON THE BROKEN PEOPLE.
I SECOND THE MOTION AND DECLARE THEM OUTCAST, THEIR DEATHS RULED TO BE IN THE DEFENSE OF STAALBREAK, AND THEREFORE JUST.
THAT MEANS JACOB THE KINSLAYER DOES NOT REQUIRE A TRIAL UNDER THE LAW. AN EXECUTION AT DAWN WILL NOT BE SOON ENOUGH.
VARIK'S DISEASED! SO IS IVAN, AND THE OTHERS HE TRAVELED WITH!
LOOK AT YOUR OWN FLESH! I CAN SEE THE SCARS FROM HERE!

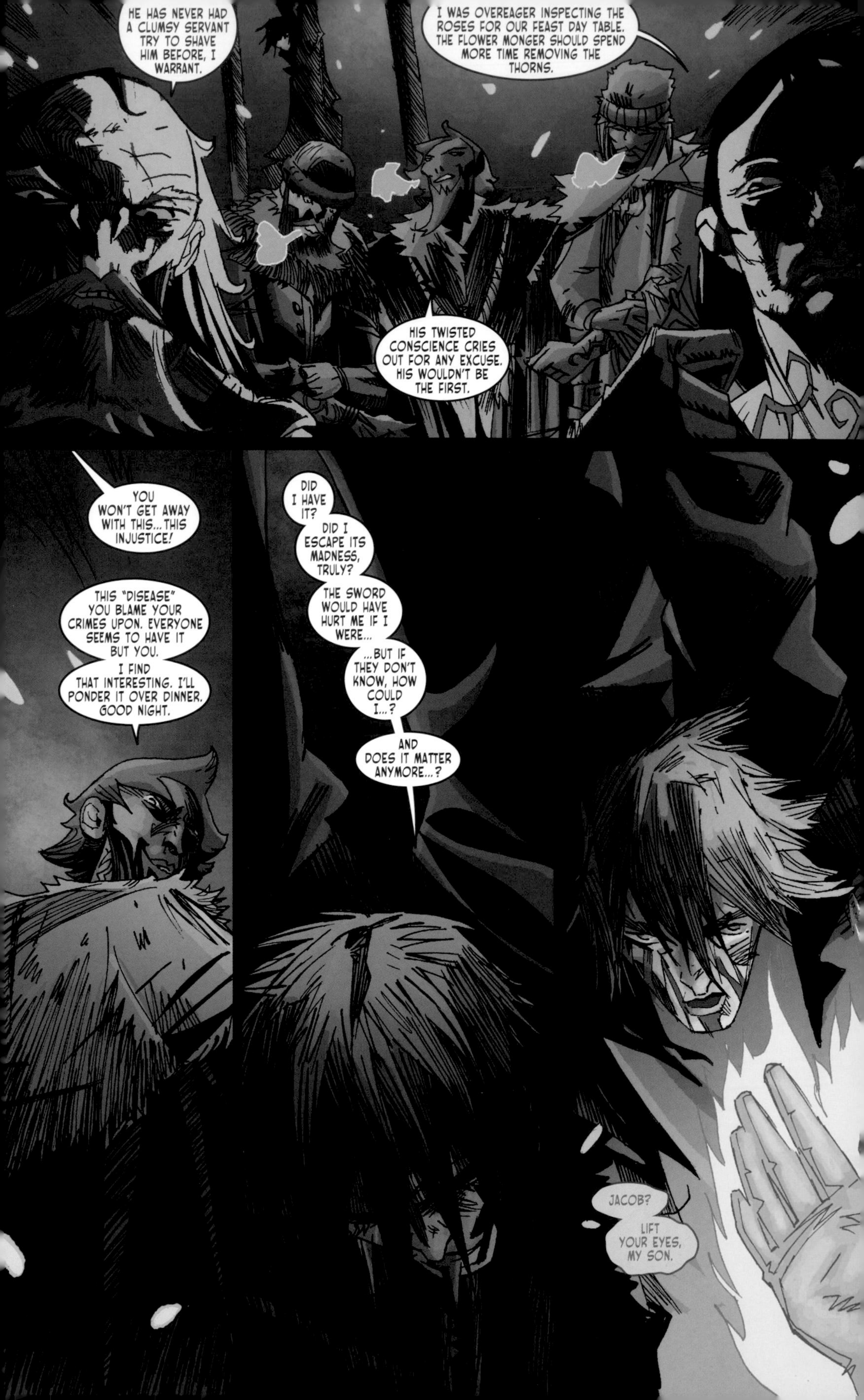
HE HAS NEVER HAD A CLUMSY SERVANT TRY TO SHAVE HIM BEFORE, I WARRANT.
I WAS OVEREAGER INSPECTING THE ROSES FOR OUR FEAST DAY TABLE. THE FLOWER MONGER SHOULD SPEND MORE TIME REMOVING THE THORNS.
HIS TWISTED CONSCIENCE CRIES OUT FOR ANY EXCUSE. HIS WOULDN'T BE THE FIRST.
YOU WON'T GET AWAY WITH THIS... THIS INJUSTICE!
THIS "DISEASE" YOU BLAME YOUR CRIMES UPON. EVERYONE SEEMS TO HAVE IT BUT YOU.
I FIND THAT INTERESTING. I'LL PONDER IT OVER DINNER. GOOD NIGHT.
DID I HAVE IT?
DID I ESCAPE ITS MADNESS, TRULY?
THE SWORD WOULD HAVE HURT ME IF I WERE...
...BUT IF THEY DON'T KNOW, HOW COULD I...?
AND DOES IT MATTER ANYMORE...?
JACOB?
LIFT YOUR EYES, MY SON.

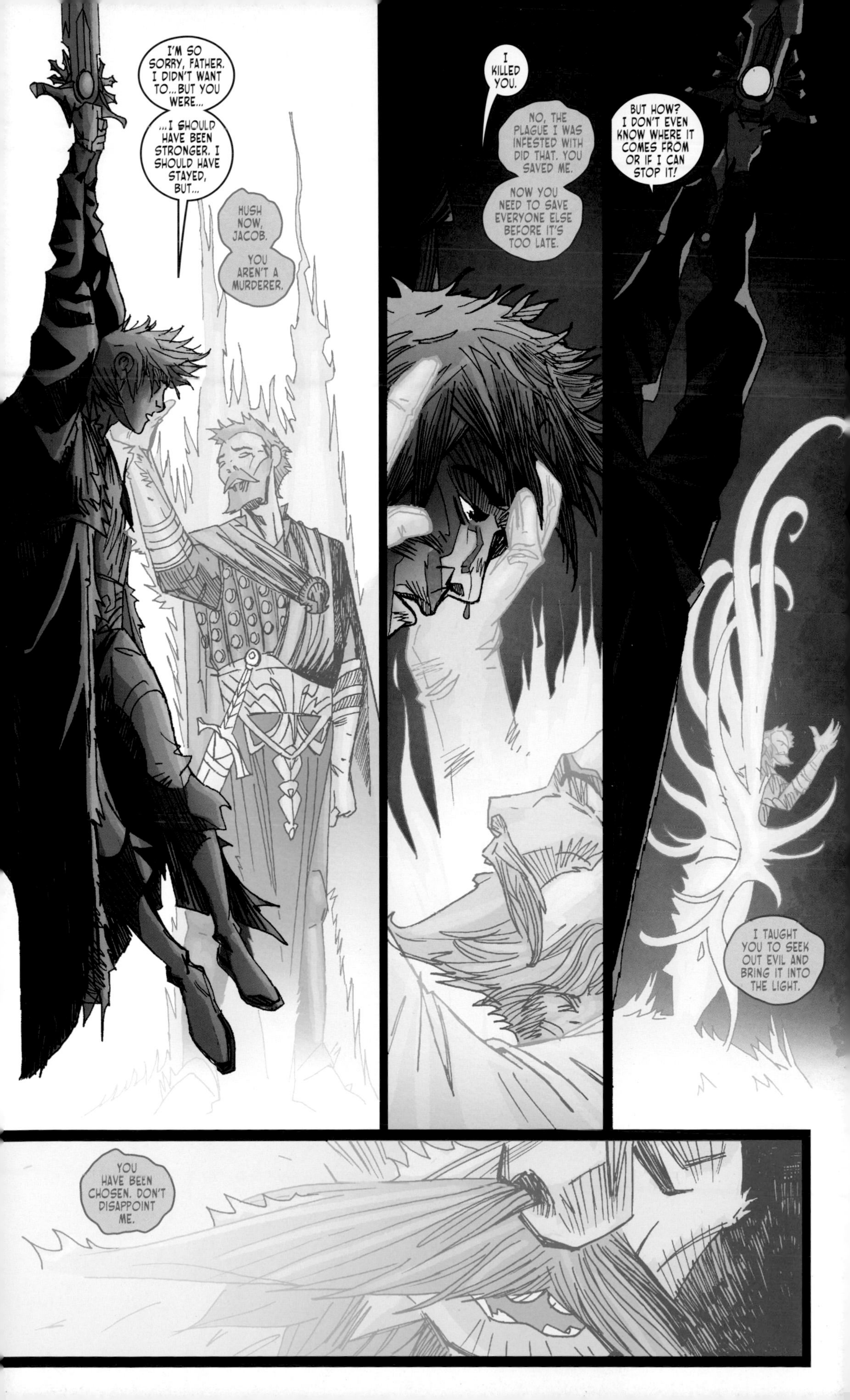
I'M SO SORRY, FATHER. I DIDN'T WANT TO...BUT YOU WERE...
...I SHOULD HAVE BEEN STRONGER. I SHOULD HAVE STAYED, BUT...
HUSH NOW, JACOB.
YOU AREN'T A MURDERER.
I KILLED YOU.
NO, THE PLAGUE I WAS INFESTED WITH DID THAT. YOU SAVED ME.
NOW YOU NEED TO SAVE EVERYONE ELSE BEFORE IT'S TOO LATE.
BUT HOW? I DON'T EVEN KNOW WHERE IT COMES FROM OR IF I CAN STOP IT!
I TAUGHT YOU TO SEEK OUT EVIL AND BRING IT INTO THE LIGHT.
YOU HAVE BEEN CHOSEN. DON'T DISAPPOINT ME.

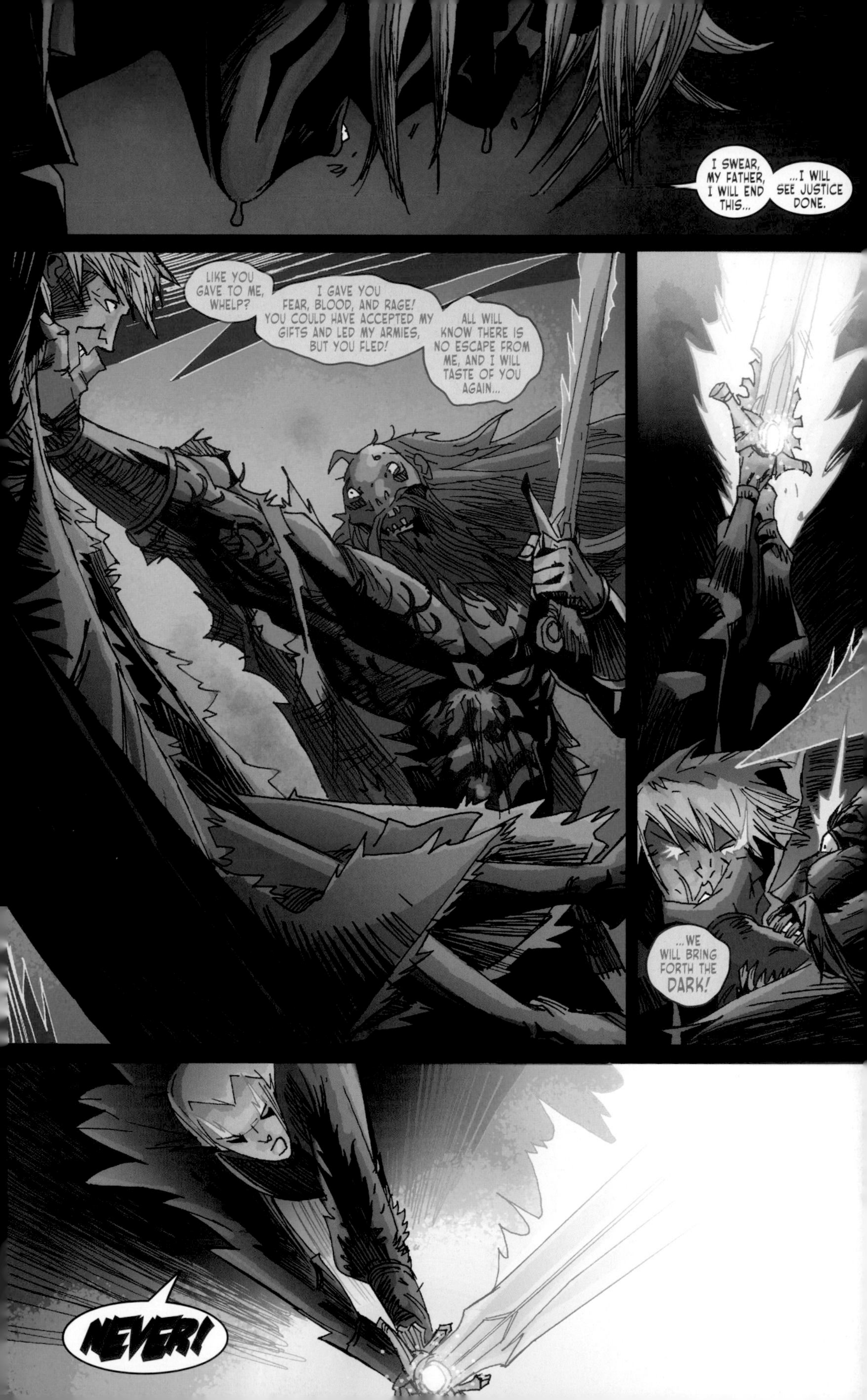
I SWEAR, MY FATHER, I WILL END THIS...
...I WILL SEE JUSTICE DONE.
LIKE YOU GAVE TO ME, WHELP?
I GAVE YOU FEAR, BLOOD, AND RAGE! YOU COULD HAVE ACCEPTED MY GIFTS AND LED MY ARMIES, BUT YOU FLED!
ALL WILL KNOW THERE IS NO ESCAPE FROM ME, AND I WILL TASTE OF YOU AGAIN...
...WE WILL BRING FORTH THE DARK!
NEVER!

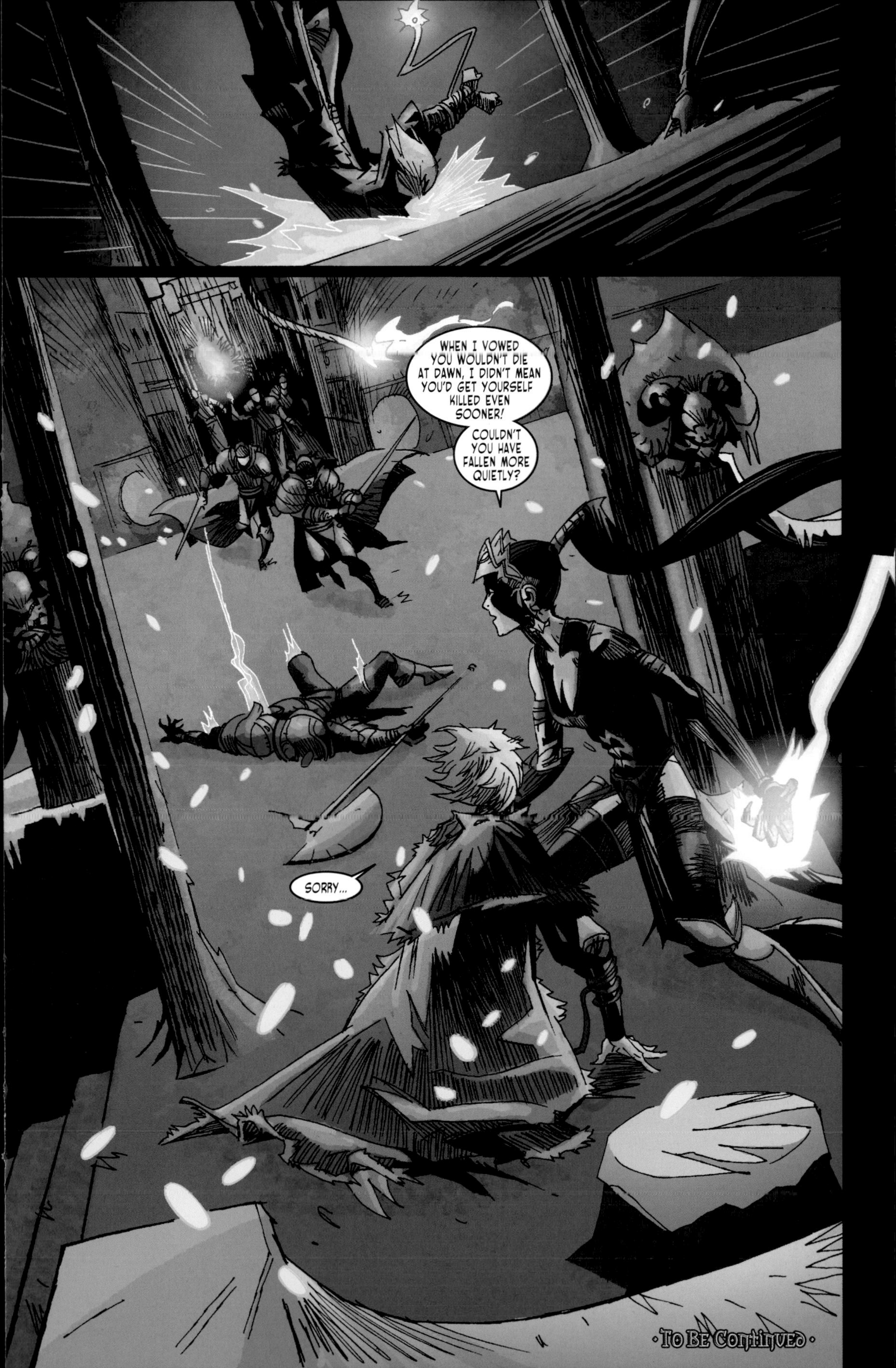
WHEN I VOWED YOU WOULDN'T DIE AT DAWN, I DIDN'T MEAN YOU'D GET YOURSELF KILLED EVEN SOONER!
COULDN'T YOU HAVE FALLEN MORE QUIETLY?
SORRY...
TO BE CONTINUED

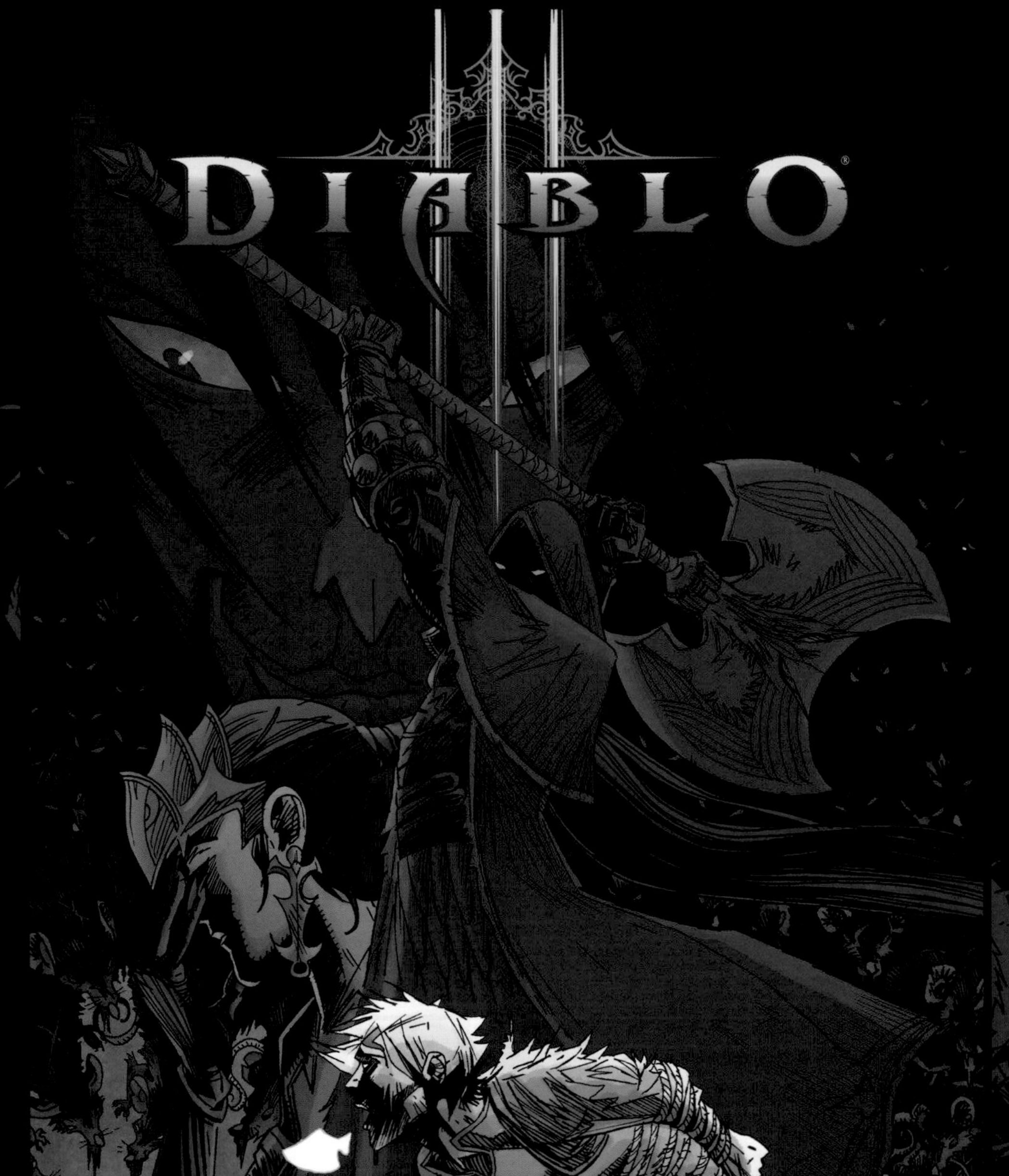
DIABLO

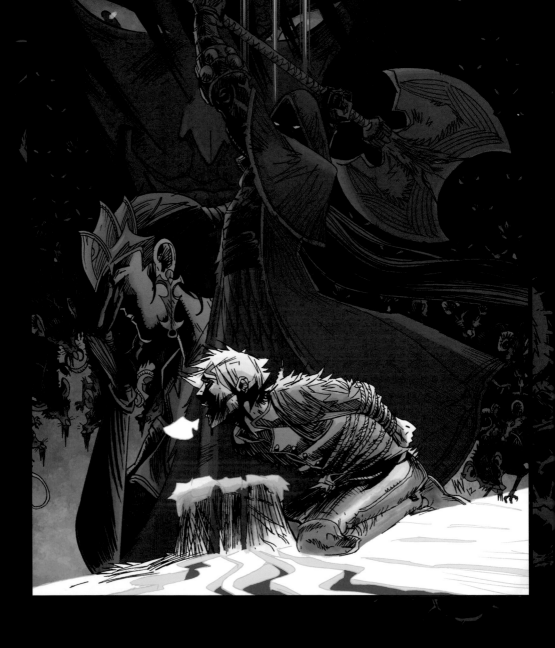

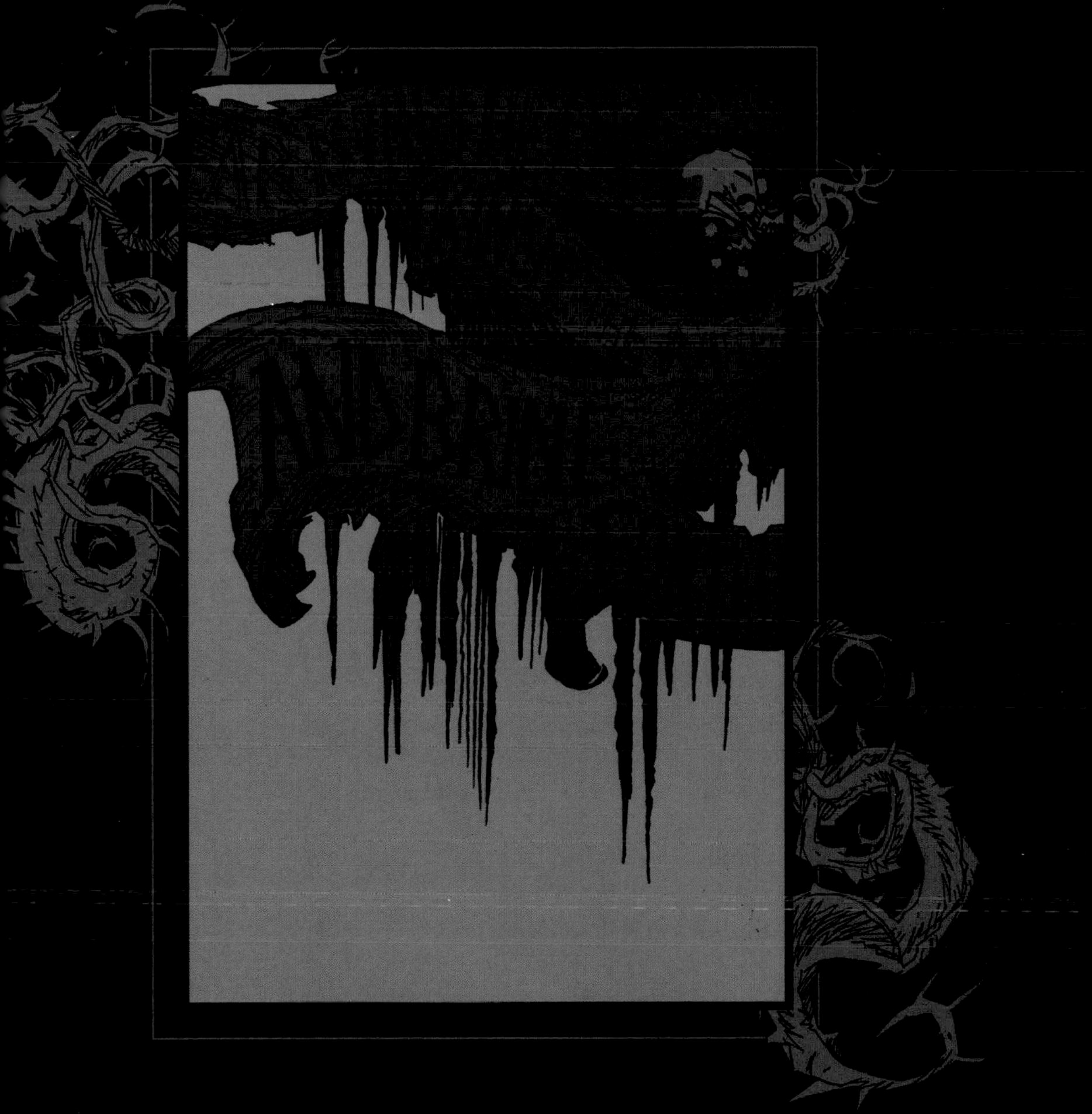

ACT IV

AARON WILLIAMS
JOSEPH LACROIX
LEE LOUGHRIDGE

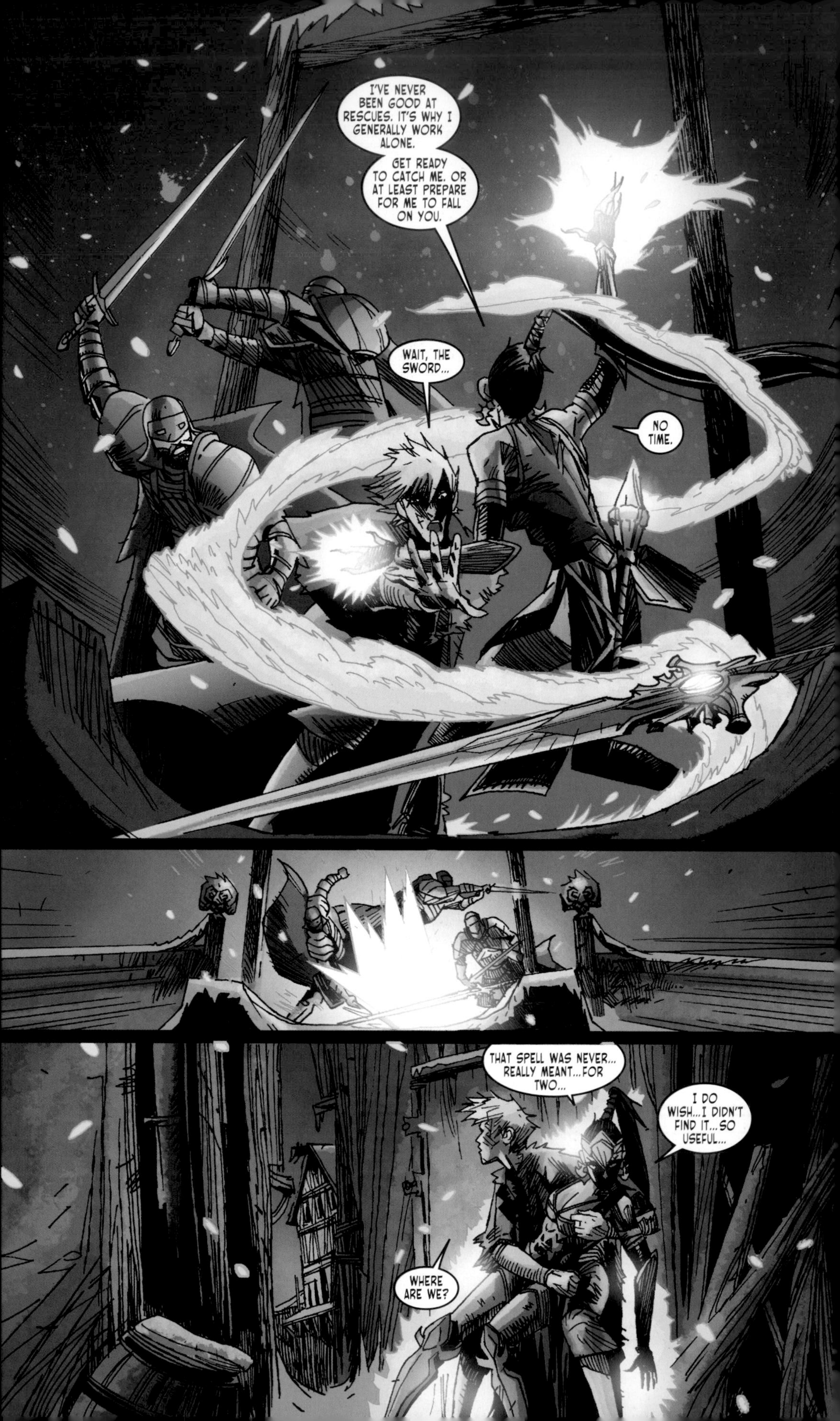
I'VE NEVER BEEN GOOD AT RESCUES. IT'S WHY I GENERALLY WORK ALONE.
GET READY TO CATCH ME. OR AT LEAST PREPARE FOR ME TO FALL ON YOU.
WAIT, THE SWORD...
NO TIME.
THAT SPELL WAS NEVER... REALLY MEANT...FOR TWO...
I DO WISH...I DIDN'T FIND IT...SO USEFUL...
WHERE ARE WE?

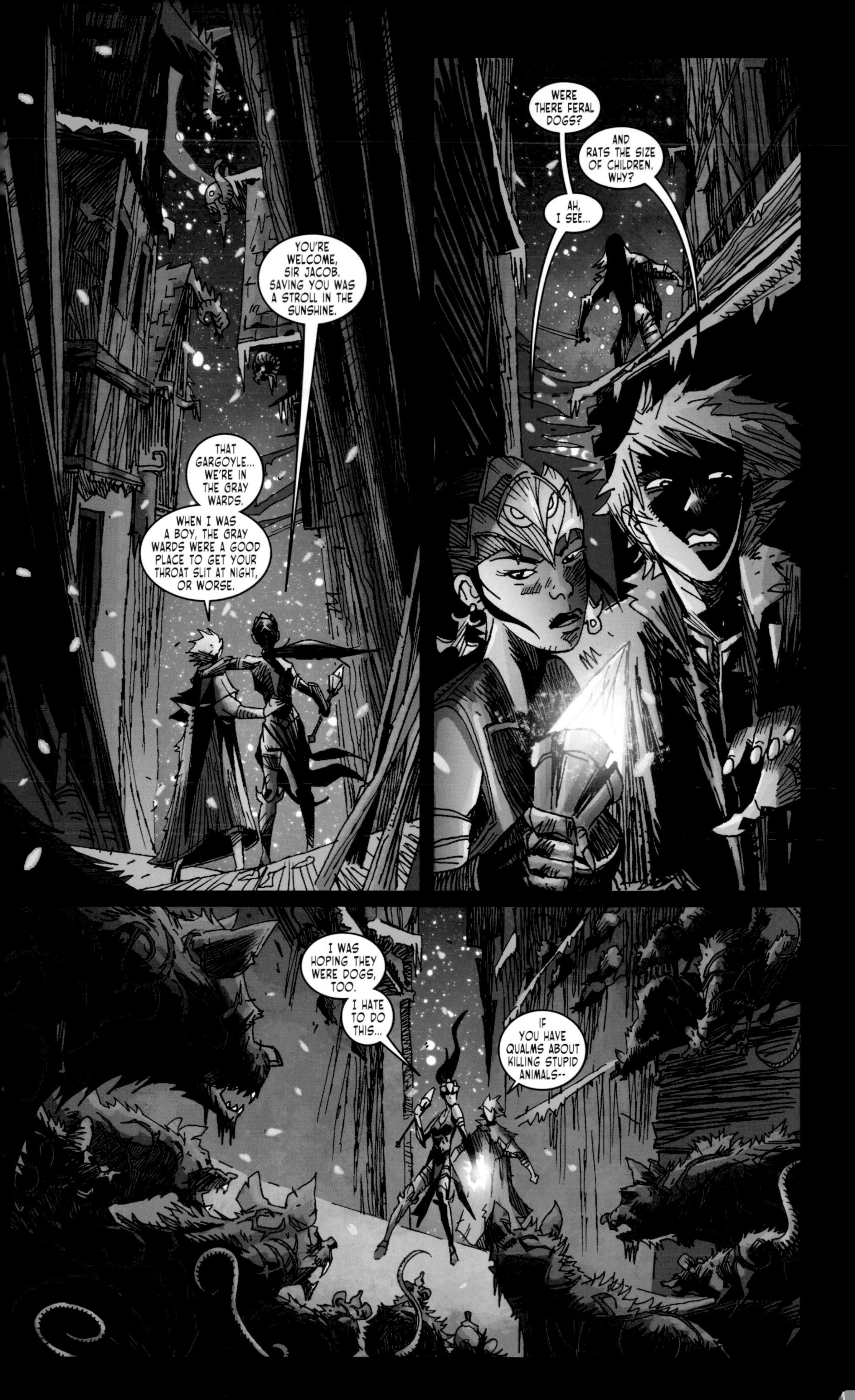
YOU'RE WELCOME, SIR JACOB. SAVING YOU WAS A STROLL IN THE SUNSHINE.
THAT GARGOYLE... WE'RE IN THE GRAY WARDS.
WHEN I WAS A BOY, THE GRAY WARDS WERE A GOOD PLACE TO GET YOUR THROAT SLIT AT NIGHT, OR WORSE.
WERE THERE FERAL DOGS?
AND RATS THE SIZE OF CHILDREN. WHY?
AH, I SEE...
I WAS HOPING THEY WERE DOGS, TOO.
I HATE TO DO THIS...
IF YOU HAVE QUALMS ABOUT KILLING STUPID ANIMALS--

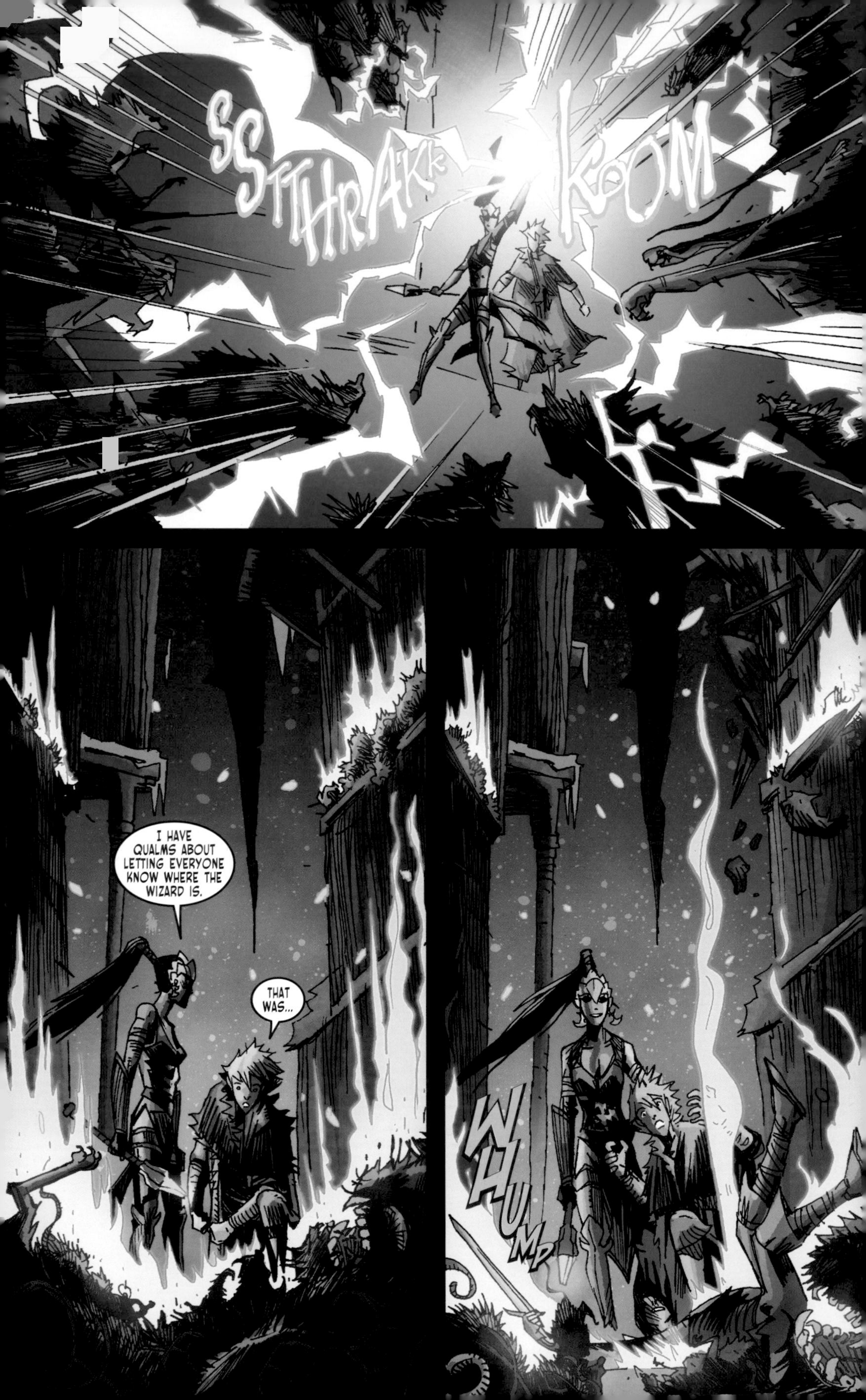
SSTTHRAKK
KOOM
I HAVE QUALMS ABOUT LETTING EVERYONE KNOW WHERE THE WIZARD IS.
THAT WAS...
WHUMP

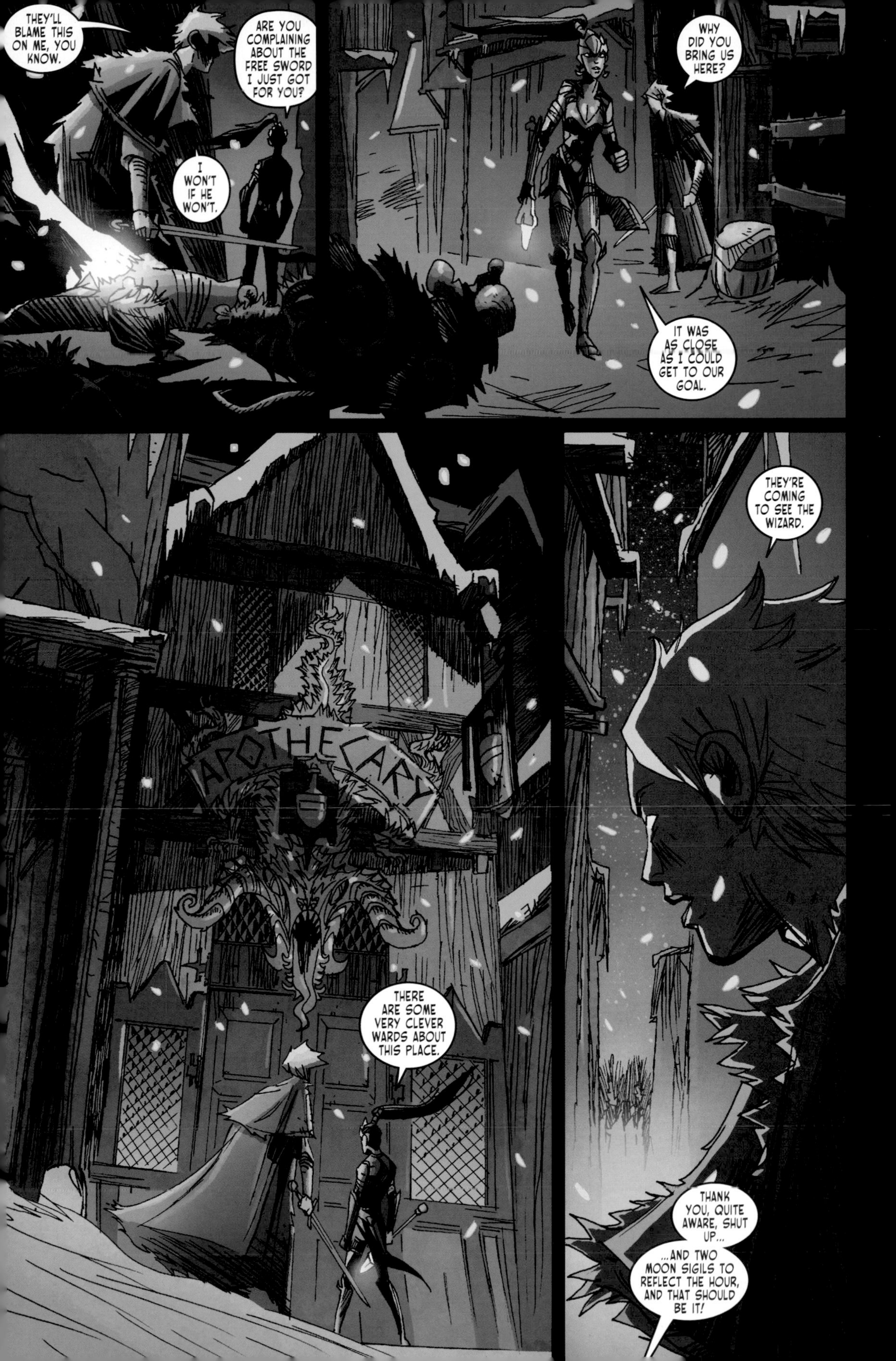
THEY'LL BLAME THIS ON ME, YOU KNOW.
ARE YOU COMPLAINING ABOUT THE FREE SWORD I JUST GOT FOR YOU?
I WON'T IF HE WON'T.
WHY DID YOU BRING US HERE?
IT WAS AS CLOSE AS I COULD GET TO OUR GOAL.
APOTHECARY
THERE ARE SOME VERY CLEVER WARDS ABOUT THIS PLACE.
THEY'RE COMING TO SEE THE WIZARD.
THANK YOU, QUITE AWARE, SHUT UP...
...AND TWO MOON SIGILS TO REFLECT THE HOUR, AND THAT SHOULD BE IT!

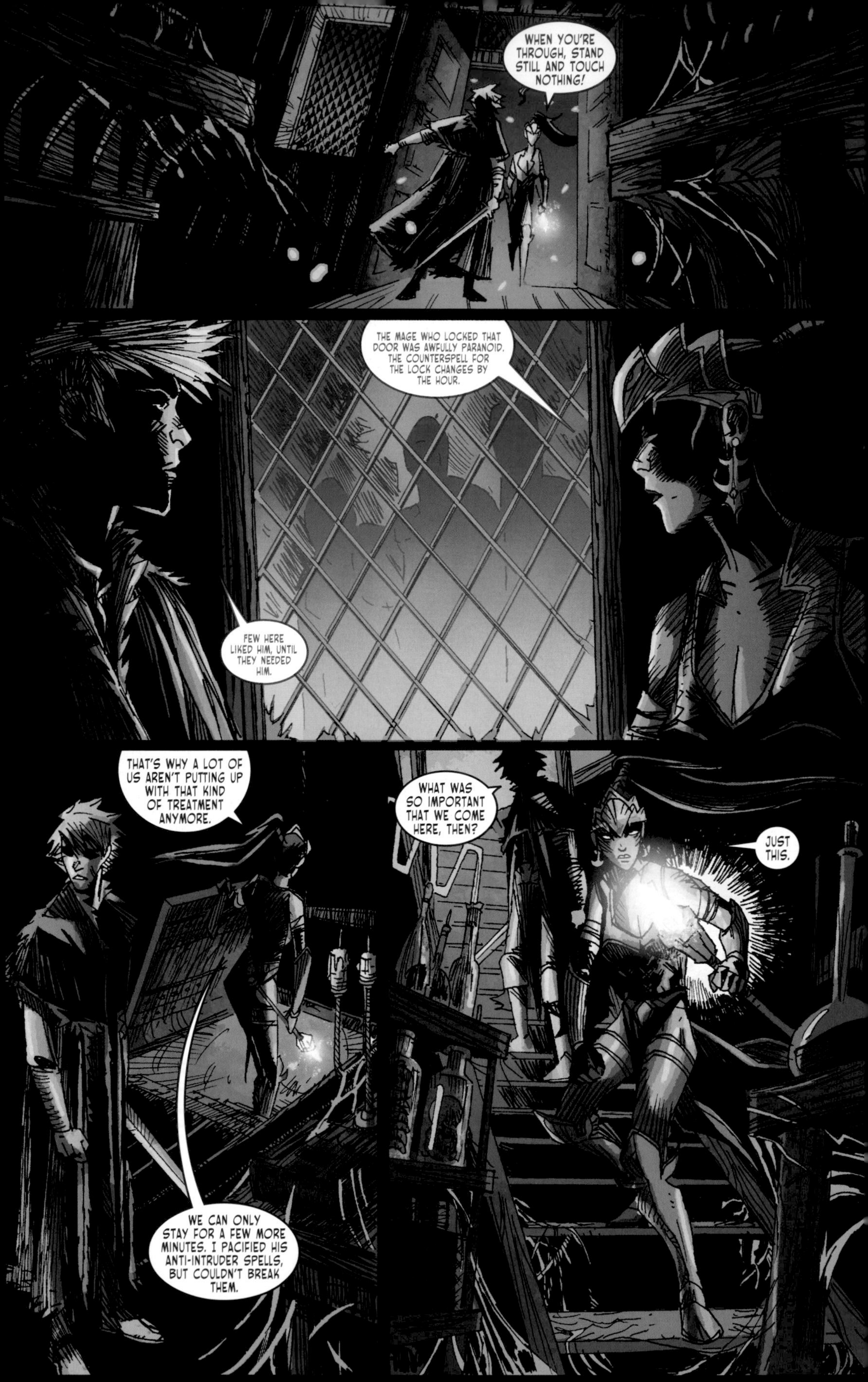
WHEN YOU'RE THROUGH, STAND STILL AND TOUCH NOTHING!
THE MAGE WHO LOCKED THAT DOOR WAS AWFULLY PARANOID. THE COUNTERSPELL FOR THE LOCK CHANGES BY THE HOUR.
FEW HERE LIKED HIM, UNTIL THEY NEEDED HIM.
THAT'S WHY A LOT OF US AREN'T PUTTING UP WITH THAT KIND OF TREATMENT ANYMORE.
WE CAN ONLY STAY FOR A FEW MORE MINUTES. I PACIFIED HIS ANTI-INTRUDER SPELLS, BUT COULDN'T BREAK THEM.
WHAT WAS SO IMPORTANT THAT WE COME HERE, THEN?
JUST THIS.

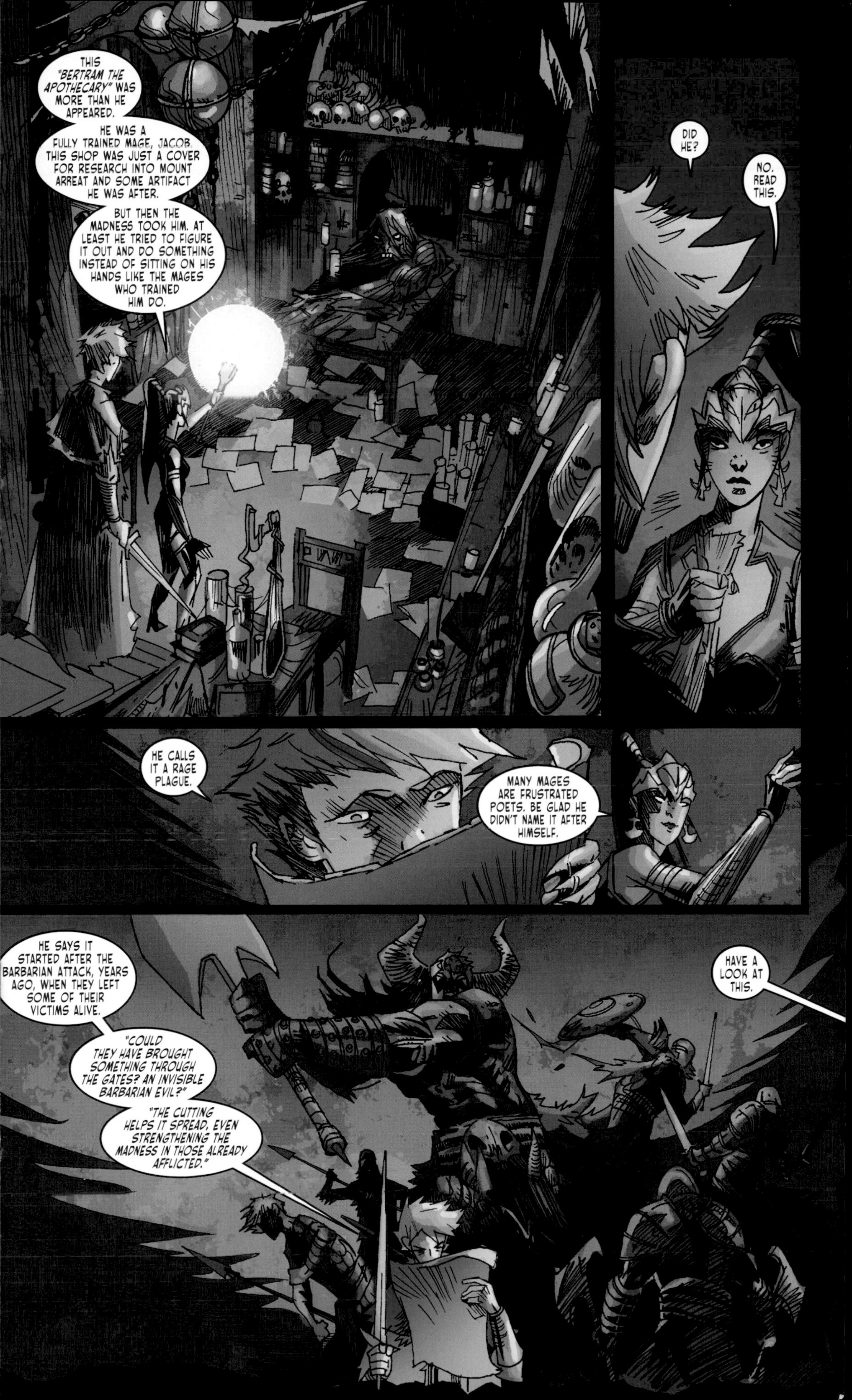

THIS "BERTRAM THE APOTHECARY" WAS MORE THAN HE APPEARED.
HE WAS A FULLY TRAINED MAGE, JACOB. THIS SHOP WAS JUST A COVER FOR RESEARCH INTO MOUNT ARREAT AND SOME ARTIFACT HE WAS AFTER.
BUT THEN THE MADNESS TOOK HIM. AT LEAST HE TRIED TO FIGURE IT OUT AND DO SOMETHING INSTEAD OF SITTING ON HIS HANDS LIKE THE MAGES WHO TRAINED HIM DO.
DID HE?
NO. READ THIS.
HE CALLS IT A RAGE PLAGUE.
MANY MAGES ARE FRUSTRATED POETS. BE GLAD HE DIDN'T NAME IT AFTER HIMSELF.
HE SAYS IT STARTED AFTER THE BARBARIAN ATTACK, YEARS AGO, WHEN THEY LEFT SOME OF THEIR VICTIMS ALIVE.
"COULD THEY HAVE BROUGHT SOMETHING THROUGH THE GATES? AN INVISIBLE BARBARIAN EVIL?"
"THE CUTTING HELPS IT SPREAD, EVEN STRENGTHENING THE MADNESS IN THOSE ALREADY AFFLICTED."
HAVE A LOOK AT THIS.

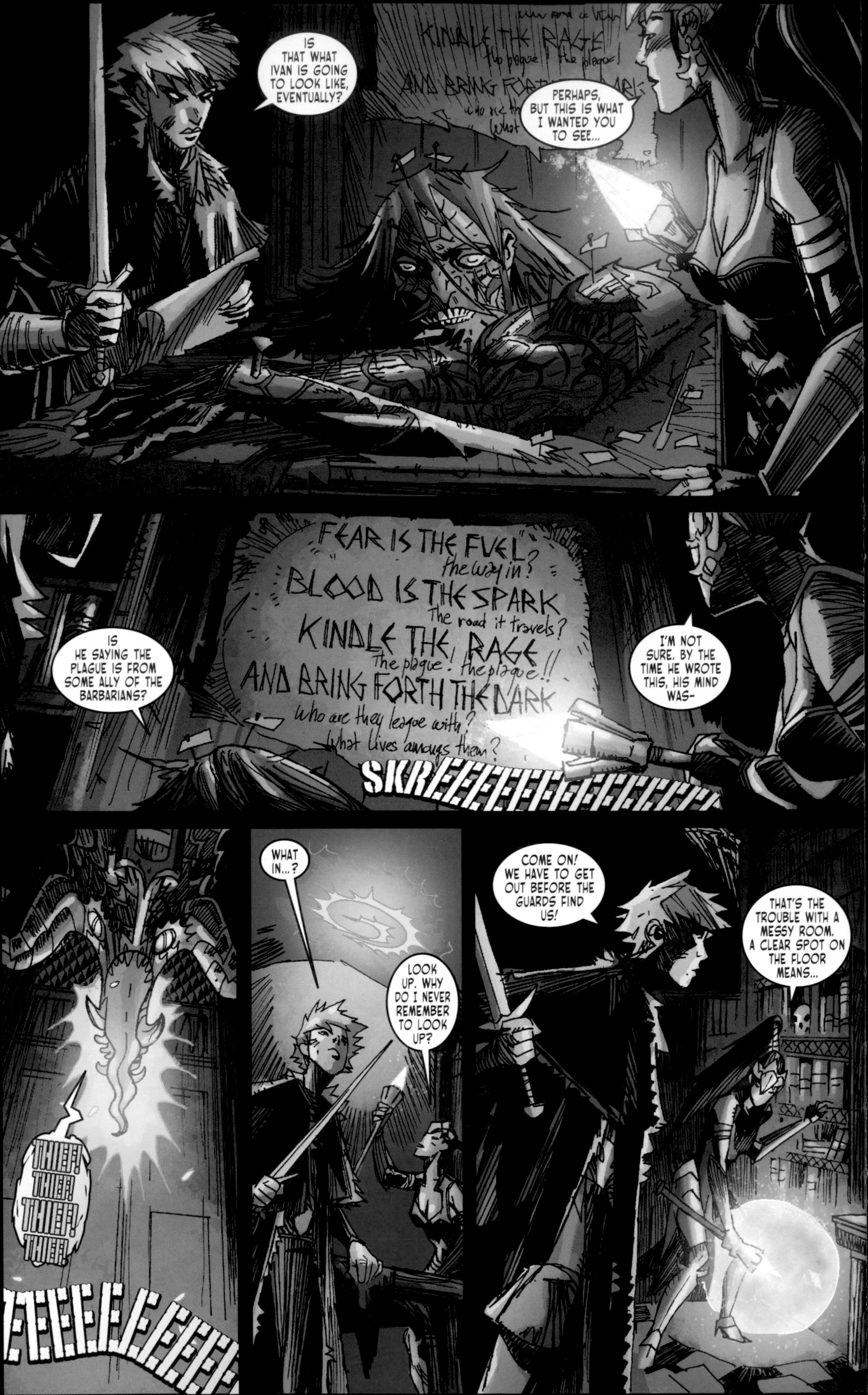

IS THAT WHAT IVAN IS GOING TO LOOK LIKE, EVENTUALLY?
PERHAPS, BUT THIS IS WHAT I WANTED YOU TO SEE...
FEAR IS THE FUEL
the way in?
BLOOD IS THE SPARK
The road it travels?
KINDLE THE RAGE
The plague! the plague!!
AND BRING FORTH THE DARK
who are they league with?
What lives amongs them?
IS HE SAYING THE PLAGUE IS FROM SOME ALLY OF THE BARBARIANS?
I'M NOT SURE. BY THE TIME HE WROTE THIS, HIS MIND WAS-
SKREEEEEEEEEEEEEEEEEEEEEEEEEEEEEE
WHAT IN...?
LOOK UP. WHY DO I NEVER REMEMBER TO LOOK UP?
COME ON! WE HAVE TO GET OUT BEFORE THE GUARDS FIND US!
THAT'S THE TROUBLE WITH A MESSY ROOM. A CLEAR SPOT ON THE FLOOR MEANS...

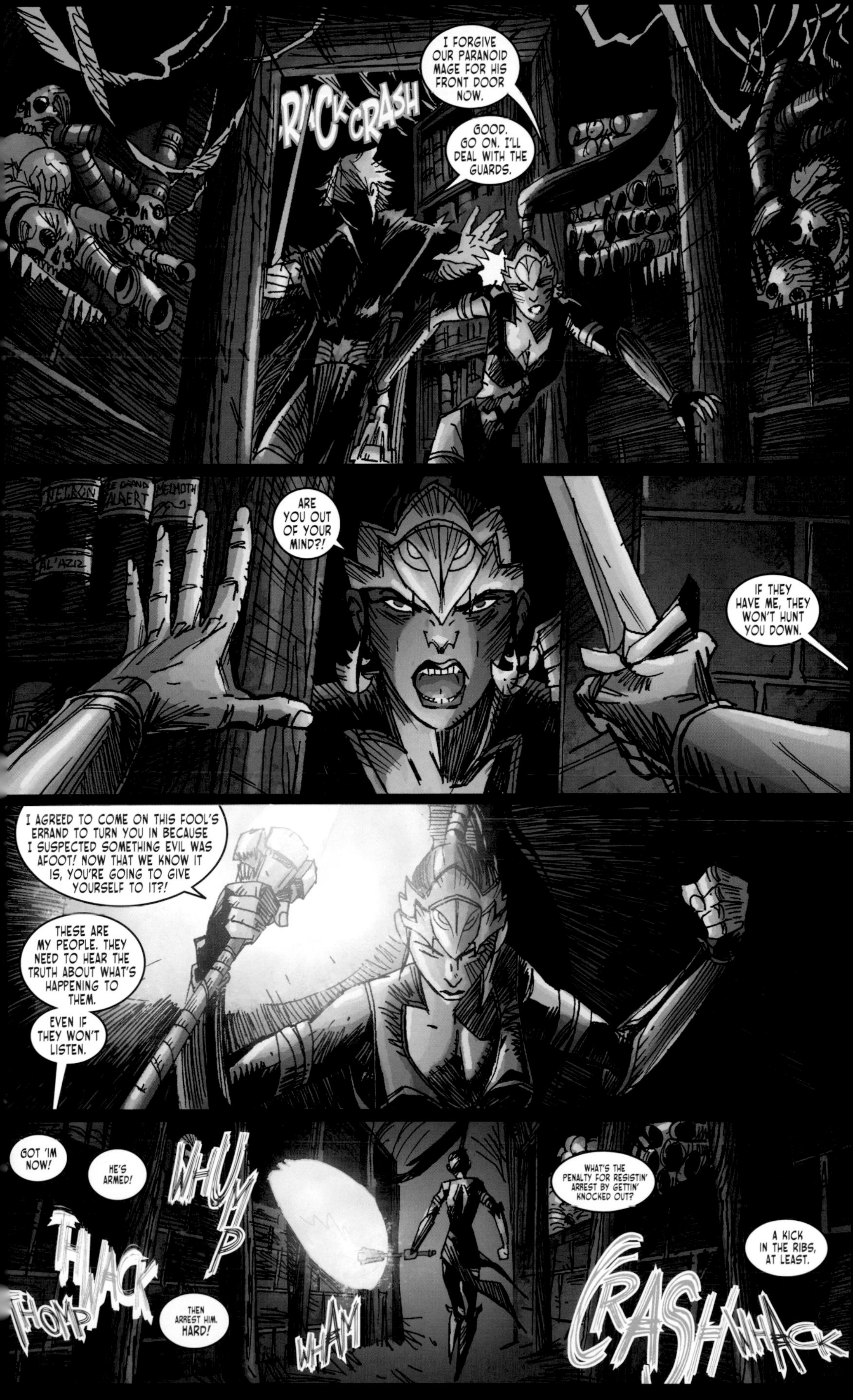
KRACK CRASH
I FORGIVE OUR PARANOID MAGE FOR HIS FRONT DOOR NOW.
GOOD. GO ON. I'LL DEAL WITH THE GUARDS.
ARE YOU OUT OF YOUR MIND?!
IF THEY HAVE ME, THEY WON'T HUNT YOU DOWN.
I AGREED TO COME ON THIS FOOL'S ERRAND TO TURN YOU IN BECAUSE I SUSPECTED SOMETHING EVIL WAS AFOOT! NOW THAT WE KNOW IT IS, YOU'RE GOING TO GIVE YOURSELF TO IT?!
THESE ARE MY PEOPLE. THEY NEED TO HEAR THE TRUTH ABOUT WHAT'S HAPPENING TO THEM.
EVEN IF THEY WON'T LISTEN.
GOT 'IM NOW!
HE'S ARMED!
WHUMP
THACK
THOMP
WHACK
THEN ARREST HIM. HARD!
WHAM
WHAT'S THE PENALTY FOR RESISTIN' ARREST BY GETTIN' KNOCKED OUT?
A KICK IN THE RIBS, AT LEAST.
CRASH
WHACK

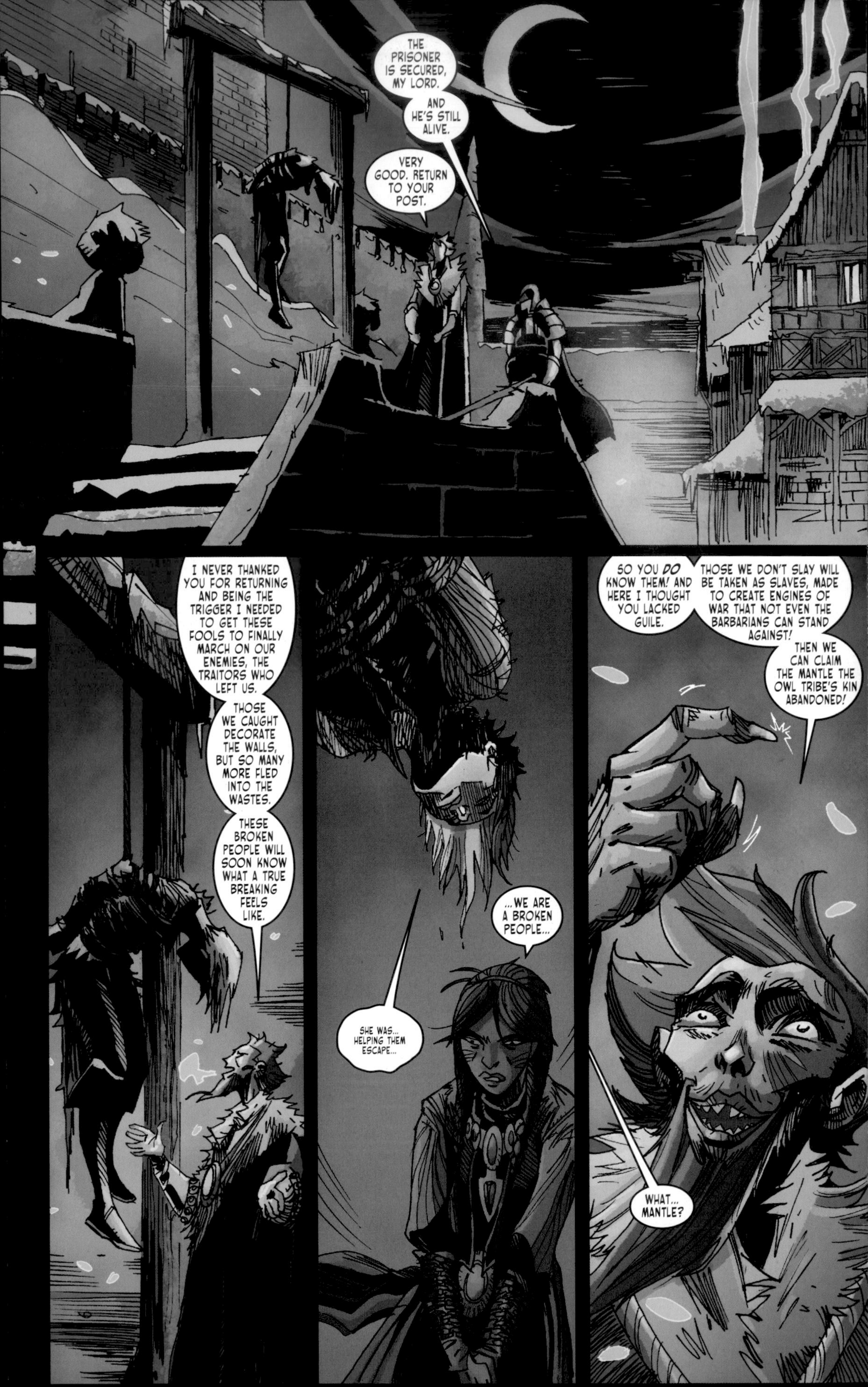
THE PRISONER IS SECURED, MY LORD.
AND HE'S STILL ALIVE.
VERY GOOD. RETURN TO YOUR POST.
I NEVER THANKED YOU FOR RETURNING AND BEING THE TRIGGER I NEEDED TO GET THESE FOOLS TO FINALLY MARCH ON OUR ENEMIES, THE TRAITORS WHO LEFT US.
THOSE WE CAUGHT DECORATE THE WALLS, BUT SO MANY MORE FLED INTO THE WASTES.
THESE BROKEN PEOPLE WILL SOON KNOW WHAT A TRUE BREAKING FEELS LIKE.
...WE ARE A BROKEN PEOPLE...
SHE WAS... HELPING THEM ESCAPE...
SO YOU DO KNOW THEM! AND HERE I THOUGHT YOU LACKED GUILE.
THOSE WE DON'T SLAY WILL BE TAKEN AS SLAVES, MADE TO CREATE ENGINES OF WAR THAT NOT EVEN THE BARBARIANS CAN STAND AGAINST!
THEN WE CAN CLAIM THE MANTLE THE OWL TRIBE'S KIN ABANDONED!
WHAT... MANTLE?

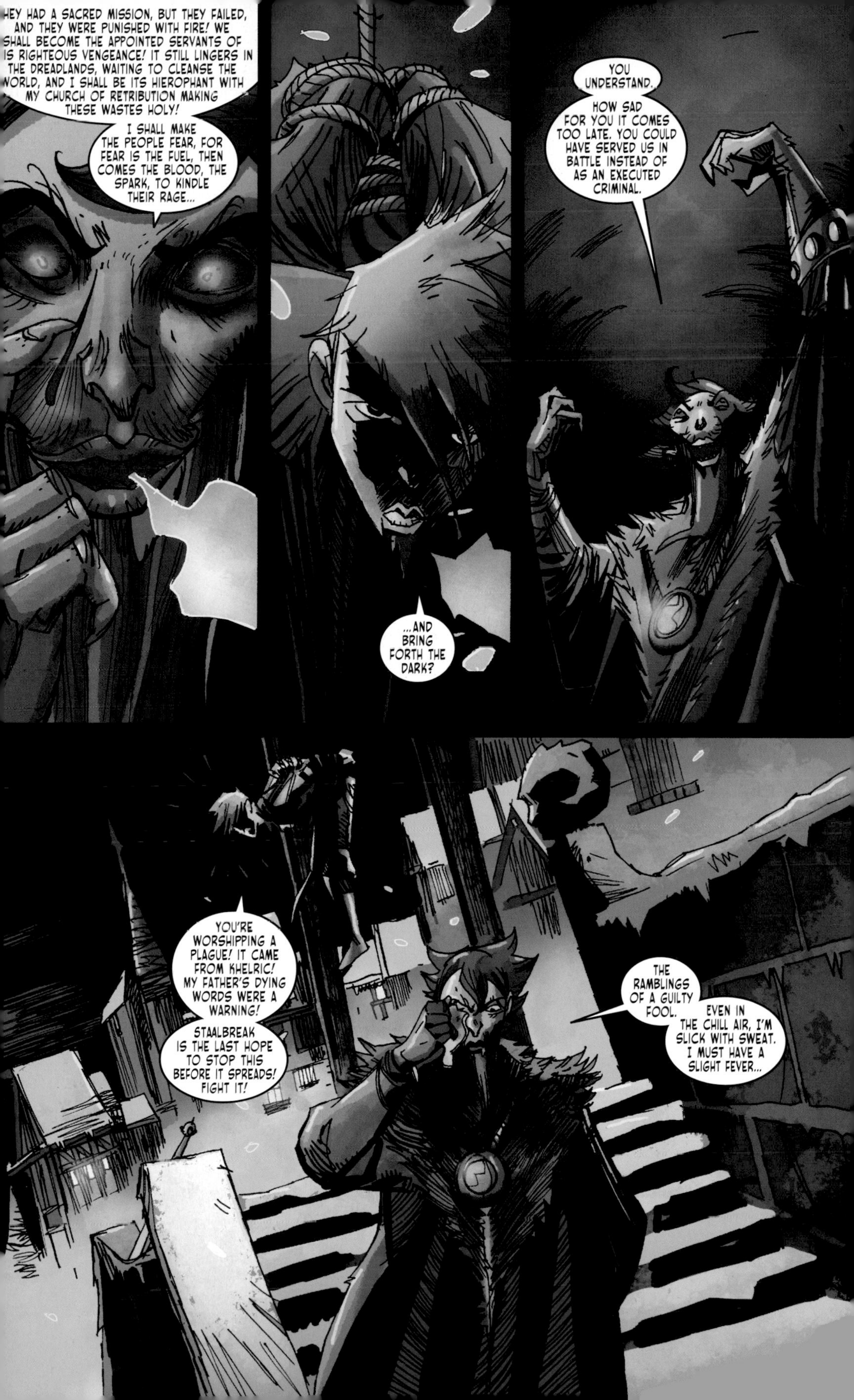
HEY HAD A SACRED MISSION, BUT THEY FAILED, AND THEY WERE PUNISHED WITH FIRE! WE SHALL BECOME THE APPOINTED SERVANTS OF IS RIGHTEOUS VENGEANCE! IT STILL LINGERS IN THE DREADLANDS, WAITING TO CLEANSE THE WORLD, AND I SHALL BE ITS HIEROPHANT WITH MY CHURCH OF RETRIBUTION MAKING THESE WASTES HOLY!
I SHALL MAKE THE PEOPLE FEAR, FOR FEAR IS THE FUEL, THEN COMES THE BLOOD, THE SPARK, TO KINDLE THEIR RAGE...
...AND BRING FORTH THE DARK?
YOU UNDERSTAND.
HOW SAD FOR YOU IT COMES TOO LATE. YOU COULD HAVE SERVED US IN BATTLE INSTEAD OF AS AN EXECUTED CRIMINAL.
YOU'RE WORSHIPPING A PLAGUE! IT CAME FROM KHELRIC! MY FATHER'S DYING WORDS WERE A WARNING!
STAALBREAK IS THE LAST HOPE TO STOP THIS BEFORE IT SPREADS! FIGHT IT!
THE RAMBLINGS OF A GUILTY FOOL.
EVEN IN THE CHILL AIR, I'M SLICK WITH SWEAT. I MUST HAVE A SLIGHT FEVER...

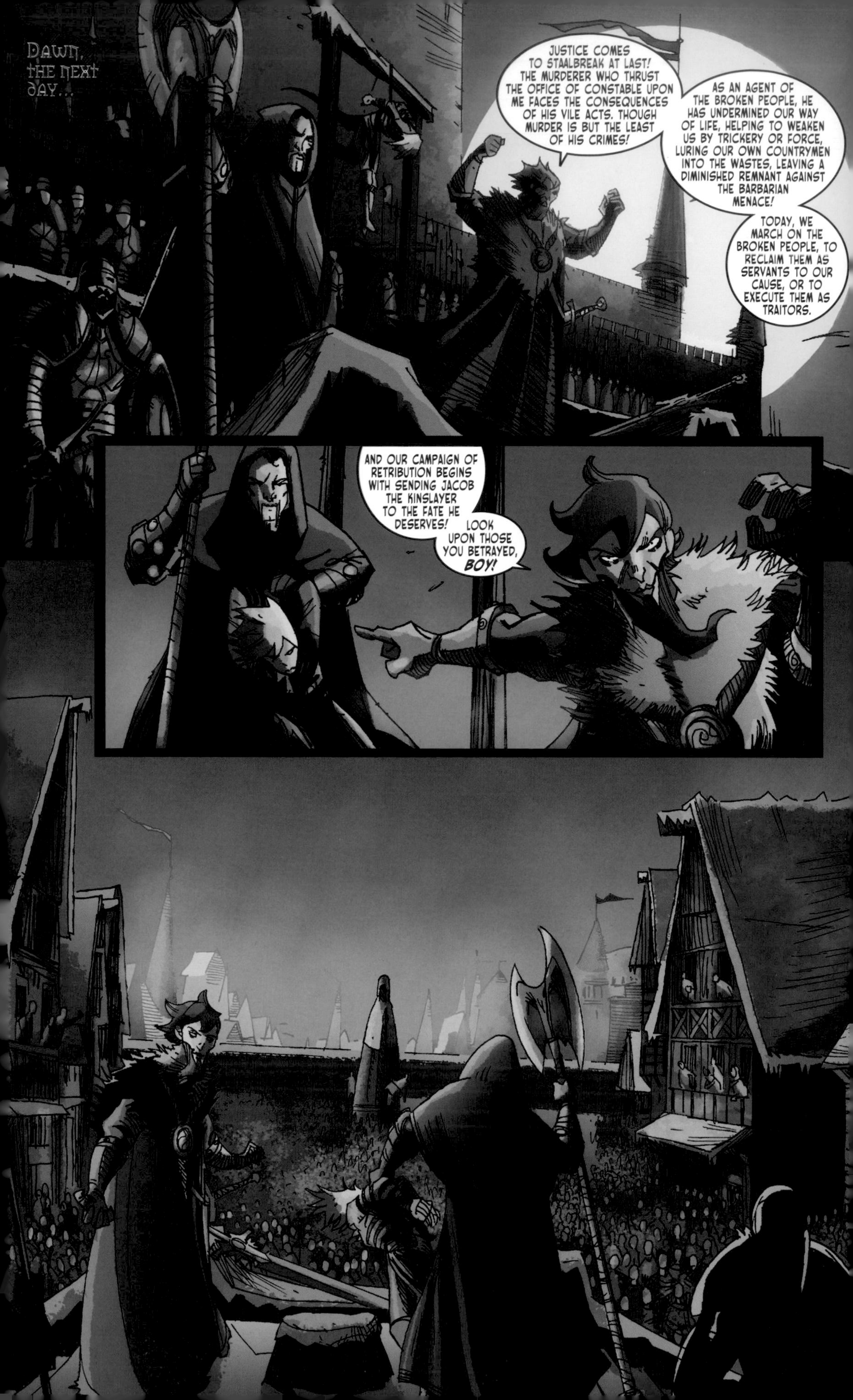
DAWN, THE NEXT DAY...
JUSTICE COMES TO STAALBREAK AT LAST! THE MURDERER WHO THRUST THE OFFICE OF CONSTABLE UPON ME FACES THE CONSEQUENCES OF HIS VILE ACTS. THOUGH MURDER IS BUT THE LEAST OF HIS CRIMES!
AS AN AGENT OF THE BROKEN PEOPLE, HE HAS UNDERMINED OUR WAY OF LIFE, HELPING TO WEAKEN US BY TRICKERY OR FORCE, LURING OUR OWN COUNTRYMEN INTO THE WASTES, LEAVING A DIMINISHED REMNANT AGAINST THE BARBARIAN MENACE!
TODAY, WE MARCH ON THE BROKEN PEOPLE, TO RECLAIM THEM AS SERVANTS TO OUR CAUSE, OR TO EXECUTE THEM AS TRAITORS.
AND OUR CAMPAIGN OF RETRIBUTION BEGINS WITH SENDING JACOB THE KINSLAYER TO THE FATE HE DESERVES!
LOOK UPON THOSE YOU BETRAYED, BOY!

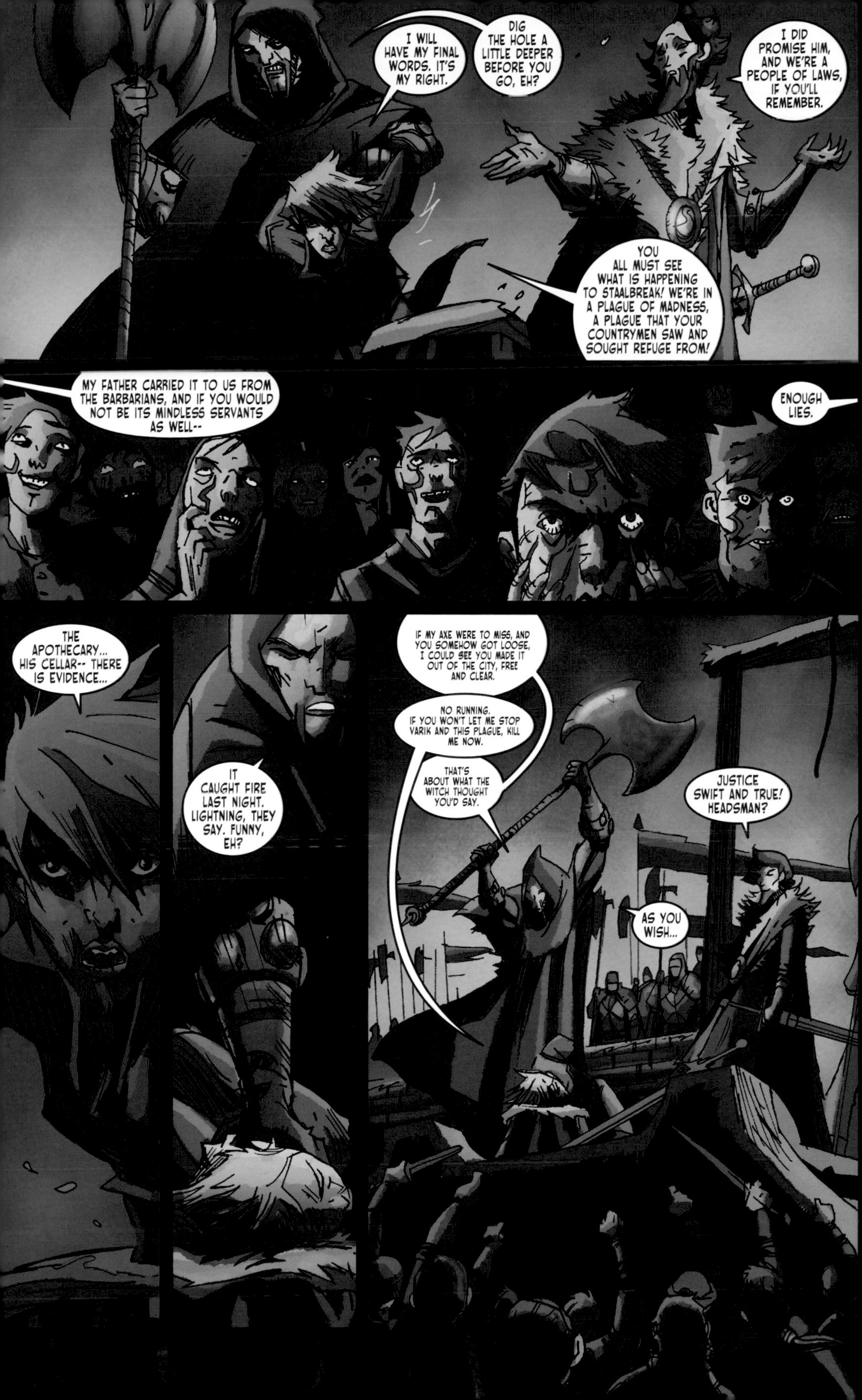
I WILL HAVE MY FINAL WORDS. IT'S MY RIGHT.
DIG THE HOLE A LITTLE DEEPER BEFORE YOU GO, EH?
I DID PROMISE HIM, AND WE'RE A PEOPLE OF LAWS, IF YOU'LL REMEMBER.
YOU ALL MUST SEE WHAT IS HAPPENING TO STAALBREAK! WE'RE IN A PLAGUE OF MADNESS, A PLAGUE THAT YOUR COUNTRYMEN SAW AND SOUGHT REFUGE FROM!
MY FATHER CARRIED IT TO US FROM THE BARBARIANS, AND IF YOU WOULD NOT BE ITS MINDLESS SERVANTS AS WELL--
ENOUGH LIES.
THE APOTHECARY... HIS CELLAR-- THERE IS EVIDENCE...
IT CAUGHT FIRE LAST NIGHT. LIGHTNING, THEY SAY. FUNNY, EH?
IF MY AXE WERE TO MISS, AND YOU SOMEHOW GOT LOOSE, I COULD SEE YOU MADE IT OUT OF THE CITY, FREE AND CLEAR.
NO RUNNING. IF YOU WON'T LET ME STOP VARIK AND THIS PLAGUE, KILL ME NOW.
THAT'S ABOUT WHAT THE WITCH THOUGHT YOU'D SAY.
JUSTICE SWIFT AND TRUE! HEADSMAN?
AS YOU WISH...

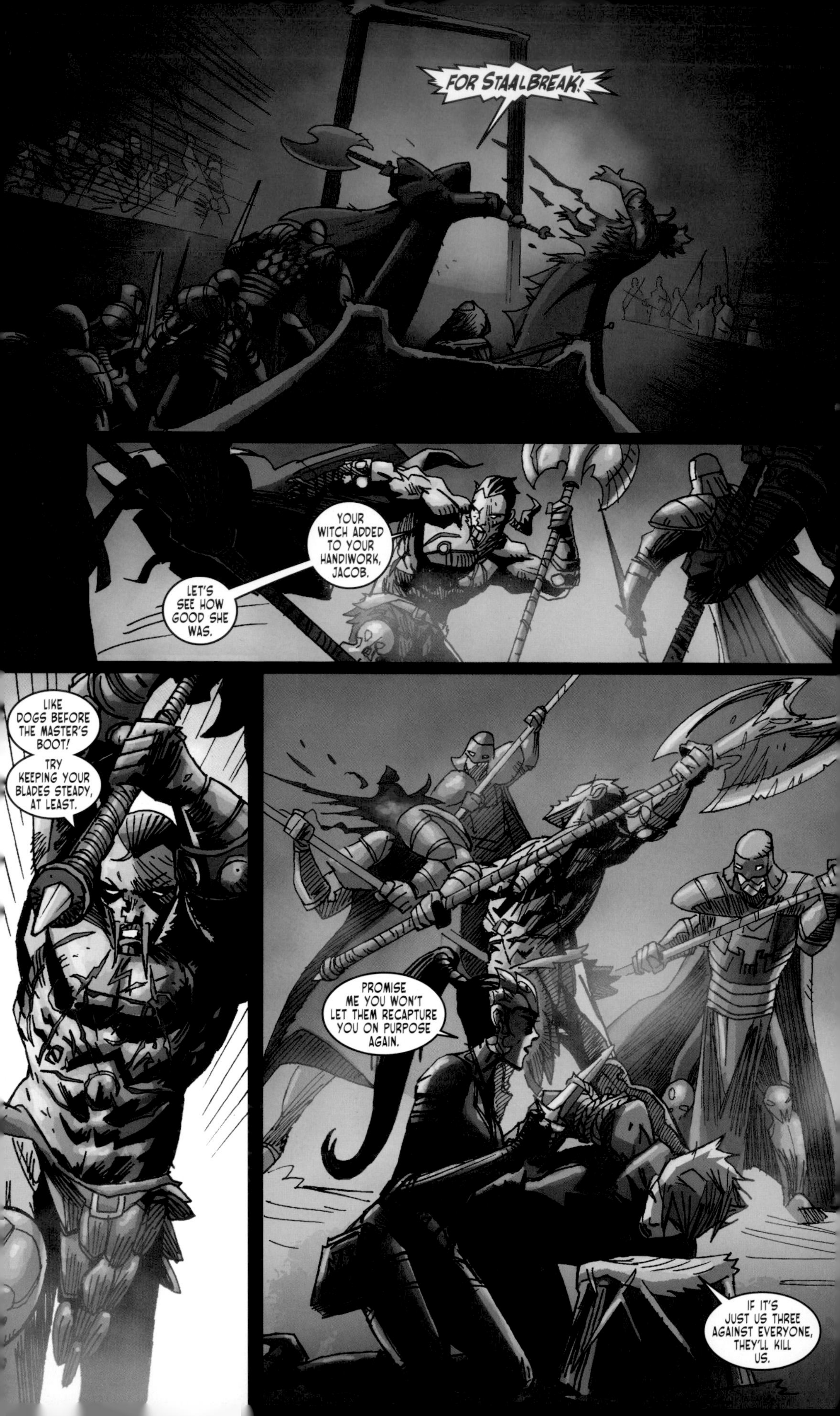
FOR STAALBREAK!
YOUR WITCH ADDED TO YOUR HANDIWORK, JACOB.
LET'S SEE HOW GOOD SHE WAS.
LIKE DOGS BEFORE THE MASTER'S BOOT!
TRY KEEPING YOUR BLADES STEADY, AT LEAST.
PROMISE ME YOU WON'T LET THEM RECAPTURE YOU ON PURPOSE AGAIN.
IF IT'S JUST US THREE AGAINST EVERYONE, THEY'LL KILL US.

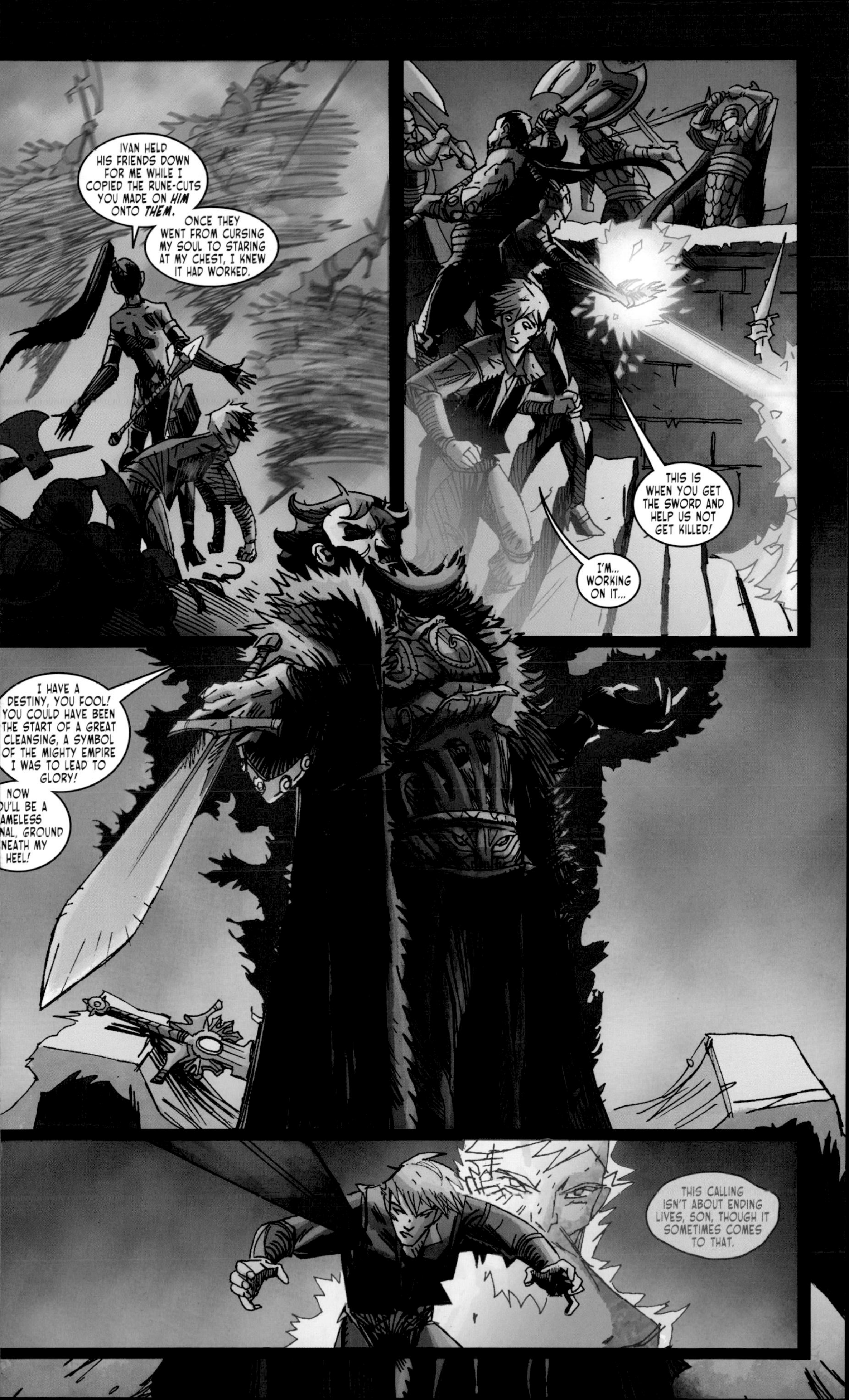
IVAN HELD HIS FRIENDS DOWN FOR ME WHILE I COPIED THE RUNE-CUTS YOU MADE ON *HIM* ONTO *THEM*.
ONCE THEY WENT FROM CURSING MY SOUL TO STARING AT MY CHEST, I KNEW IT HAD WORKED.
THIS IS WHEN YOU GET THE SWORD AND HELP US NOT GET KILLED!
I'M... WORKING ON IT...
I HAVE A DESTINY, YOU FOOL! YOU COULD HAVE BEEN THE START OF A GREAT CLEANSING, A SYMBOL OF THE MIGHTY EMPIRE I WAS TO LEAD TO GLORY!
NOW OU'LL BE A AMELESS NAL, GROUND NEATH MY HEEL!
THIS CALLING ISN'T ABOUT ENDING LIVES, SON, THOUGH IT SOMETIMES COMES TO THAT.

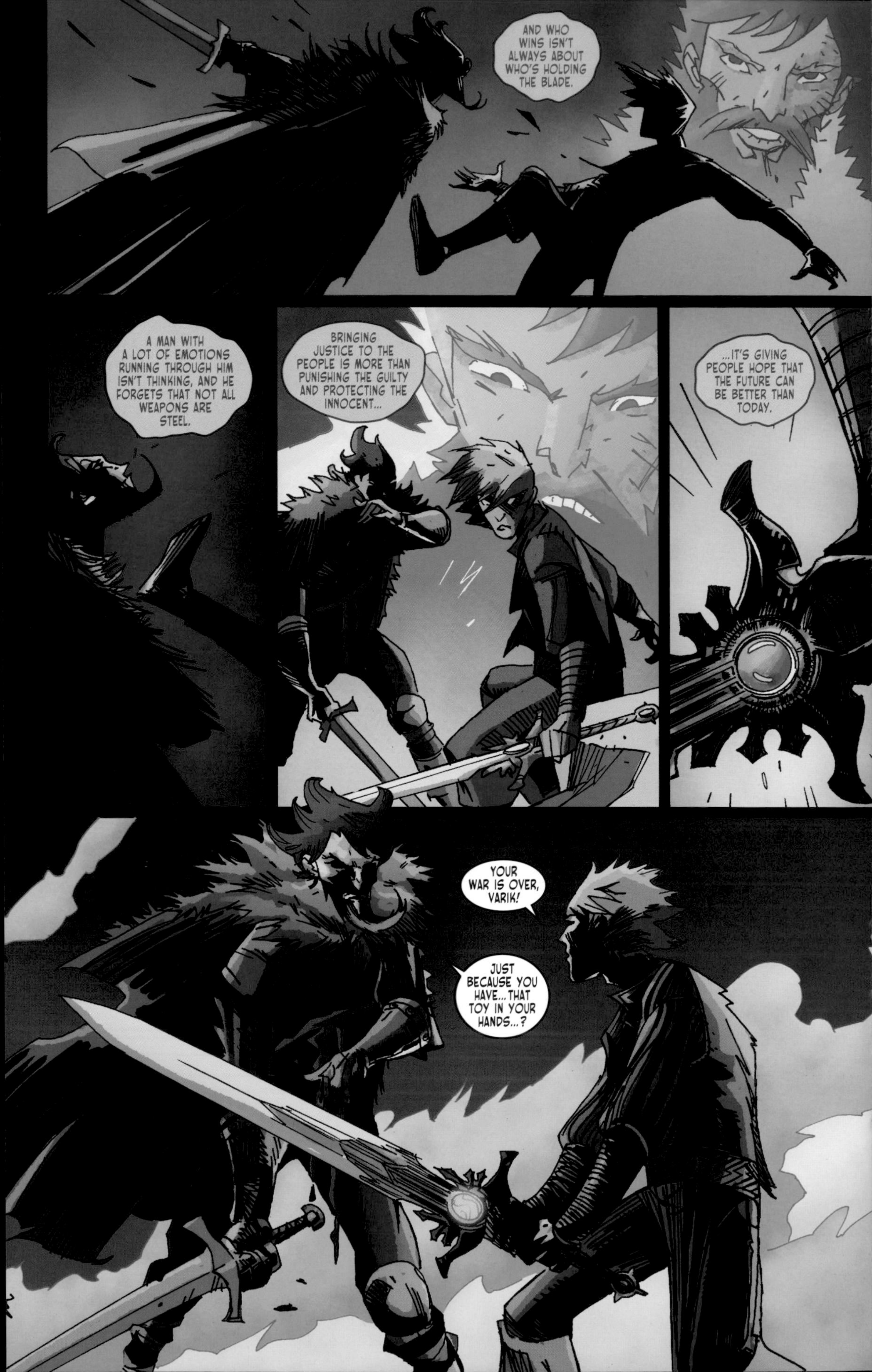
AND WHO WINS ISN'T ALWAYS ABOUT WHO'S HOLDING THE BLADE.
A MAN WITH A LOT OF EMOTIONS RUNNING THROUGH HIM ISN'T THINKING, AND HE FORGETS THAT NOT ALL WEAPONS ARE STEEL.
BRINGING JUSTICE TO THE PEOPLE IS MORE THAN PUNISHING THE GUILTY AND PROTECTING THE INNOCENT...
...IT'S GIVING PEOPLE HOPE THAT THE FUTURE CAN BE BETTER THAN TODAY.
YOUR WAR IS OVER, VARIK!
JUST BECAUSE YOU HAVE... THAT TOY IN YOUR HANDS...?

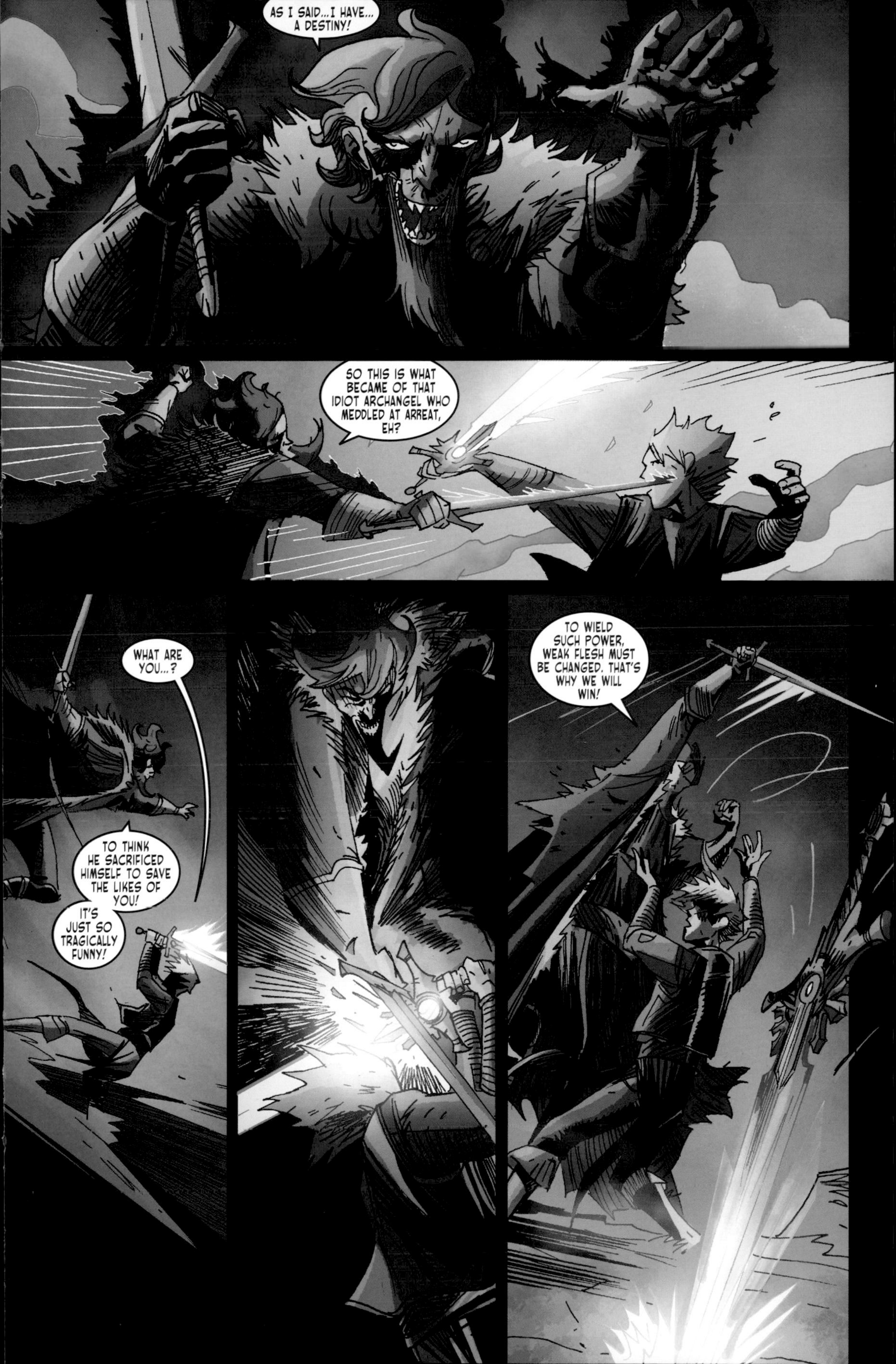
AS I SAID...I HAVE... A DESTINY!
SO THIS IS WHAT BECAME OF THAT IDIOT ARCHANGEL WHO MEDDLED AT ARREAT, EH?
WHAT ARE YOU...?
TO THINK HE SACRIFICED HIMSELF TO SAVE THE LIKES OF YOU!
IT'S JUST SO TRAGICALLY FUNNY!
TO WIELD SUCH POWER, WEAK FLESH MUST BE CHANGED. THAT'S WHY WE WILL WIN!

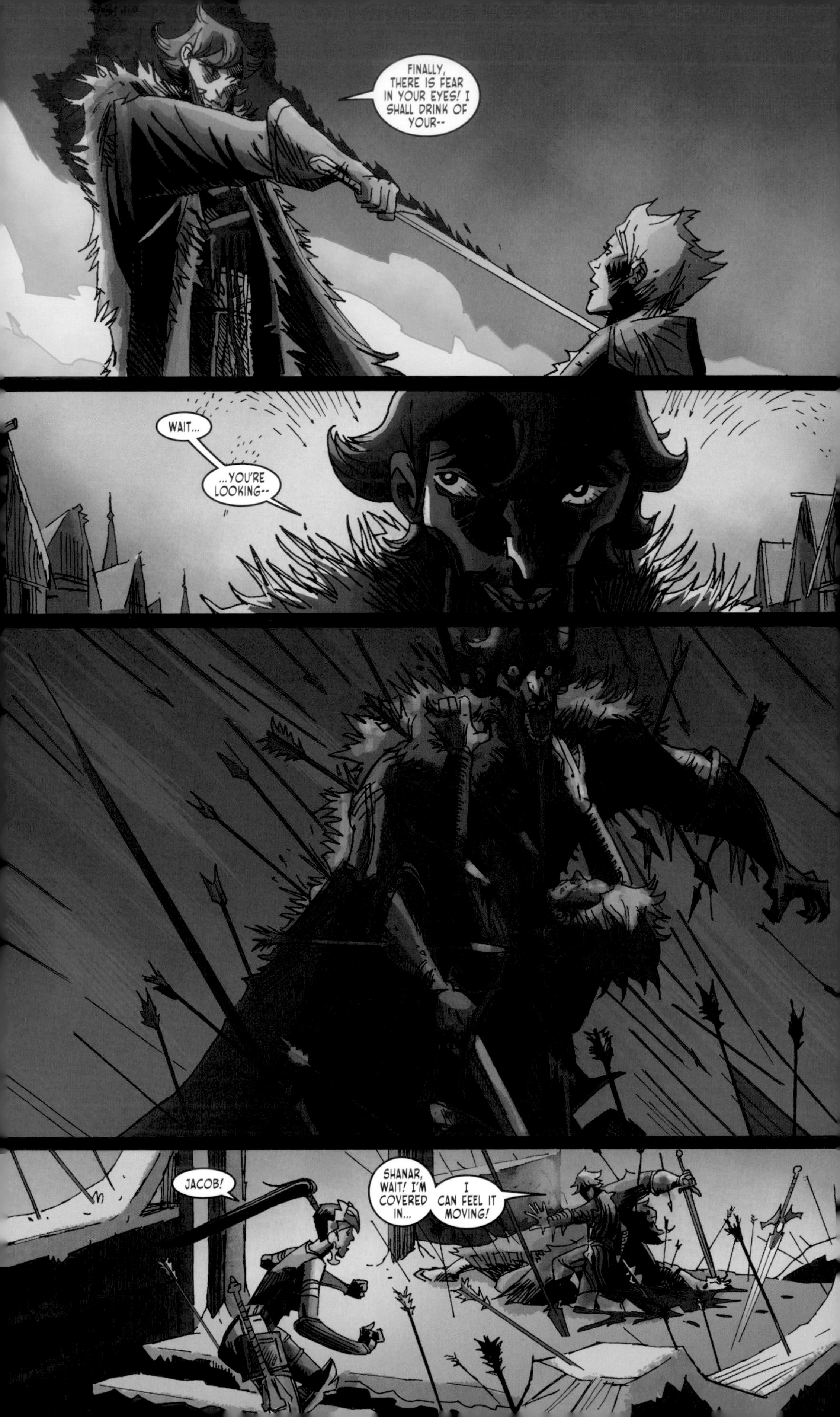
FINALLY, THERE IS FEAR IN YOUR EYES! I SHALL DRINK OF YOUR--
WAIT...
...YOU'RE LOOKING--
JACOB!
SHANAR, WAIT! I'M COVERED IN...
I CAN FEEL IT MOVING!

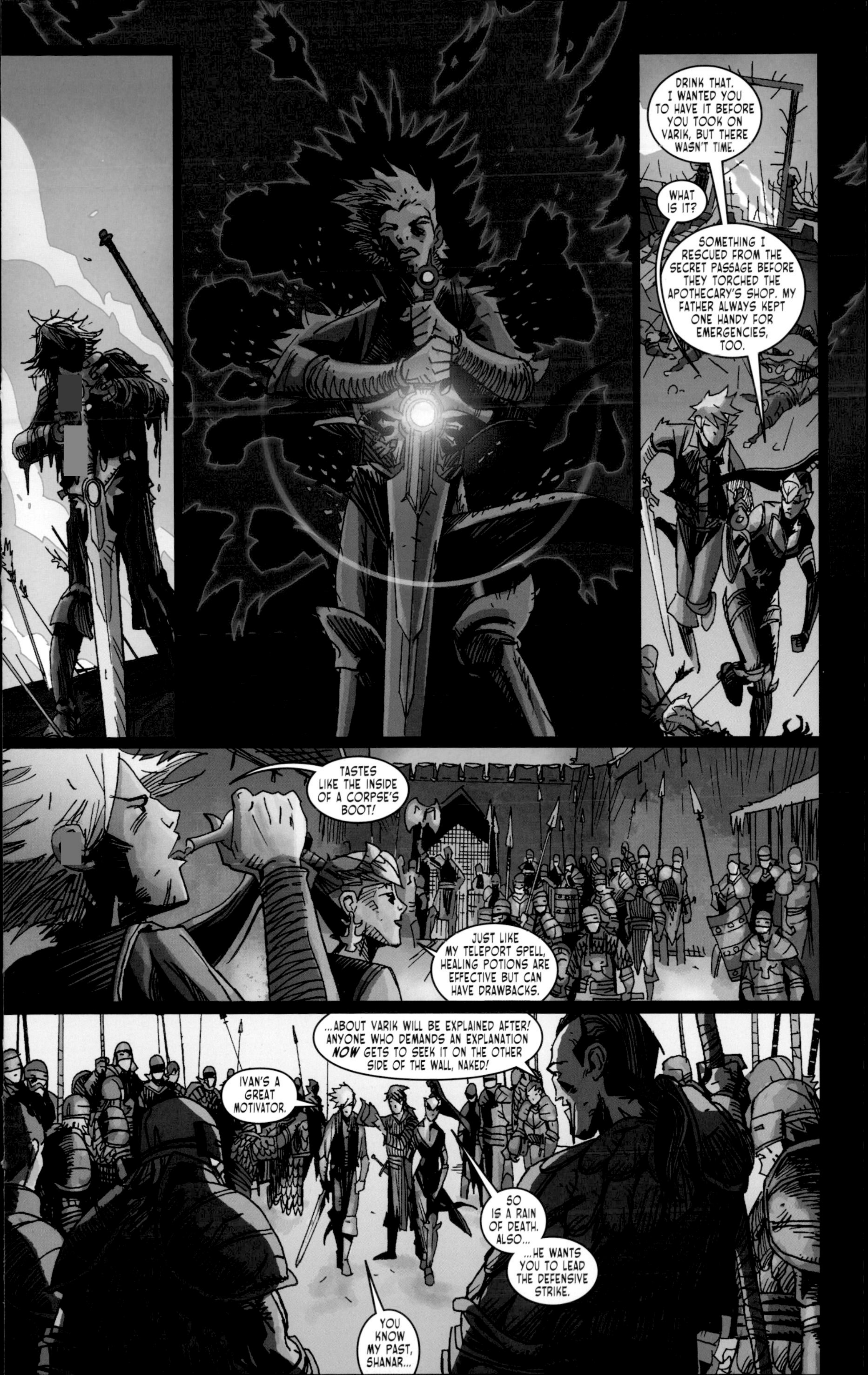
DRINK THAT. I WANTED YOU TO HAVE IT BEFORE YOU TOOK ON VARIK, BUT THERE WASN'T TIME.
WHAT IS IT?
SOMETHING I RESCUED FROM THE SECRET PASSAGE BEFORE THEY TORCHED THE APOTHECARY'S SHOP. MY FATHER ALWAYS KEPT ONE HANDY FOR EMERGENCIES, TOO.
TASTES LIKE THE INSIDE OF A CORPSE'S BOOT!
JUST LIKE MY TELEPORT SPELL, HEALING POTIONS ARE EFFECTIVE BUT CAN HAVE DRAWBACKS.
...ABOUT VARIK WILL BE EXPLAINED AFTER! ANYONE WHO DEMANDS AN EXPLANATION NOW GETS TO SEEK IT ON THE OTHER SIDE OF THE WALL, NAKED!
IVAN'S A GREAT MOTIVATOR.
SO IS A RAIN OF DEATH. ALSO...
...HE WANTS YOU TO LEAD THE DEFENSIVE STRIKE.
YOU KNOW MY PAST, SHANAR...

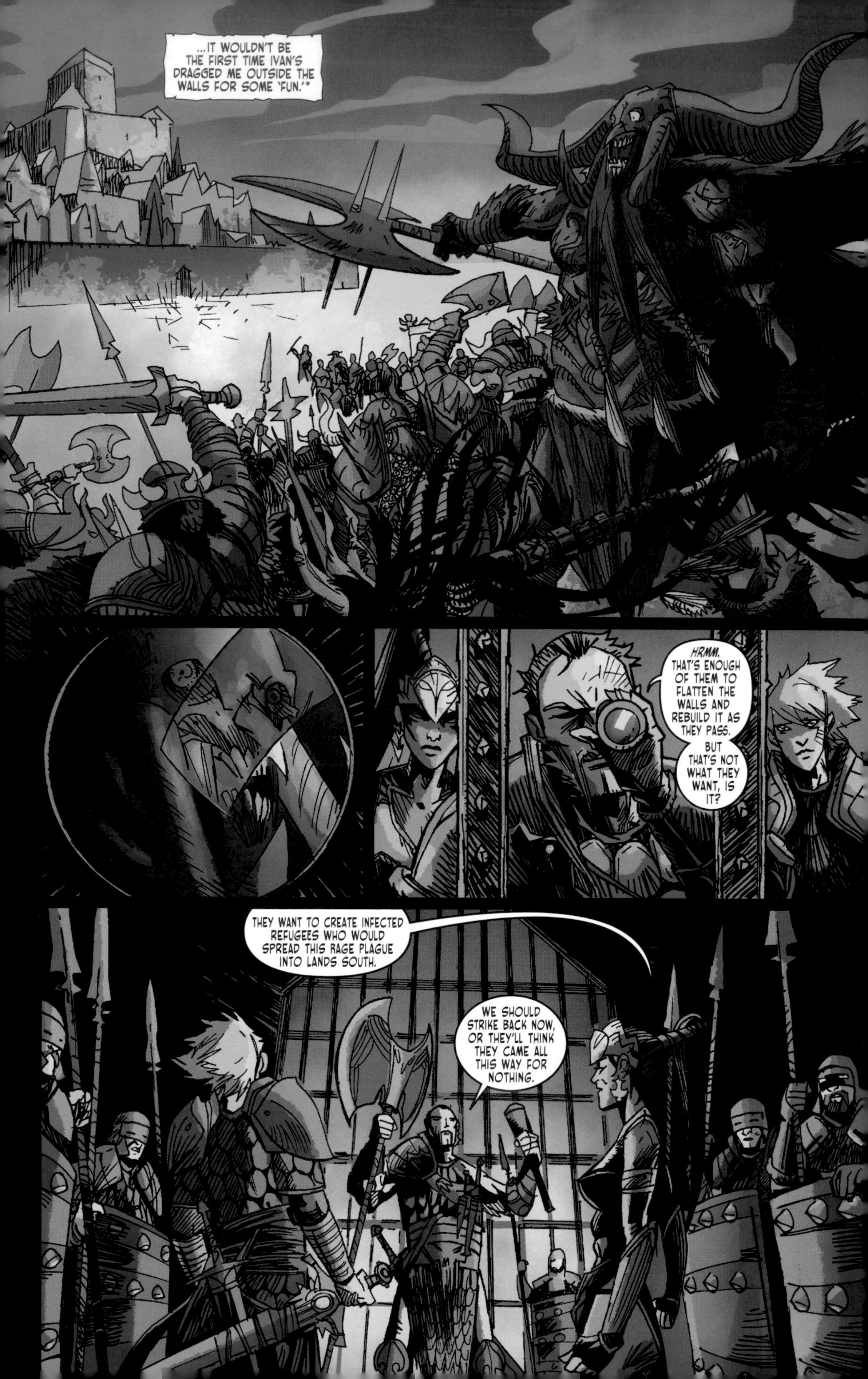
...IT WOULDN'T BE THE FIRST TIME IVAN'S DRAGGED ME OUTSIDE THE WALLS FOR SOME 'FUN.'"
HRMM. THAT'S ENOUGH OF THEM TO FLATTEN THE WALLS AND REBUILD IT AS THEY PASS.
BUT THAT'S NOT WHAT THEY WANT, IS IT?
THEY WANT TO CREATE INFECTED REFUGEES WHO WOULD SPREAD THIS RAGE PLAGUE INTO LANDS SOUTH.
WE SHOULD STRIKE BACK NOW, OR THEY'LL THINK THEY CAME ALL THIS WAY FOR NOTHING.

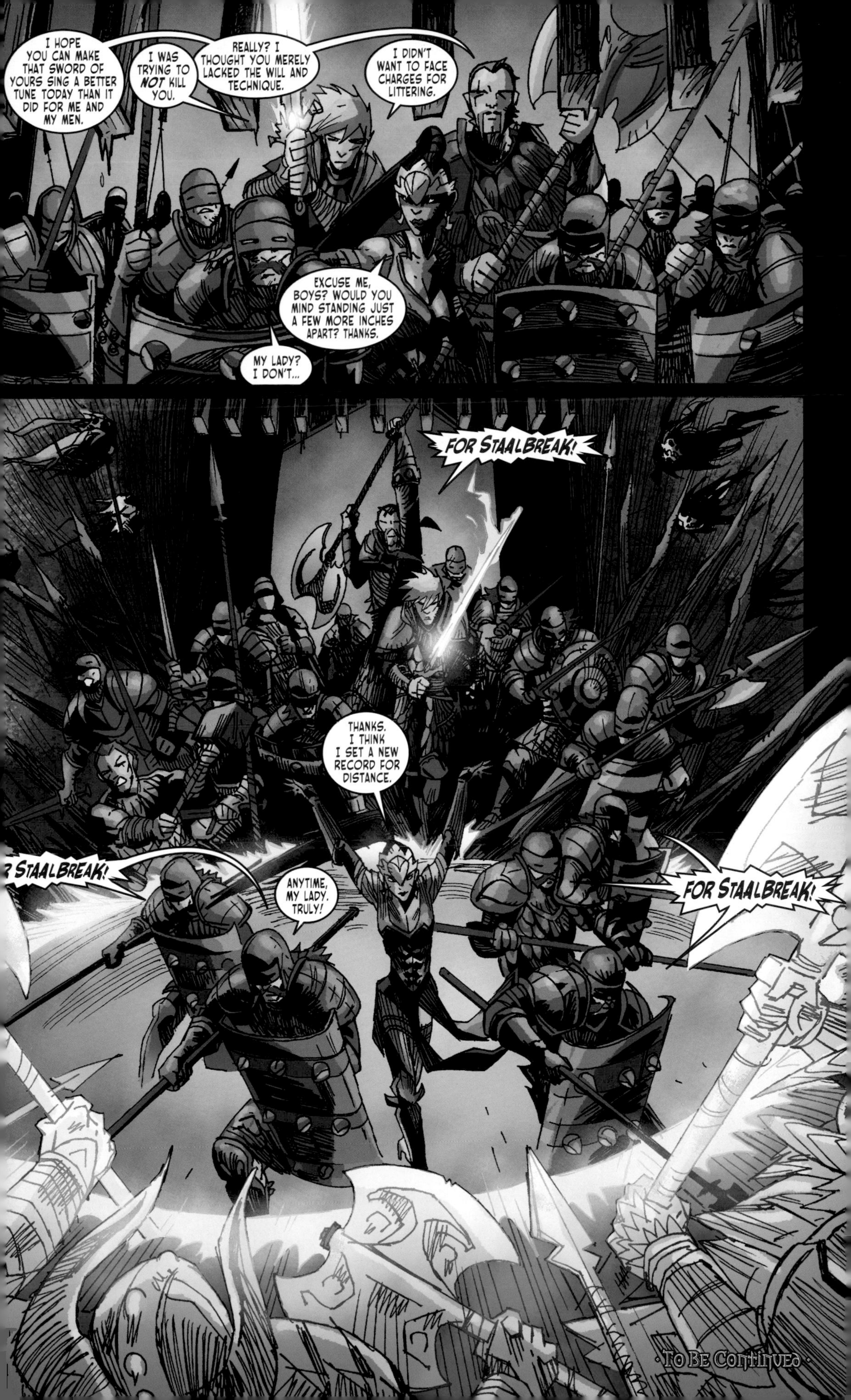
I HOPE YOU CAN MAKE THAT SWORD OF YOURS SING A BETTER TUNE TODAY THAN IT DID FOR ME AND MY MEN.
I WAS TRYING TO NOT KILL YOU.
REALLY? I THOUGHT YOU MERELY LACKED THE WILL AND TECHNIQUE.
I DIDN'T WANT TO FACE CHARGES FOR LITTERING.
EXCUSE ME, BOYS? WOULD YOU MIND STANDING JUST A FEW MORE INCHES APART? THANKS.
MY LADY? I DON'T...
FOR STAALBREAK!
THANKS. I THINK I SET A NEW RECORD FOR DISTANCE.
R STAALBREAK!
ANYTIME, MY LADY. TRULY!
FOR STAALBREAK!
To Be Continued

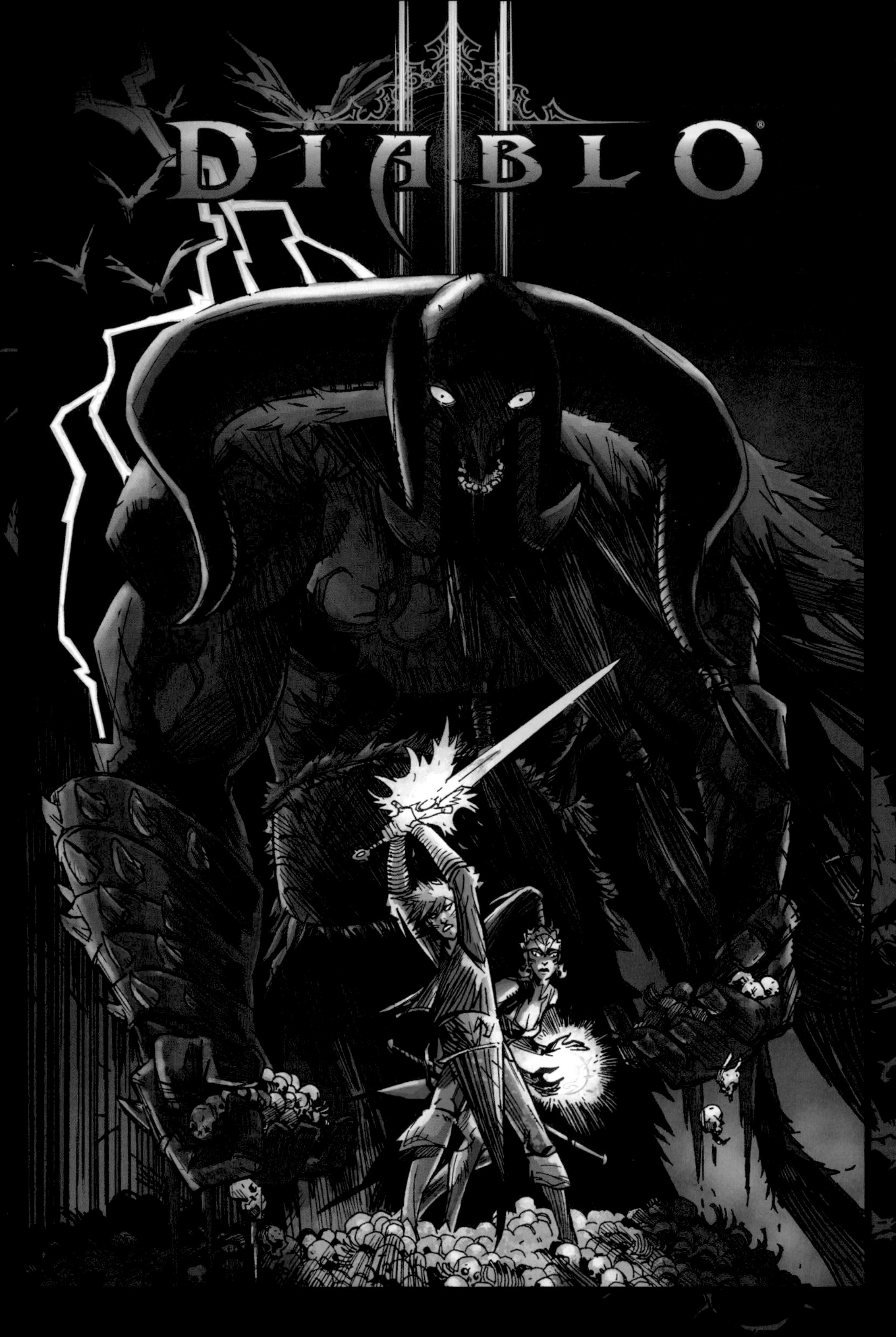
DIABLO

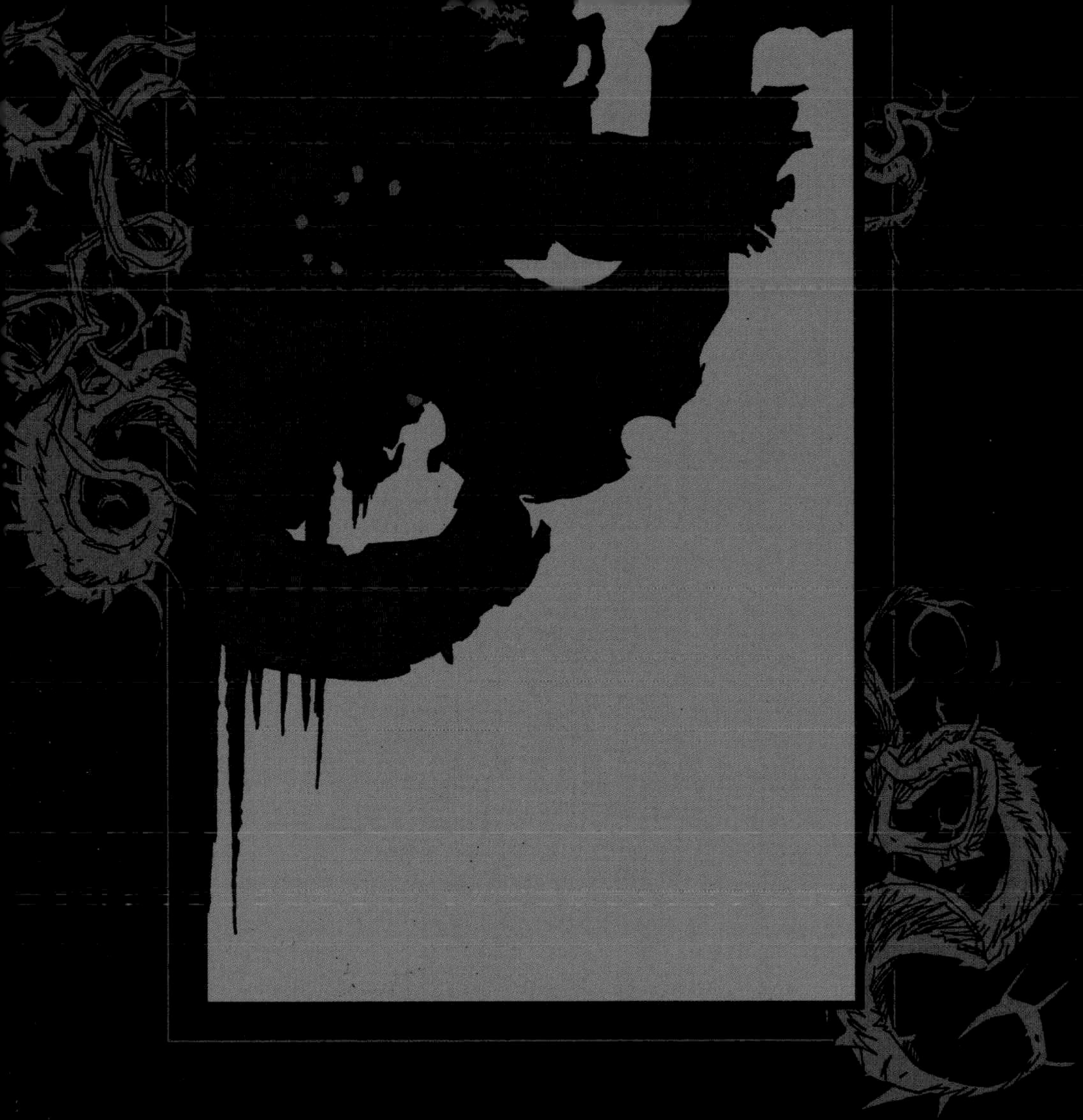

ACT V

AARON WILLIAMS
JOSEPH LACROIX
LEE LOUGHRIDGE

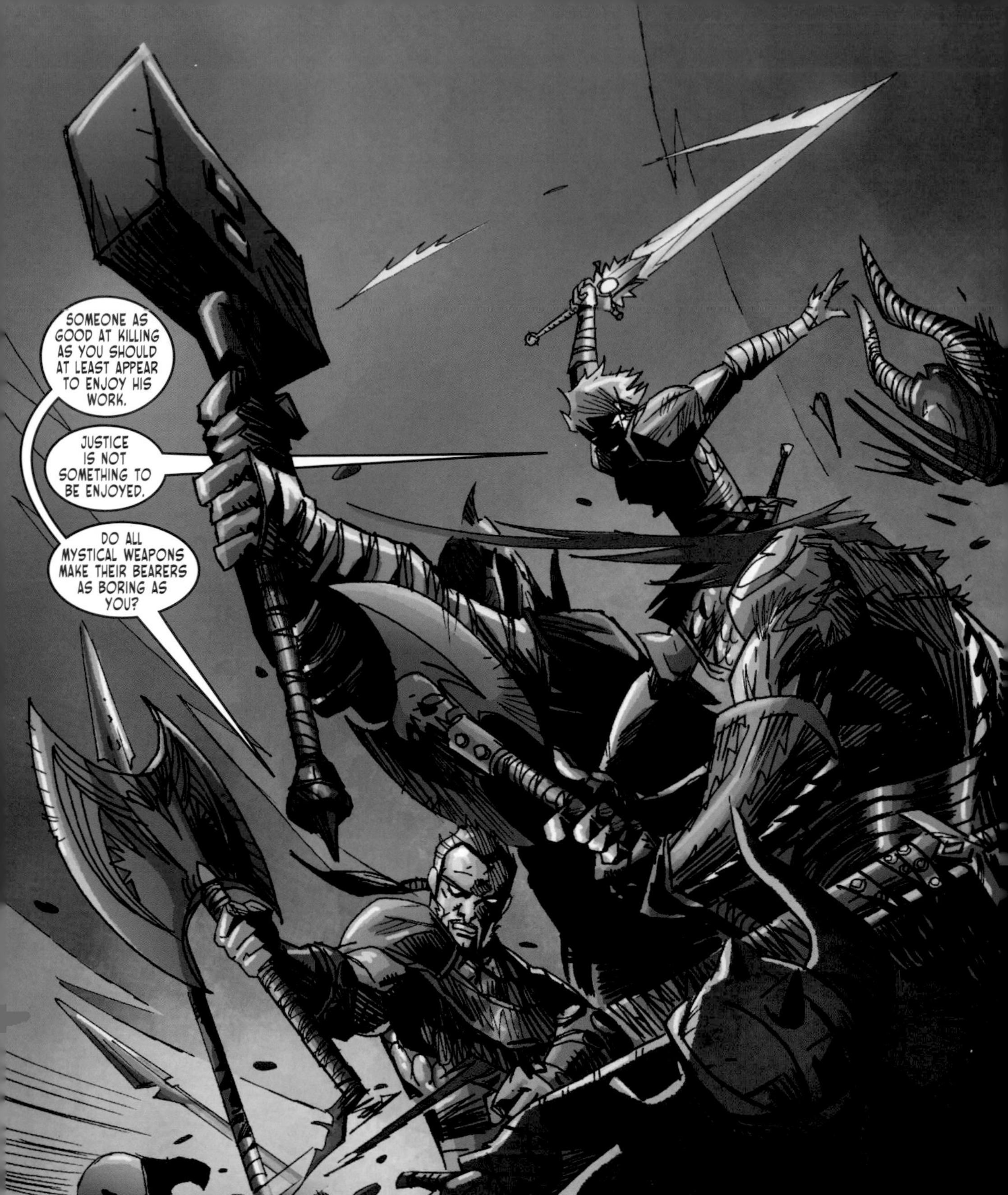
SOMEONE AS GOOD AT KILLING AS YOU SHOULD AT LEAST APPEAR TO ENJOY HIS WORK.
JUSTICE IS NOT SOMETHING TO BE ENJOYED.
DO ALL MYSTICAL WEAPONS MAKE THEIR BEARERS AS BORING AS YOU?

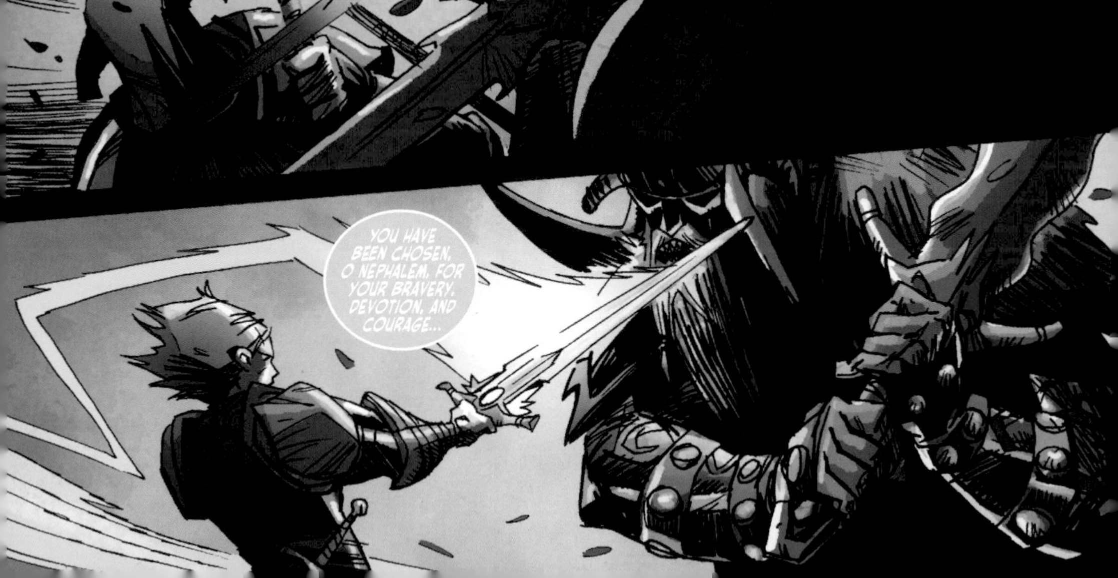
YOU HAVE BEEN CHOSEN, O NEPHALEM, FOR YOUR BRAVERY, DEVOTION, AND COURAGE...

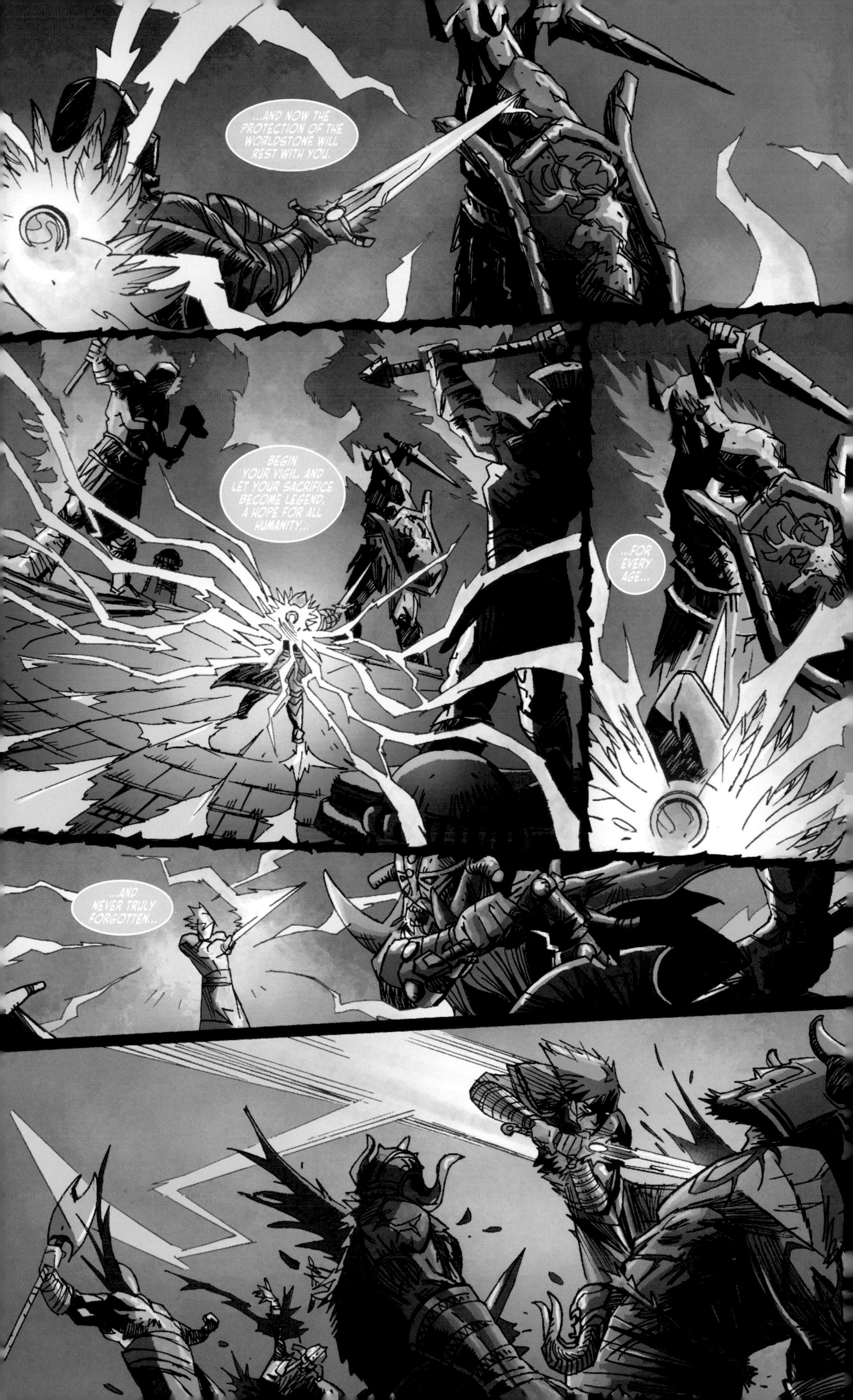
...AND NOW THE PROTECTION OF THE WORLDSTONE WILL REST WITH YOU.
BEGIN YOUR VIGIL, AND LET YOUR SACRIFICE BECOME LEGEND, A HOPE FOR ALL HUMANITY...
...FOR EVERY AGE...
...AND NEVER TRULY FORGOTTEN...

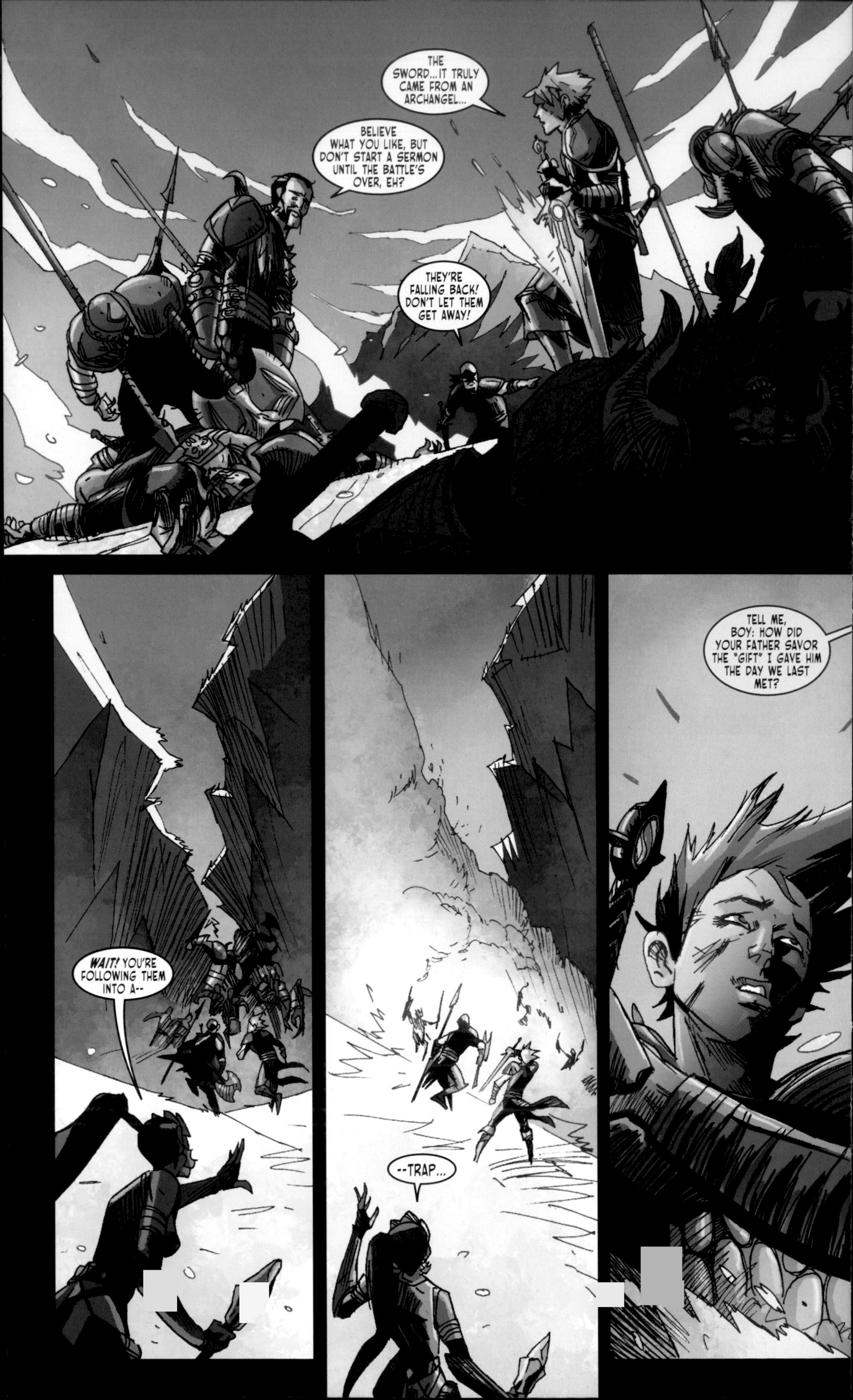
THE SWORD...IT TRULY CAME FROM AN ARCHANGEL...
BELIEVE WHAT YOU LIKE, BUT DON'T START A SERMON UNTIL THE BATTLE'S OVER, EH?
THEY'RE FALLING BACK! DON'T LET THEM GET AWAY!
WAIT! YOU'RE FOLLOWING THEM INTO A--
--TRAP...
TELL ME, BOY: HOW DID YOUR FATHER SAVOR THE "GIFT" I GAVE HIM THE DAY WE LAST MET?

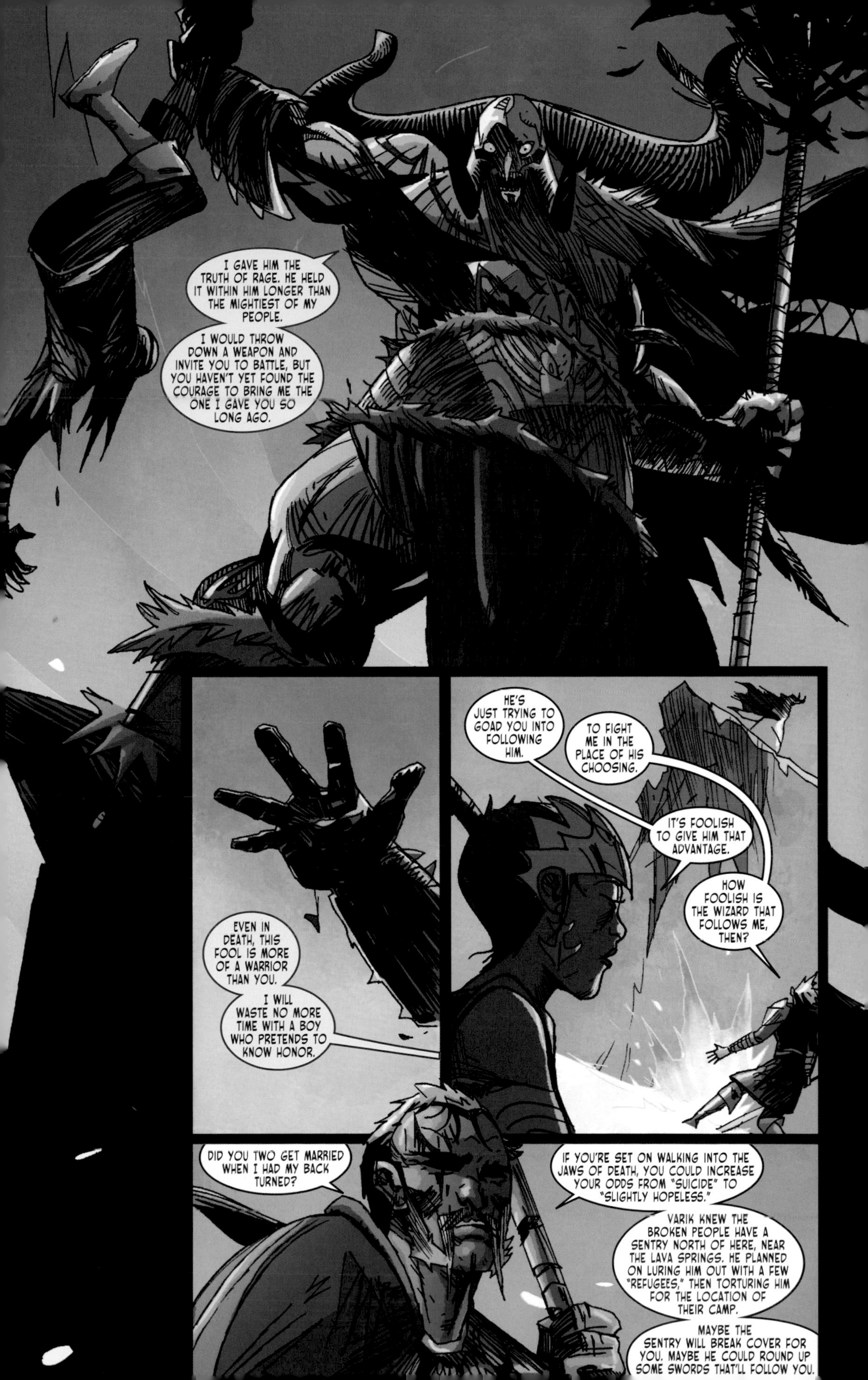
I GAVE HIM THE TRUTH OF RAGE. HE HELD IT WITHIN HIM LONGER THAN THE MIGHTIEST OF MY PEOPLE.
I WOULD THROW DOWN A WEAPON AND INVITE YOU TO BATTLE, BUT YOU HAVEN'T YET FOUND THE COURAGE TO BRING ME THE ONE I GAVE YOU SO LONG AGO.
EVEN IN DEATH, THIS FOOL IS MORE OF A WARRIOR THAN YOU.
I WILL WASTE NO MORE TIME WITH A BOY WHO PRETENDS TO KNOW HONOR.
HE'S JUST TRYING TO GOAD YOU INTO FOLLOWING HIM.
TO FIGHT ME IN THE PLACE OF HIS CHOOSING.
IT'S FOOLISH TO GIVE HIM THAT ADVANTAGE.
HOW FOOLISH IS THE WIZARD THAT FOLLOWS ME, THEN?
DID YOU TWO GET MARRIED WHEN I HAD MY BACK TURNED?
IF YOU'RE SET ON WALKING INTO THE JAWS OF DEATH, YOU COULD INCREASE YOUR ODDS FROM "SUICIDE" TO "SLIGHTLY HOPELESS."
VARIK KNEW THE BROKEN PEOPLE HAVE A SENTRY NORTH OF HERE, NEAR THE LAVA SPRINGS. HE PLANNED ON LURING HIM OUT WITH A FEW "REFUGEES," THEN TORTURING HIM FOR THE LOCATION OF THEIR CAMP.
MAYBE THE SENTRY WILL BREAK COVER FOR YOU. MAYBE HE COULD ROUND UP SOME SWORDS THAT'LL FOLLOW YOU.

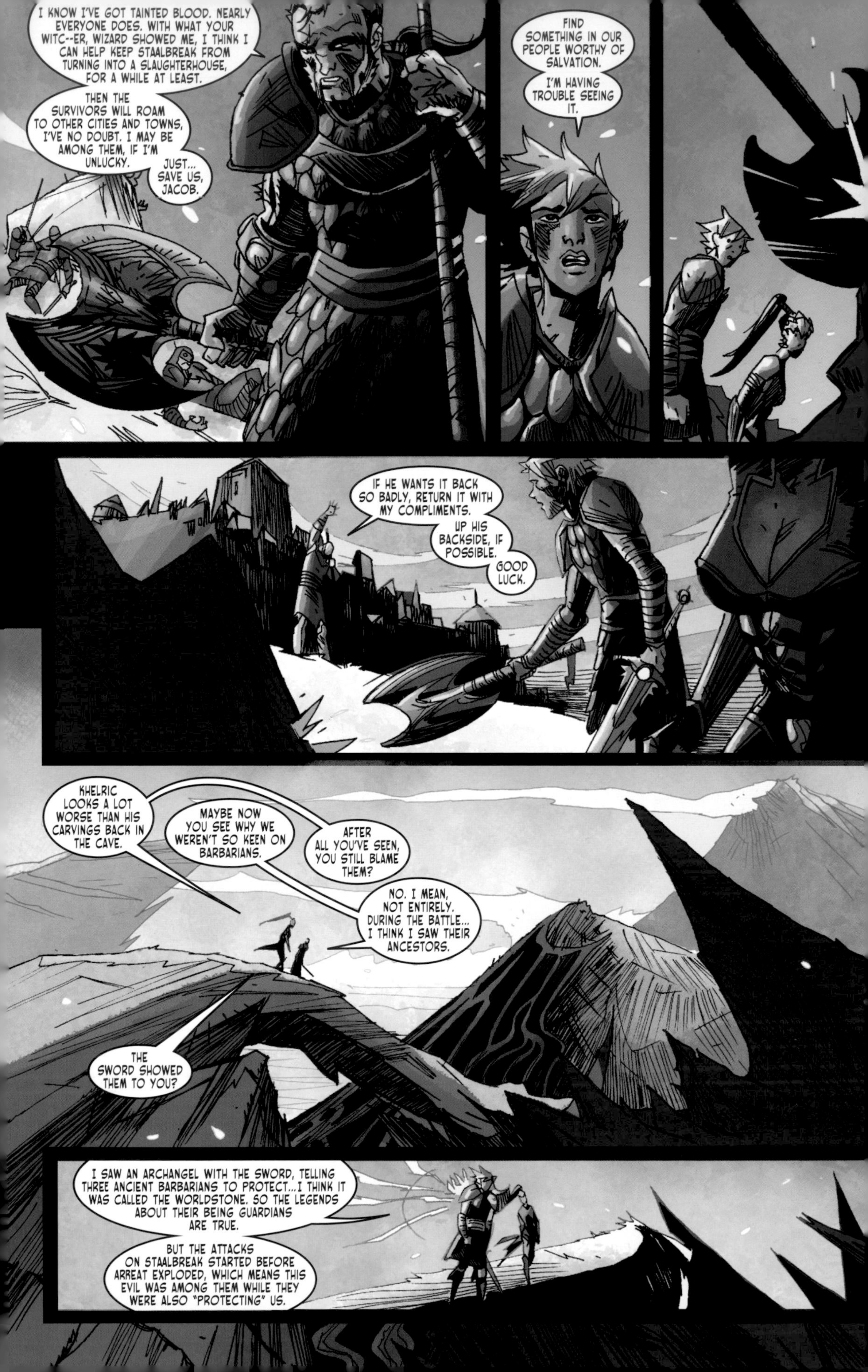
I KNOW I'VE GOT TAINTED BLOOD. NEARLY EVERYONE DOES. WITH WHAT YOUR WITC--ER, WIZARD SHOWED ME, I THINK I CAN HELP KEEP STAALBREAK FROM TURNING INTO A SLAUGHTERHOUSE, FOR A WHILE AT LEAST.
THEN THE SURVIVORS WILL ROAM TO OTHER CITIES AND TOWNS, I'VE NO DOUBT. I MAY BE AMONG THEM, IF I'M UNLUCKY.
JUST... SAVE US, JACOB.
FIND SOMETHING IN OUR PEOPLE WORTHY OF SALVATION.
I'M HAVING TROUBLE SEEING IT.
IF HE WANTS IT BACK SO BADLY, RETURN IT WITH MY COMPLIMENTS.
UP HIS BACKSIDE, IF POSSIBLE.
GOOD LUCK.
KHELRIC LOOKS A LOT WORSE THAN HIS CARVINGS BACK IN THE CAVE.
MAYBE NOW YOU SEE WHY WE WEREN'T SO KEEN ON BARBARIANS.
AFTER ALL YOU'VE SEEN, YOU STILL BLAME THEM?
NO. I MEAN, NOT ENTIRELY. DURING THE BATTLE... I THINK I SAW THEIR ANCESTORS.
THE SWORD SHOWED THEM TO YOU?
I SAW AN ARCHANGEL WITH THE SWORD, TELLING THREE ANCIENT BARBARIANS TO PROTECT...I THINK IT WAS CALLED THE WORLDSTONE. SO THE LEGENDS ABOUT THEIR BEING GUARDIANS ARE TRUE.
BUT THE ATTACKS ON STAALBREAK STARTED BEFORE ARREAT EXPLODED, WHICH MEANS THIS EVIL WAS AMONG THEM WHILE THEY WERE ALSO "PROTECTING" US.

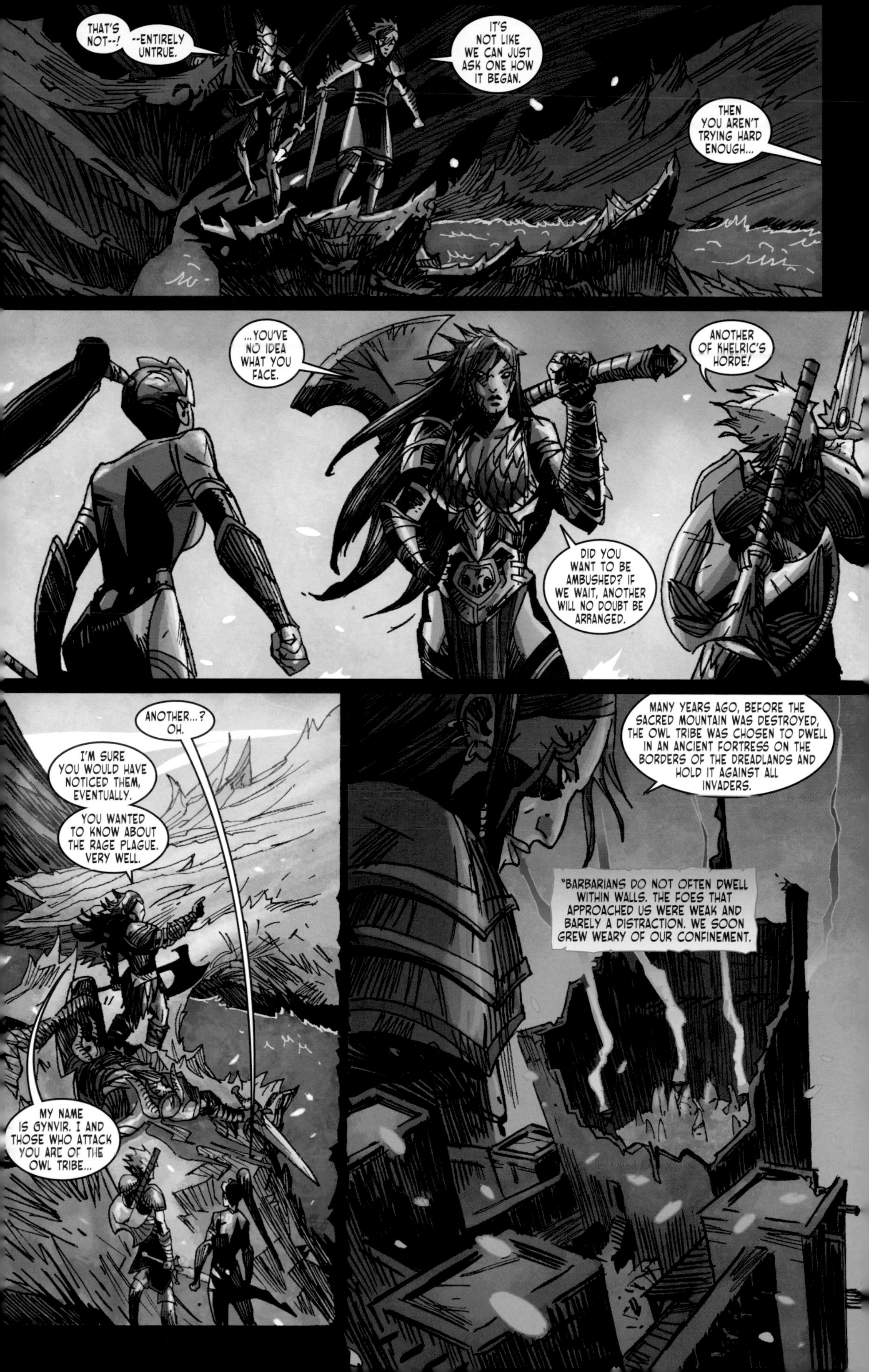
THAT'S NOT--!
--ENTIRELY UNTRUE.
IT'S NOT LIKE WE CAN JUST ASK ONE HOW IT BEGAN.
THEN YOU AREN'T TRYING HARD ENOUGH...
...YOU'VE NO IDEA WHAT YOU FACE.
ANOTHER OF KHELRIC'S HORDE!
DID YOU WANT TO BE AMBUSHED? IF WE WAIT, ANOTHER WILL NO DOUBT BE ARRANGED.
ANOTHER...? OH.
I'M SURE YOU WOULD HAVE NOTICED THEM, EVENTUALLY.
YOU WANTED TO KNOW ABOUT THE RAGE PLAGUE. VERY WELL.
MY NAME IS GYNVIR. I AND THOSE WHO ATTACK YOU ARE OF THE OWL TRIBE...
MANY YEARS AGO, BEFORE THE SACRED MOUNTAIN WAS DESTROYED, THE OWL TRIBE WAS CHOSEN TO DWELL IN AN ANCIENT FORTRESS ON THE BORDERS OF THE DREADLANDS AND HOLD IT AGAINST ALL INVADERS.
"BARBARIANS DO NOT OFTEN DWELL WITHIN WALLS. THE FOES THAT APPROACHED US WERE WEAK AND BARELY A DISTRACTION. WE SOON GREW WEARY OF OUR CONFINEMENT.

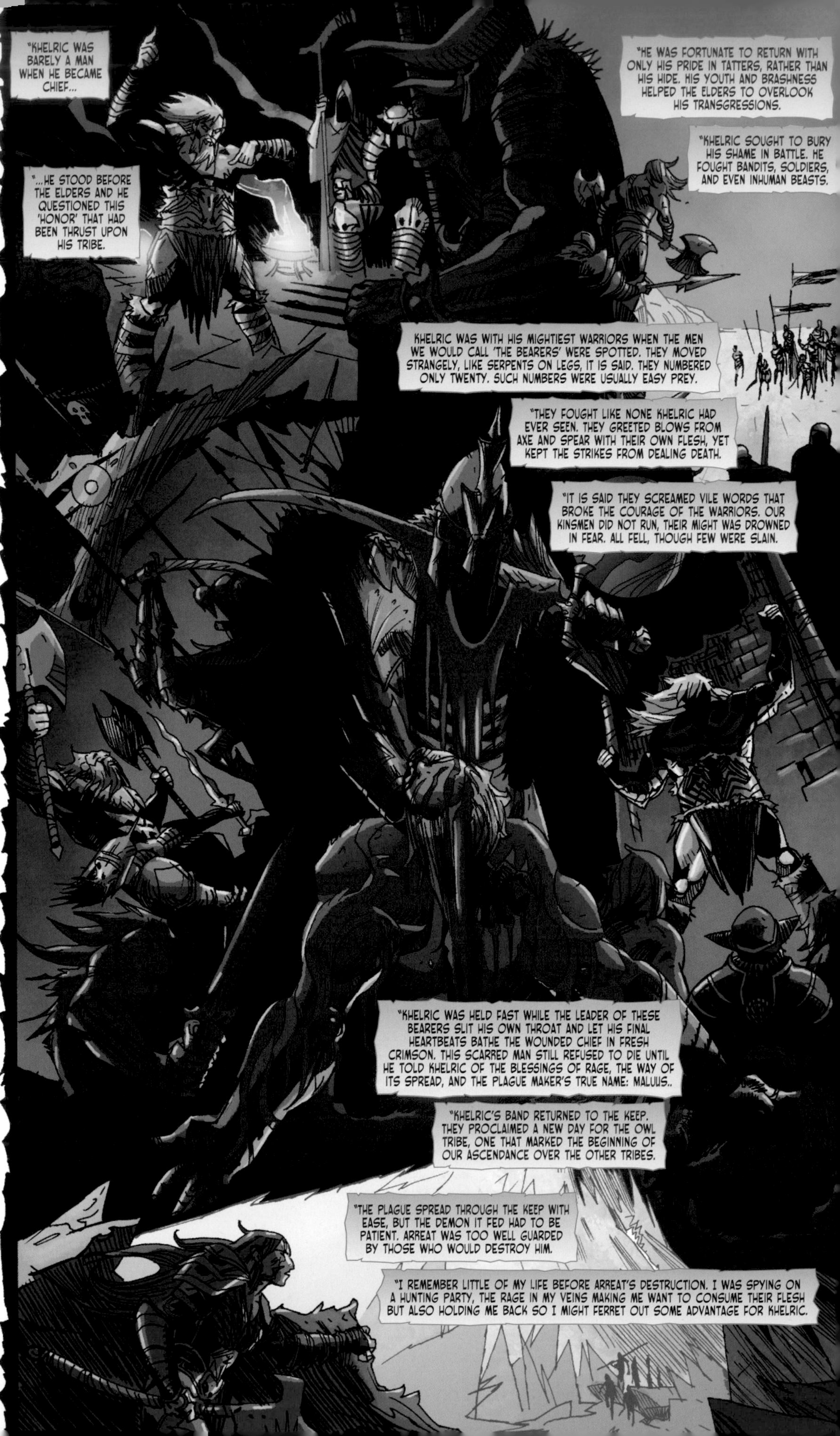
"KHELRIC WAS BARELY A MAN WHEN HE BECAME CHIEF...
"...HE STOOD BEFORE THE ELDERS AND HE QUESTIONED THIS 'HONOR' THAT HAD BEEN THRUST UPON HIS TRIBE.
"HE WAS FORTUNATE TO RETURN WITH ONLY HIS PRIDE IN TATTERS, RATHER THAN HIS HIDE. HIS YOUTH AND BRASHNESS HELPED THE ELDERS TO OVERLOOK HIS TRANSGRESSIONS.
"KHELRIC SOUGHT TO BURY HIS SHAME IN BATTLE. HE FOUGHT BANDITS, SOLDIERS, AND EVEN INHUMAN BEASTS.
KHELRIC WAS WITH HIS MIGHTIEST WARRIORS WHEN THE MEN WE WOULD CALL 'THE BEARERS' WERE SPOTTED. THEY MOVED STRANGELY, LIKE SERPENTS ON LEGS, IT IS SAID. THEY NUMBERED ONLY TWENTY. SUCH NUMBERS WERE USUALLY EASY PREY.
"THEY FOUGHT LIKE NONE KHELRIC HAD EVER SEEN. THEY GREETED BLOWS FROM AXE AND SPEAR WITH THEIR OWN FLESH, YET KEPT THE STRIKES FROM DEALING DEATH.
"IT IS SAID THEY SCREAMED VILE WORDS THAT BROKE THE COURAGE OF THE WARRIORS. OUR KINSMEN DID NOT RUN, THEIR MIGHT WAS DROWNED IN FEAR. ALL FELL, THOUGH FEW WERE SLAIN.
"KHELRIC WAS HELD FAST WHILE THE LEADER OF THESE BEARERS SLIT HIS OWN THROAT AND LET HIS FINAL HEARTBEATS BATHE THE WOUNDED CHIEF IN FRESH CRIMSON. THIS SCARRED MAN STILL REFUSED TO DIE UNTIL HE TOLD KHELRIC OF THE BLESSINGS OF RAGE, THE WAY OF ITS SPREAD, AND THE PLAGUE MAKER'S TRUE NAME: MALUUS..
"KHELRIC'S BAND RETURNED TO THE KEEP. THEY PROCLAIMED A NEW DAY FOR THE OWL TRIBE, ONE THAT MARKED THE BEGINNING OF OUR ASCENDANCE OVER THE OTHER TRIBES.
"THE PLAGUE SPREAD THROUGH THE KEEP WITH EASE, BUT THE DEMON IT FED HAD TO BE PATIENT. ARREAT WAS TOO WELL GUARDED BY THOSE WHO WOULD DESTROY HIM.
"I REMEMBER LITTLE OF MY LIFE BEFORE ARREAT'S DESTRUCTION. I WAS SPYING ON A HUNTING PARTY, THE RAGE IN MY VEINS MAKING ME WANT TO CONSUME THEIR FLESH BUT ALSO HOLDING ME BACK SO I MIGHT FERRET OUT SOME ADVANTAGE FOR KHELRIC.

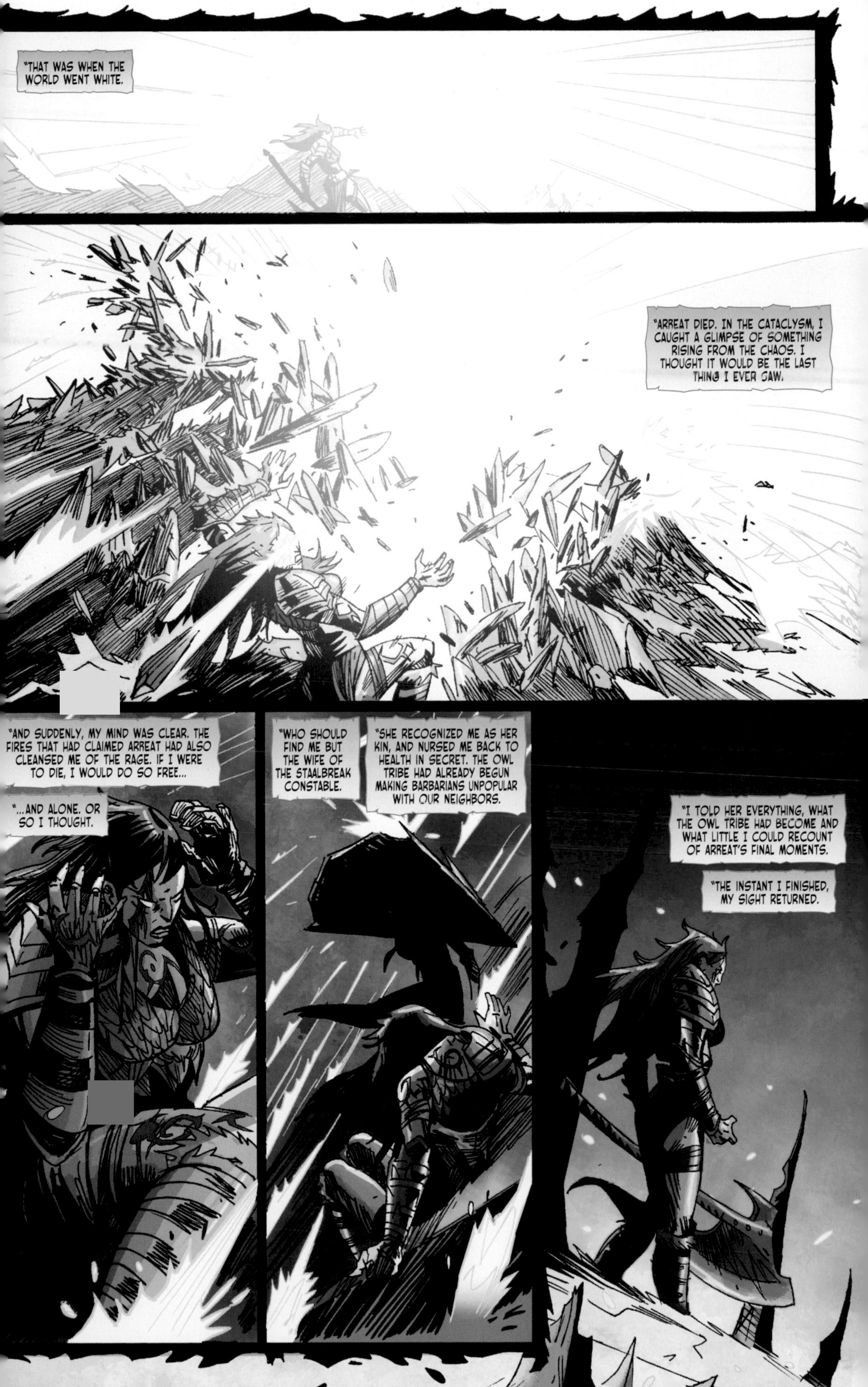
"THAT WAS WHEN THE WORLD WENT WHITE.
"ARREAT DIED. IN THE CATACLYSM, I CAUGHT A GLIMPSE OF SOMETHING RISING FROM THE CHAOS. I THOUGHT IT WOULD BE THE LAST THING I EVER SAW.
"AND SUDDENLY, MY MIND WAS CLEAR. THE FIRES THAT HAD CLAIMED ARREAT HAD ALSO CLEANSED ME OF THE RAGE. IF I WERE TO DIE, I WOULD DO SO FREE...
"...AND ALONE. OR SO I THOUGHT.
"WHO SHOULD FIND ME BUT THE WIFE OF THE STAALBREAK CONSTABLE.
"SHE RECOGNIZED ME AS HER KIN, AND NURSED ME BACK TO HEALTH IN SECRET. THE OWL TRIBE HAD ALREADY BEGUN MAKING BARBARIANS UNPOPULAR WITH OUR NEIGHBORS.
"I TOLD HER EVERYTHING, WHAT THE OWL TRIBE HAD BECOME AND WHAT LITTLE I COULD RECOUNT OF ARREAT'S FINAL MOMENTS.
"THE INSTANT I FINISHED, MY SIGHT RETURNED.

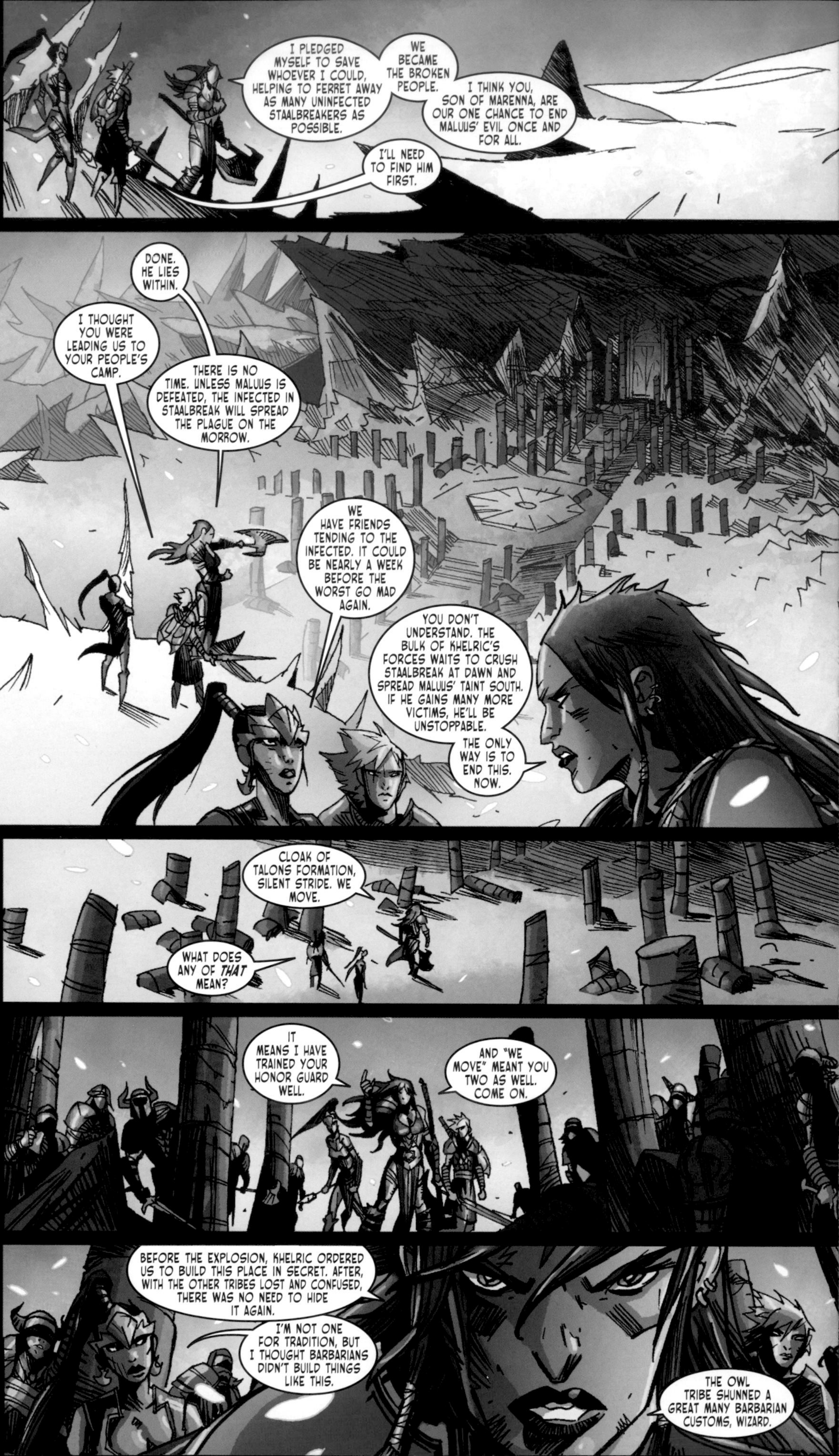
I PLEDGED MYSELF TO SAVE WHOEVER I COULD, HELPING TO FERRET AWAY AS MANY UNINFECTED STAALBREAKERS AS POSSIBLE.
WE BECAME THE BROKEN PEOPLE.
I THINK YOU, SON OF MARENNA, ARE OUR ONE CHANCE TO END MALUUS' EVIL ONCE AND FOR ALL.
I'LL NEED TO FIND HIM FIRST.
DONE. HE LIES WITHIN.
I THOUGHT YOU WERE LEADING US TO YOUR PEOPLE'S CAMP.
THERE IS NO TIME. UNLESS MALUUS IS DEFEATED, THE INFECTED IN STAALBREAK WILL SPREAD THE PLAGUE ON THE MORROW.
WE HAVE FRIENDS TENDING TO THE INFECTED. IT COULD BE NEARLY A WEEK BEFORE THE WORST GO MAD AGAIN.
YOU DON'T UNDERSTAND. THE BULK OF KHELRIC'S FORCES WAITS TO CRUSH STAALBREAK AT DAWN AND SPREAD MALUUS' TAINT SOUTH. IF HE GAINS MANY MORE VICTIMS, HE'LL BE UNSTOPPABLE.
THE ONLY WAY IS TO END THIS. NOW.
CLOAK OF TALONS FORMATION, SILENT STRIDE. WE MOVE.
WHAT DOES ANY OF *THAT* MEAN?
IT MEANS I HAVE TRAINED YOUR HONOR GUARD WELL.
AND "WE MOVE" MEANT YOU TWO AS WELL. COME ON.
BEFORE THE EXPLOSION, KHELRIC ORDERED US TO BUILD THIS PLACE IN SECRET. AFTER, WITH THE OTHER TRIBES LOST AND CONFUSED, THERE WAS NO NEED TO HIDE IT AGAIN.
I'M NOT ONE FOR TRADITION, BUT I THOUGHT BARBARIANS DIDN'T BUILD THINGS LIKE THIS.
THE OWL TRIBE SHUNNED A GREAT MANY BARBARIAN CUSTOMS, WIZARD.

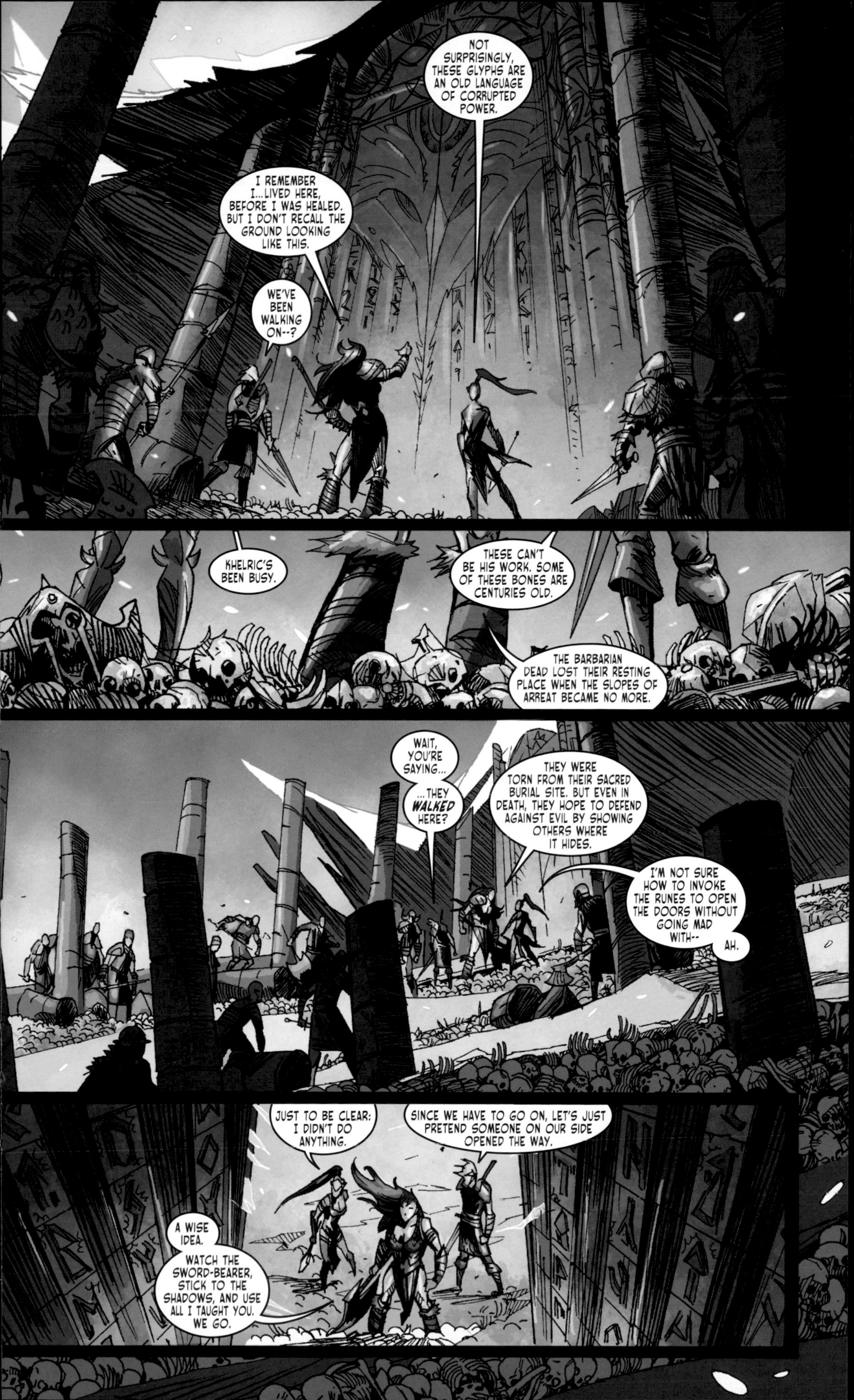
NOT SURPRISINGLY, THESE GLYPHS ARE AN OLD LANGUAGE OF CORRUPTED POWER.
I REMEMBER I...LIVED HERE, BEFORE I WAS HEALED. BUT I DON'T RECALL THE GROUND LOOKING LIKE THIS.
WE'VE BEEN WALKING ON--?
KHELRIC'S BEEN BUSY.
THESE CAN'T BE HIS WORK. SOME OF THESE BONES ARE CENTURIES OLD.
THE BARBARIAN DEAD LOST THEIR RESTING PLACE WHEN THE SLOPES OF ARREAT BECAME NO MORE.
WAIT, YOU'RE SAYING...
...THEY *WALKED* HERE?
THEY WERE TORN FROM THEIR SACRED BURIAL SITE. BUT EVEN IN DEATH, THEY HOPE TO DEFEND AGAINST EVIL BY SHOWING OTHERS WHERE IT HIDES.
I'M NOT SURE HOW TO INVOKE THE RUNES TO OPEN THE DOORS WITHOUT GOING MAD WITH--
AH.
JUST TO BE CLEAR: I DIDN'T DO ANYTHING.
SINCE WE HAVE TO GO ON, LET'S JUST PRETEND SOMEONE ON OUR SIDE OPENED THE WAY.
A WISE IDEA.
WATCH THE SWORD-BEARER, STICK TO THE SHADOWS, AND USE ALL I TAUGHT YOU. WE GO.

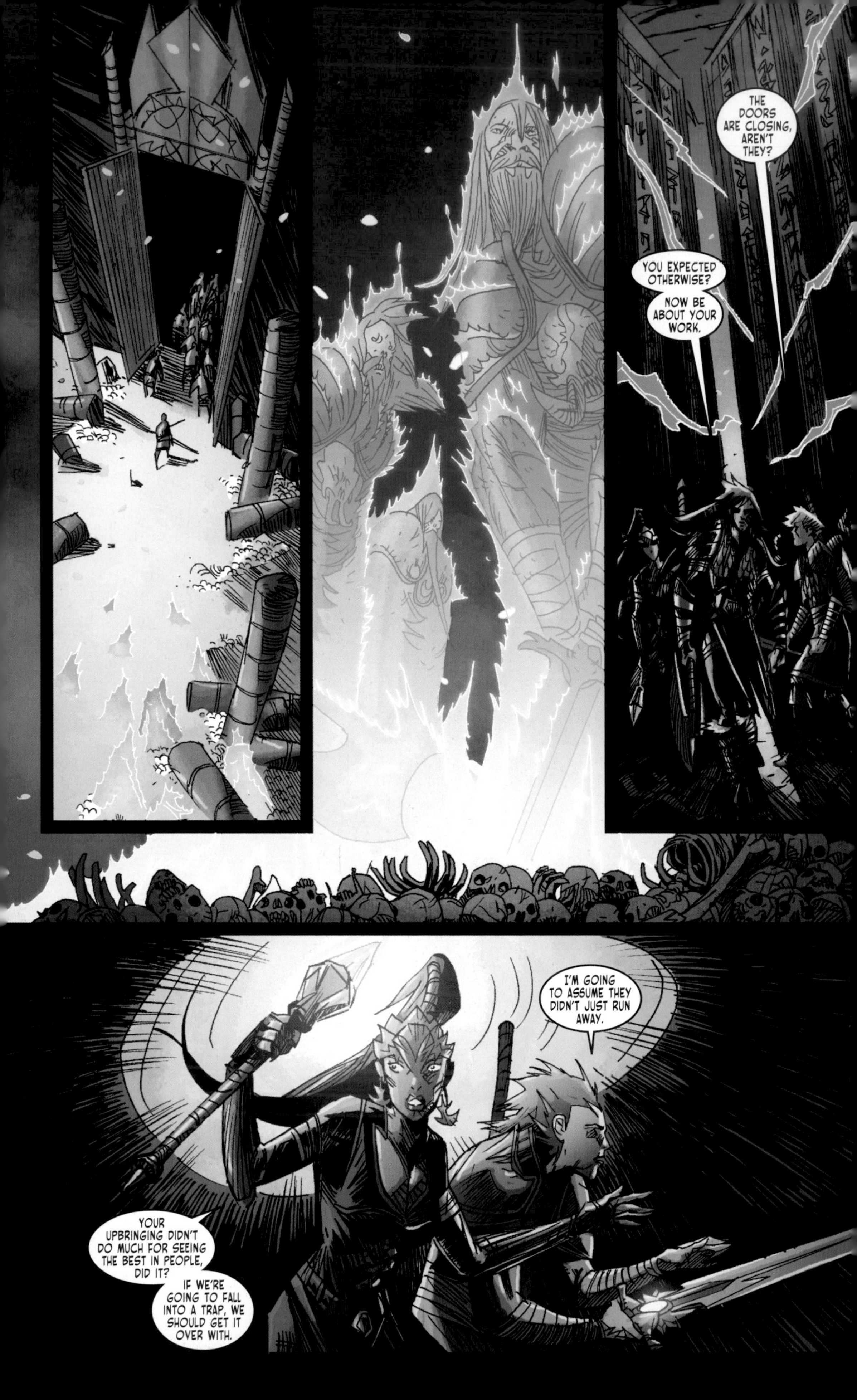
THE DOORS ARE CLOSING, AREN'T THEY?
YOU EXPECTED OTHERWISE?
NOW BE ABOUT YOUR WORK.
I'M GOING TO ASSUME THEY DIDN'T JUST RUN AWAY.
YOUR UPBRINGING DIDN'T DO MUCH FOR SEEING THE BEST IN PEOPLE, DID IT?
IF WE'RE GOING TO FALL INTO A TRAP, WE SHOULD GET IT OVER WITH.

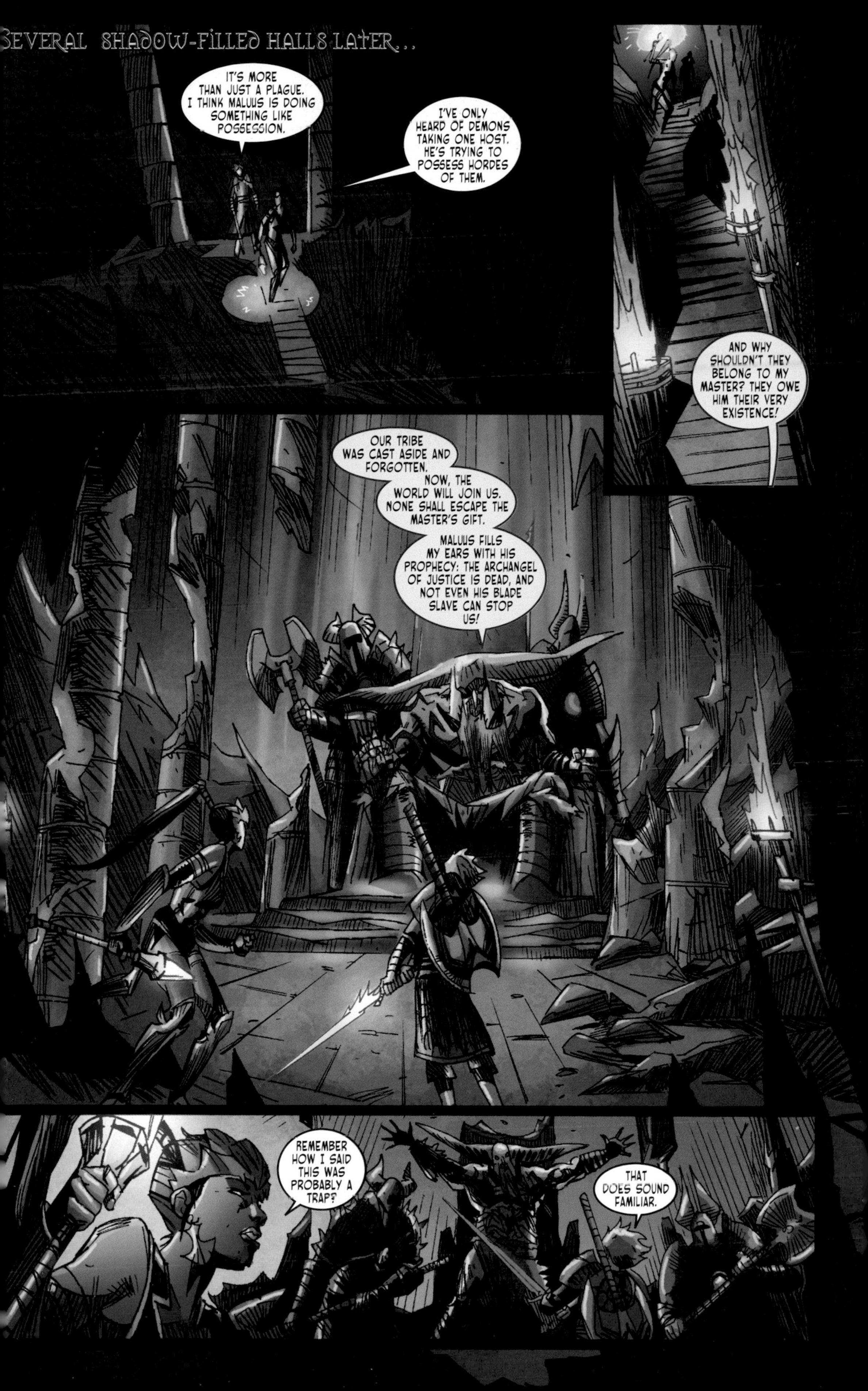
SEVERAL SHADOW-FILLED HALLS LATER...
IT'S MORE THAN JUST A PLAGUE. I THINK MALUUS IS DOING SOMETHING LIKE POSSESSION.
I'VE ONLY HEARD OF DEMONS TAKING ONE HOST. HE'S TRYING TO POSSESS HORDES OF THEM.
AND WHY SHOULDN'T THEY BELONG TO MY MASTER? THEY OWE HIM THEIR VERY EXISTENCE!
OUR TRIBE WAS CAST ASIDE AND FORGOTTEN.
NOW, THE WORLD WILL JOIN US. NONE SHALL ESCAPE THE MASTER'S GIFT.
MALUUS FILLS MY EARS WITH HIS PROPHECY: THE ARCHANGEL OF JUSTICE IS DEAD, AND NOT EVEN HIS BLADE SLAVE CAN STOP US!
REMEMBER HOW I SAID THIS WAS PROBABLY A TRAP?
THAT DOES SOUND FAMILIAR.

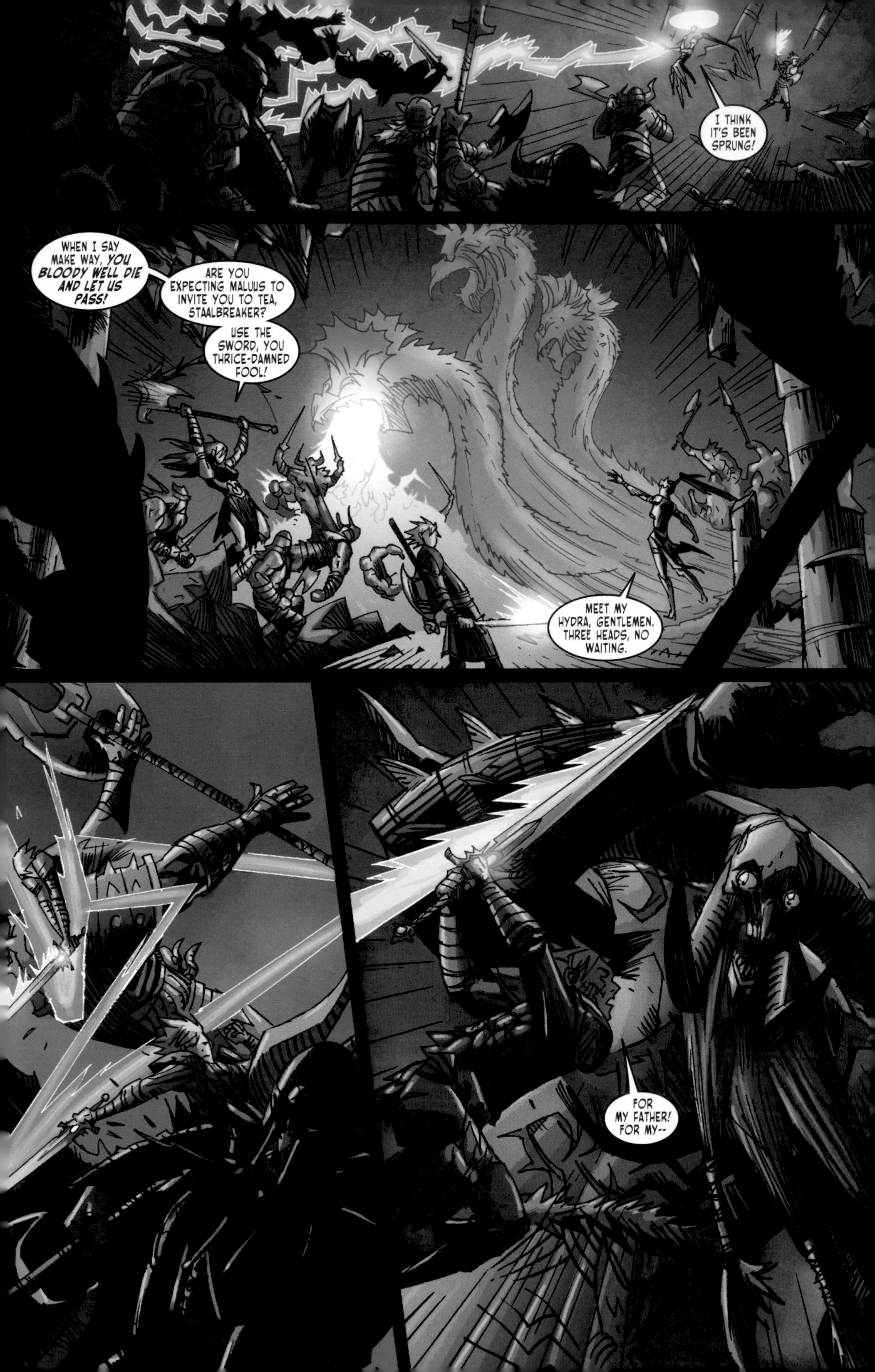
I THINK IT'S BEEN SPRUNG!
WHEN I SAY MAKE WAY, YOU BLOODY WELL DIE AND LET US PASS!
ARE YOU EXPECTING MALUUS TO INVITE YOU TO TEA, STAALBREAKER?
USE THE SWORD, YOU THRICE-DAMNED FOOL!
MEET MY HYDRA, GENTLEMEN. THREE HEADS, NO WAITING.
FOR MY FATHER! FOR MY--

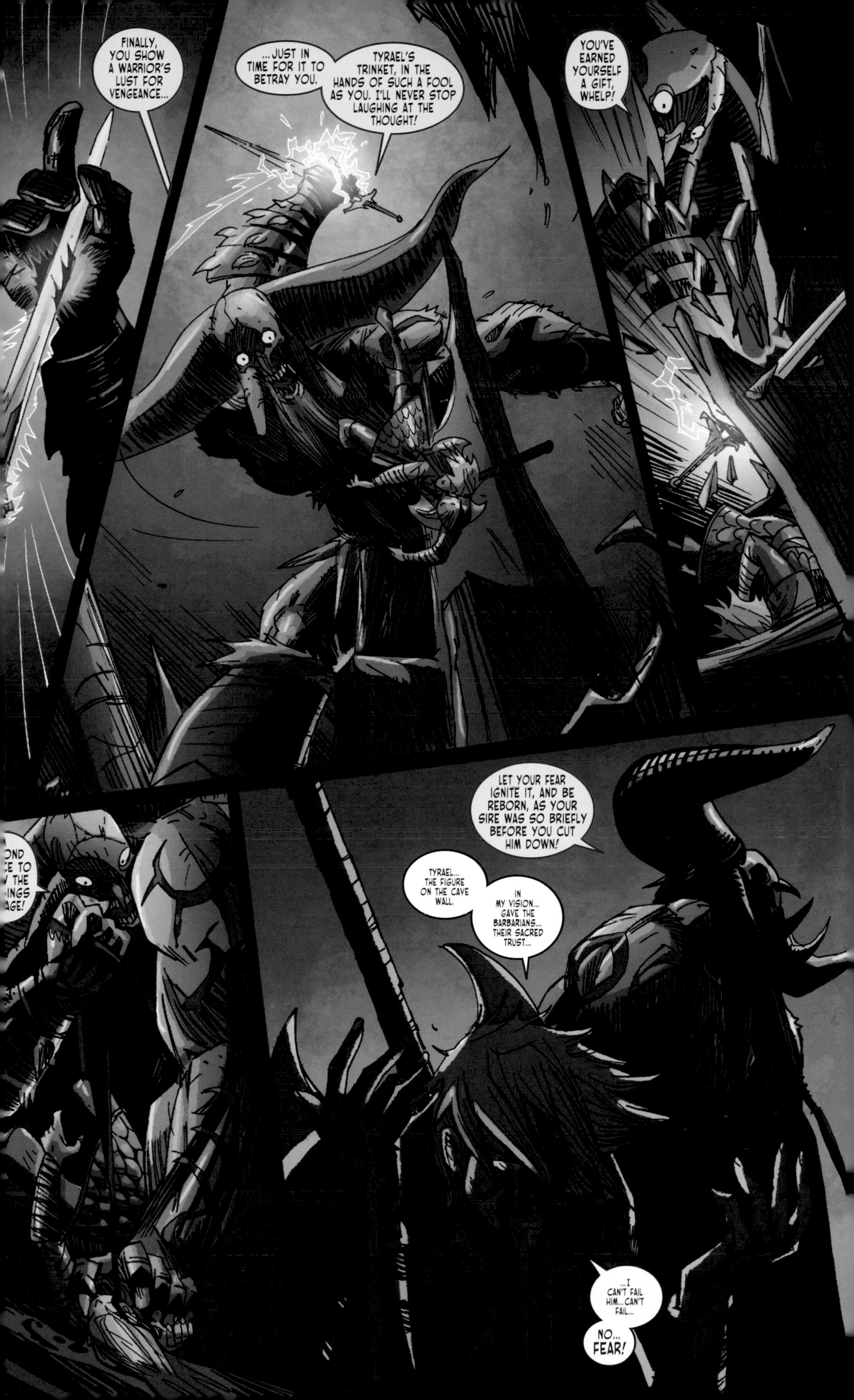
FINALLY, YOU SHOW A WARRIOR'S LUST FOR VENGEANCE...
...JUST IN TIME FOR IT TO BETRAY YOU.
TYRAEL'S TRINKET, IN THE HANDS OF SUCH A FOOL AS YOU. I'LL NEVER STOP LAUGHING AT THE THOUGHT!
YOU'VE EARNED YOURSELF A GIFT, WHELP!
LET YOUR FEAR IGNITE IT, AND BE REBORN, AS YOUR SIRE WAS SO BRIEFLY BEFORE YOU CUT HIM DOWN!
TYRAEL... THE FIGURE ON THE CAVE WALL.
IN MY VISION... GAVE THE BARBARIANS... THEIR SACRED TRUST...
...I CAN'T FAIL HIM...CAN'T FAIL...
NO... FEAR!

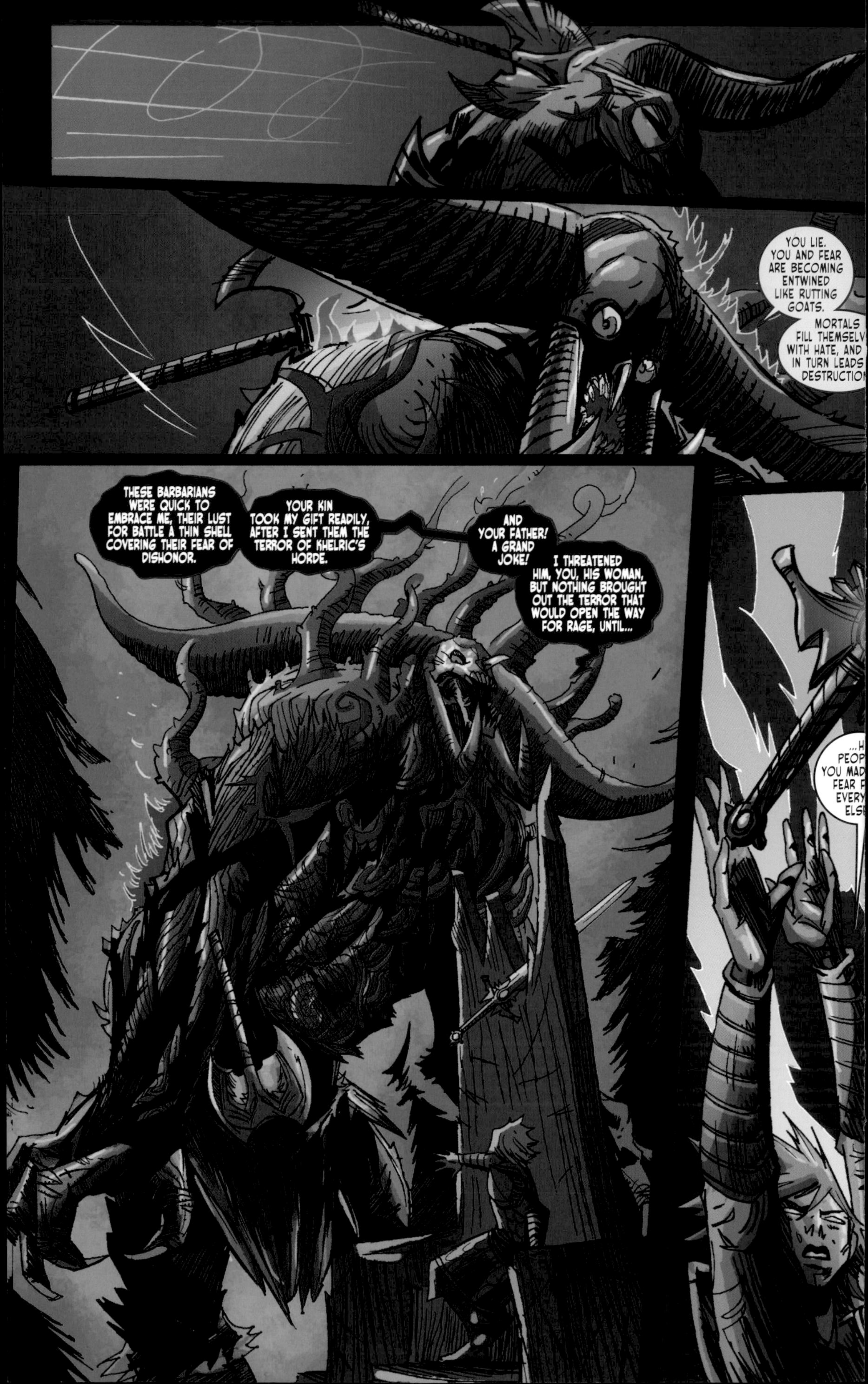
YOU LIE. YOU AND FEAR ARE BECOMING ENTWINED LIKE RUTTING GOATS.
MORTALS FILL THEMSELV WITH HATE, AND IN TURN LEADS DESTRUCTIO
THESE BARBARIANS WERE QUICK TO EMBRACE ME, THEIR LUST FOR BATTLE A THIN SHELL COVERING THEIR FEAR OF DISHONOR.
YOUR KIN TOOK MY GIFT READILY, AFTER I SENT THEM THE TERROR OF KHELRIC'S HORDE.
AND YOUR FATHER! A GRAND JOKE!
I THREATENED HIM, YOU, HIS WOMAN, BUT NOTHING BROUGHT OUT THE TERROR THAT WOULD OPEN THE WAY FOR RAGE, UNTIL...
...H PEOP YOU MAD FEAR F EVERY ELSE

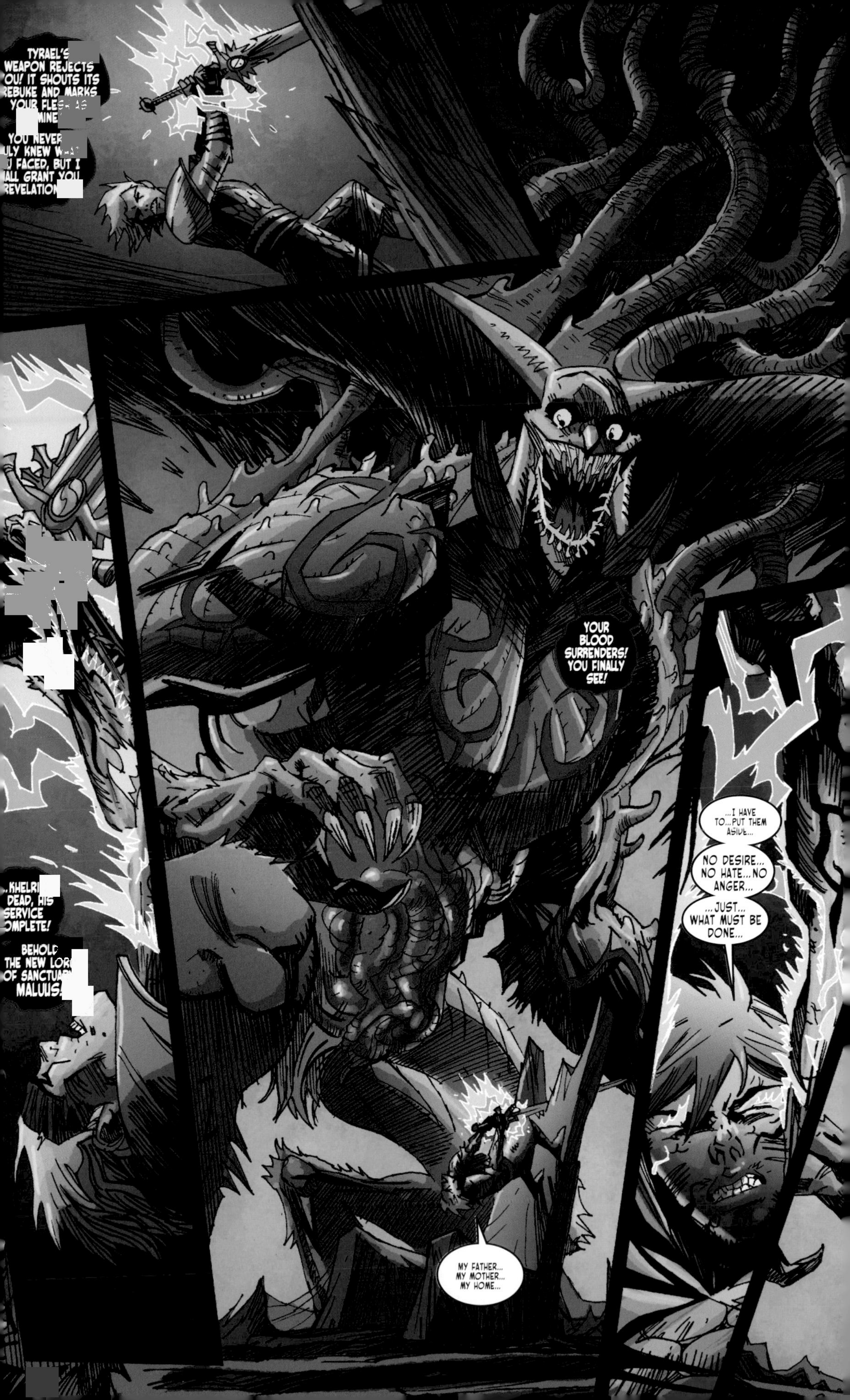

TYRAEL'S WEAPON REJECTS OU! IT SHOUTS ITS REBUKE AND MARKS YOUR FLE
YOU NEVER ULY KNEW W J FACED, BUT I ALL GRANT YOU REVELATION
YOUR BLOOD SURRENDERS! YOU FINALLY SEE!
..KHELRI DEAD, HIS SERVICE OMPLETE!
BEHOLD THE NEW LOR OF SANCTUA MALUUS
MY FATHER... MY MOTHER... MY HOME...
...I HAVE TO...PUT THEM ASIDE...
NO DESIRE... NO HATE...NO ANGER...
...JUST... WHAT MUST BE DONE...

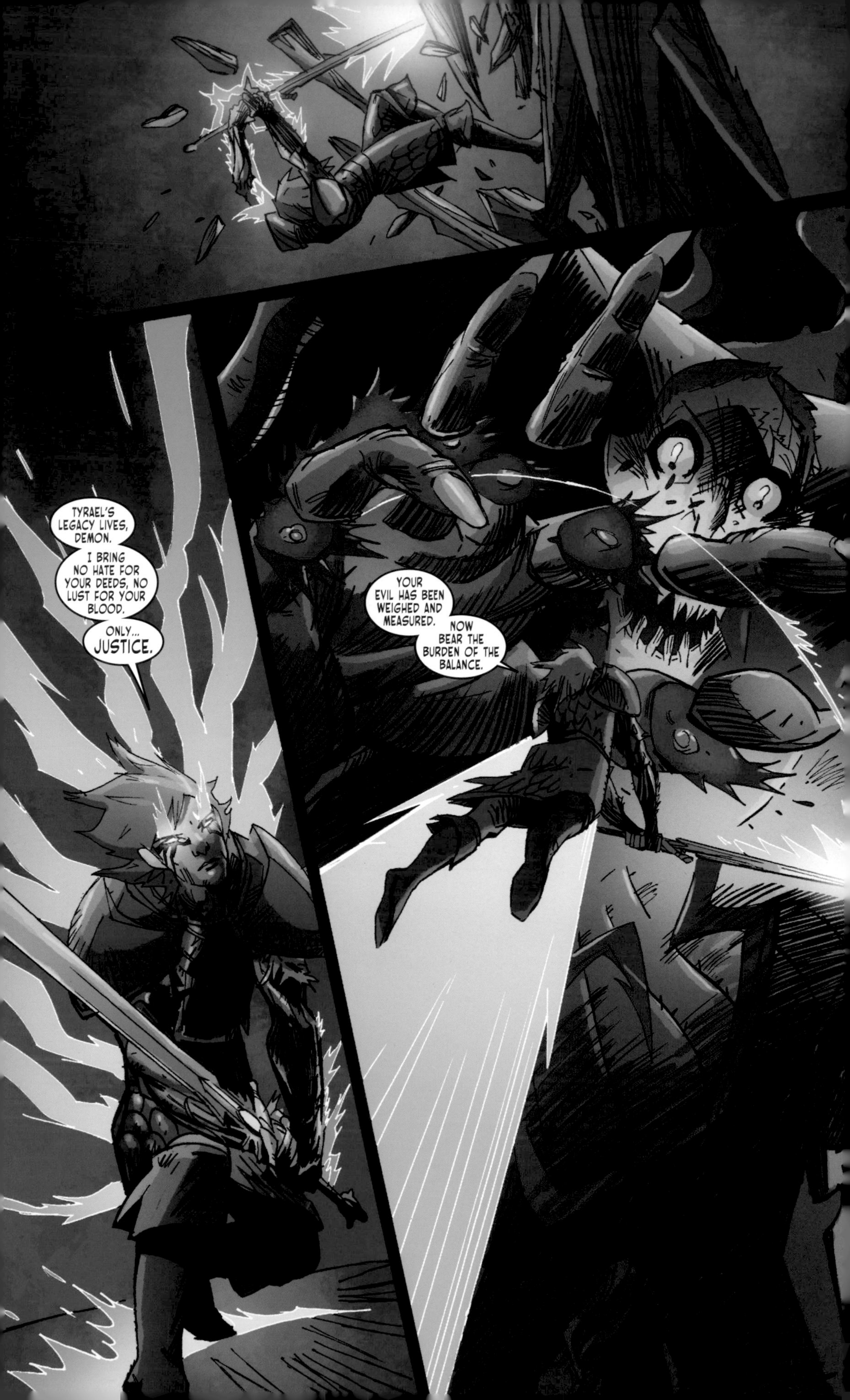
TYRAEL'S LEGACY LIVES, DEMON.
I BRING NO HATE FOR YOUR DEEDS, NO LUST FOR YOUR BLOOD.
ONLY... JUSTICE.
YOUR EVIL HAS BEEN WEIGHED AND MEASURED.
NOW BEAR THE BURDEN OF THE BALANCE.

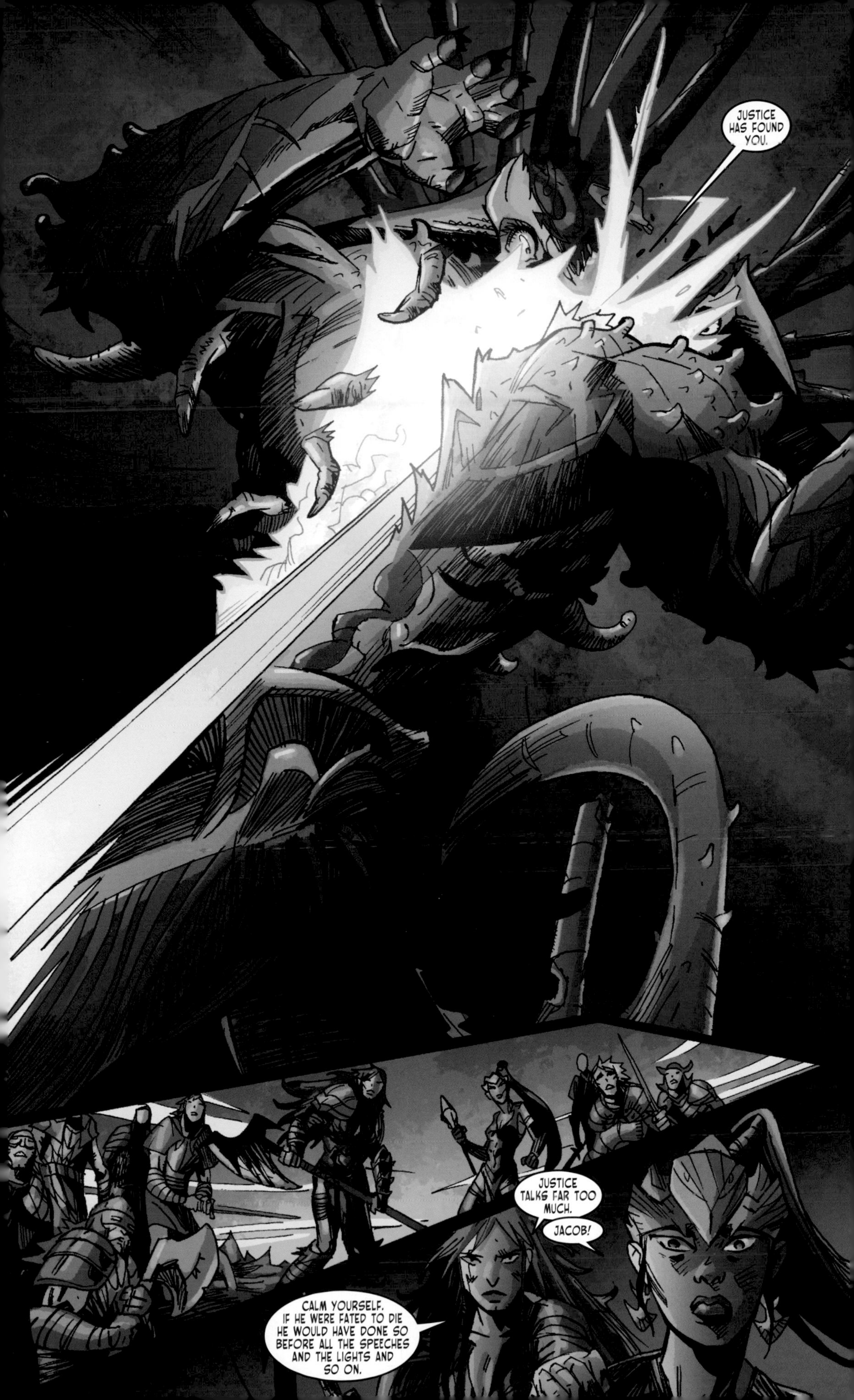
JUSTICE HAS FOUND YOU.
JUSTICE TALKS FAR TOO MUCH.
JACOB!
CALM YOURSELF. IF HE WERE FATED TO DIE HE WOULD HAVE DONE SO BEFORE ALL THE SPEECHES AND THE LIGHTS AND SO ON.

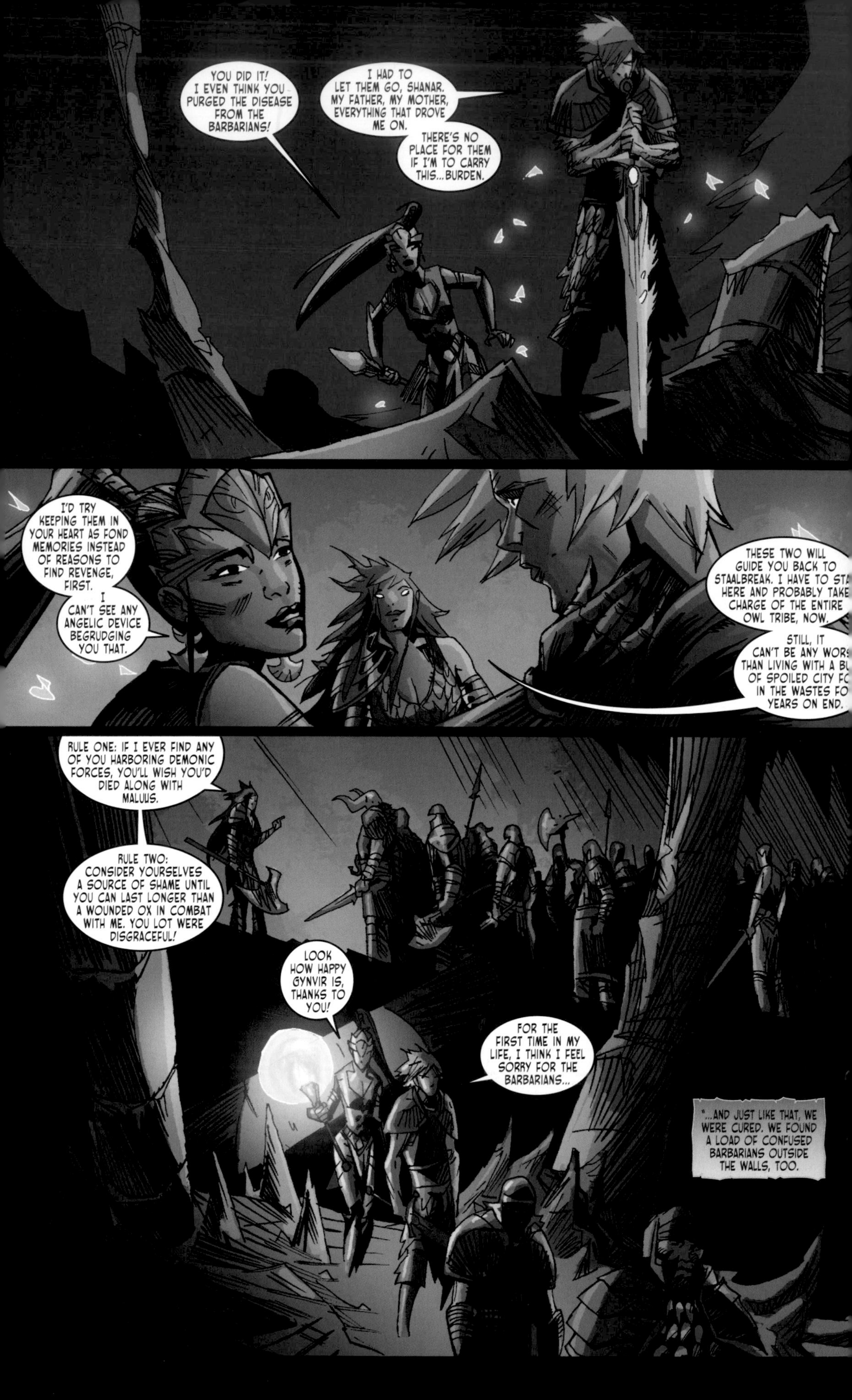
YOU DID IT! I EVEN THINK YOU PURGED THE DISEASE FROM THE BARBARIANS!
I HAD TO LET THEM GO, SHANAR. MY FATHER, MY MOTHER, EVERYTHING THAT DROVE ME ON.
THERE'S NO PLACE FOR THEM IF I'M TO CARRY THIS...BURDEN.
I'D TRY KEEPING THEM IN YOUR HEART AS FOND MEMORIES INSTEAD OF REASONS TO FIND REVENGE, FIRST.
I CAN'T SEE ANY ANGELIC DEVICE BEGRUDGING YOU THAT.
THESE TWO WILL GUIDE YOU BACK TO STAALBREAK. I HAVE TO STA HERE AND PROBABLY TAKE CHARGE OF THE ENTIRE OWL TRIBE, NOW.
STILL, IT CAN'T BE ANY WORS THAN LIVING WITH A BU OF SPOILED CITY FO IN THE WASTES FO YEARS ON END.
RULE ONE: IF I EVER FIND ANY OF YOU HARBORING DEMONIC FORCES, YOU'LL WISH YOU'D DIED ALONG WITH MALUUS.
RULE TWO: CONSIDER YOURSELVES A SOURCE OF SHAME UNTIL YOU CAN LAST LONGER THAN A WOUNDED OX IN COMBAT WITH ME. YOU LOT WERE DISGRACEFUL!
LOOK HOW HAPPY GYNVIR IS, THANKS TO YOU!
FOR THE FIRST TIME IN MY LIFE, I THINK I FEEL SORRY FOR THE BARBARIANS...
"...AND JUST LIKE THAT, WE WERE CURED. WE FOUND A LOAD OF CONFUSED BARBARIANS OUTSIDE THE WALLS, TOO.

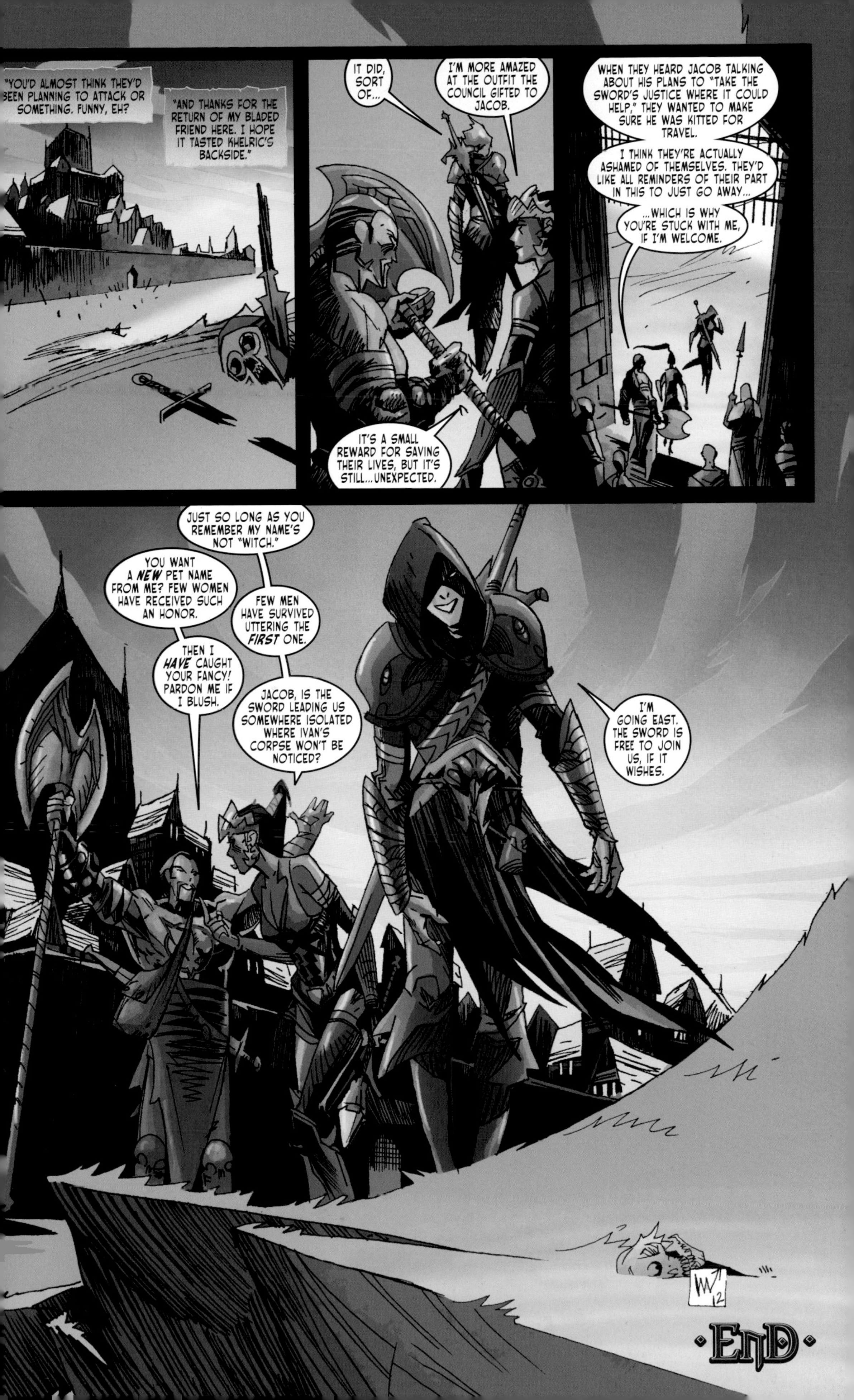
"YOU'D ALMOST THINK THEY'D BEEN PLANNING TO ATTACK OR SOMETHING. FUNNY, EH?
"AND THANKS FOR THE RETURN OF MY BLADED FRIEND HERE. I HOPE IT TASTED KHELRIC'S BACKSIDE."
IT DID, SORT OF...
I'M MORE AMAZED AT THE OUTFIT THE COUNCIL GIFTED TO JACOB.
IT'S A SMALL REWARD FOR SAVING THEIR LIVES, BUT IT'S STILL...UNEXPECTED.
WHEN THEY HEARD JACOB TALKING ABOUT HIS PLANS TO "TAKE THE SWORD'S JUSTICE WHERE IT COULD HELP," THEY WANTED TO MAKE SURE HE WAS KITTED FOR TRAVEL.
I THINK THEY'RE ACTUALLY ASHAMED OF THEMSELVES. THEY'D LIKE ALL REMINDERS OF THEIR PART IN THIS TO JUST GO AWAY...
...WHICH IS WHY YOU'RE STUCK WITH ME, IF I'M WELCOME.
JUST SO LONG AS YOU REMEMBER MY NAME'S NOT "WITCH."
YOU WANT A NEW PET NAME FROM ME? FEW WOMEN HAVE RECEIVED SUCH AN HONOR.
FEW MEN HAVE SURVIVED UTTERING THE FIRST ONE.
THEN I HAVE CAUGHT YOUR FANCY! PARDON ME IF I BLUSH.
JACOB, IS THE SWORD LEADING US SOMEWHERE ISOLATED WHERE IVAN'S CORPSE WON'T BE NOTICED?
I'M GOING EAST. THE SWORD IS FREE TO JOIN US, IF IT WISHES.
WT '12
END